Man in the Landscape

NUMBER 11
THE ENVIRONMENTAL HISTORY SERIES
Martin V. Melosi, General Editor

MAN IN THE
LANDSCAPE

A Historic View of the Esthetics of Nature

by

Paul Shepard

Foreword by Michael Martin McCarthy

Texas A&M University Press
College Station

LIBRARY OF CONGRESS CATALOGING-IN-PUBLICATION DATA
Shepard, Paul, 1925–
    Man in the landscape : a historic view of
    the esthetics of nature / by Paul Shepard ;
    foreword by Michael Martin McCarthy.
    — 2nd ed.
        p. cm. — (Environmental history
    series ; no. 11)
    Includes bibliographical references and
    index.
    ISBN 0-89096-421-1 (alk. paper)
    1. Nature (Aesthetics)   I. Title.
    II. Series.
    BH301.N3S45   1991
    111'.85—dc20   90–43864
                                        CIP

TO
Clara Grigsby Shepard

Contents

CHAPTER FOUR

THE ITINERANT EYE, *wherein travel is considered to be responsible for the idea of scenery— an abstraction necessary before some men could destroy nature or others could find it beautiful* 119

CHAPTER FIVE

THE VIRGIN DREAM, *or requiem for the now unfashionable idea that nature loves us, and will love us best when it comes to us undefiled* 157

CHAPTER SIX

FELLOW CREATURES, *an argument for killing them for their own good and ours* 190

CHAPTER SEVEN

VARIETIES OF NATURE HATING, *a chronicle of the times, an account of some of the ideas which, when pooled in one society, inspire sufficient motive for doing to our environment what we are doing* 214

CHAPTER EIGHT

THE AMERICAN WEST, *a case history holding that there is a value in the American wilderness discovered by some gentlemen who thought it looked like something else* 238

SOURCES AND REFERENCES

275

INDEX

follows page 290

Illustrations

follow page 170

Foreword

✿

O N   T H E   T H I R T E E N T H   O F   J A N U A R Y ,   1802,   two
ships, the *Geographe* and the *Naturaliste*, commanded by
Nicolas Baudin anchored off the coast of Tasmania. During
their explorations they recorded an unusual event. And it is
this observation that I wish to use in introduction of Paul
Shepard's *Man in the Landscape*.

Rising waters of Bass Strait isolated the Tasmanian Aborigines from interaction with mainland Australia and other
human populations for twelve thousand years.[1] Before the
island of Tasmania was settled by the British in 1803, three
French expeditions conducted scientific investigations and
these reports are the only accounts of the Tasmanian Aborigines prior to their subsequent extinction.[2] Of these, only the
Baudin expedition spent two months in deliberate pre-settle-
ment study. Their reports reveal a nomadic, isolated people
with a very simple culture by European standards.[3] Francis
Peron was the principal zoologist of the expedition. On the
19th of February, 1802, while exploring Maria Island (about
five kilometers off the coast), he wrote:

I made my way towards the north side of the bay and
pushed my way inland. My progress was slow at first
because of the long wiry grass which covered the ground;
and in some places even the shrubs, thicker and stronger,
blocked all passage. I was about to turn back when I saw
a path made by the natives a short distance away. I fol-

lowed it. Soon the trees became more sparse, and in less
than half an hour I arrived at the summit of a little hill
from where I had in view both the bays of Maria Island,
the isthmus separating them and the mountains of Van
Diemen's Land. . . .

While I was giving myself up to the delightful sensations,
so full of charm, which such a spot must inspire, going
around lazily, I perceived at a short distance a monument
whose construction both surprised and interested me. I
hurried towards it, and this is what I saw.[4]

In this idyllic, scenic setting Francis Peron came upon a
burial monument, a temporary tomb constructed carefully of
bark and lashed poles that surrounded cremated remains lying
in a shallow depression. And he asked himself: "What could
have been the origin here of this custom of burning the dead?
Isolated from the rest of the world, thrust towards the very
ends of the earth. . . ."[5]

Most revealing, however, are the words he used to describe the illustrations made by the expedition's artists: "The
drawing of this tomb, made with great exactness by Mr. Petit
and completed by Mr. Lesveur leaves nothing to be desired as
to the details of the monument and *for the agreeable perspective from the bluff on whose summit it was found*" (italics
added).[6] In the course of their explorations, other burial sites
were discovered that also had outstanding scenic views.

Why would these supposedly isolated and primitive people select the most scenic areas for their memorials? What is
so strongly felt by the living about views of scenery that they
are sanctified as sites for the dead? Is there an undeniable
human need for scenic views and beauty that exists in all
cultures? Why is natural beauty important to us?

These are the questions that Paul Shepard's book *Man in
the Landscape: A Historic View of the Esthetics of Nature*
begins to answer. What gives landscapes special meanings?
What effect has our cultural tradition had on beliefs about
nature? My belief, and Paul Shepard's, is that there exists in
all people a basic need for nature and for views of nature—

that is, human nature. Traditions imposed by history affect our appreciation of the esthetic experience.

Yet, canoeing along Australia's Murray River some years ago, Paul Shepard said to me: "The ideas in *Man in the Landscape* are an inadequate model. I tried to examine the traditions created from landscape painting, literature, gardening, and the notion of paradise and to reconcile these with an ecological perspective, but it left a hollow of incompleteness and I moved past that."

He was wrong in his asssessment. I argued then and continue to believe that *Man in the Landscape* is the foundation work of a collection of important books. Each of Paul Shepard's books represents part of a continuous odyssey towards an understanding of human ecology.

I hesitate to use the phrase human ecology because of the layers of interpretation that are possible. Yet, it is the correct term, and Paul Shepard has been providing pioneering insights on this subject since *Man in the Landscape*'s initial publication in 1967. That book, and each successive book he wrote, peels back another layer in helping us better understand what is conveyed by an ecology of humans.

Today my copy is worn with years of use, its value increased by underlinings and column notations. Each reading is provoking, and contains insights that make it more appreciated today than when it first appeared. *Man in the Landscape* is about a complex subject. It is better understood after successive readings and better after reading all of Paul Shepard's other books and returning to reread it again. For full understanding of his odyssey and explorations of human ecology, each book should be read as if one were reading chapters, rather than books, comprising a single volume.[7]

In one of his later books, *Nature and Madness*, Shepard argues that if we truly understood an ecology of man, our society would reflect a different situation than the one we know so well: "Among people, the effects of stress and anxiety associated with the conditions of urban life have manifold symptoms including virtually every physical complaint and emotional twitch, sexual deviation and chaotic child raising. The 'tendency to paranoia,' a persuasive feeling of fear, provokes the individual into spurious explanations with perceptual and ideological consequences."

I believe that as humans, as very adaptable and tolerant beings, we can live in a variety of ways, most of which are not so bad that they cause immediate ill health. The answers Paul Shepard is seeking would not guarantee a better life; however, I do believe they would enhance the probability of achieving a higher quality of life. His books offer insights into how we could live in environments planned and designed for perceptual and phenological richness.

The foundation for this understanding can be found in *Man in the Landscape*. What is meant by the esthetics of nature? What is our relationship to nature and viewing natural scenes?

He begins this exploration by ranging across a complex set of topics. Each chapter is both a search for connections outward from his central theme and a foreshadowing of the books yet to be written. In *Man in the Landscape* I find the younger Paul Shepard beginning to understand the literature on hunting and gathering people that would lead to *The Tender Carnivore and the Sacred Game*. There are other passages that indicate his developing interest in normative ontogeny and the symbolism of animals in child development that resulted in *Thinking Animals*, *Nature and Madness*, and *The Sacred Paw*. This multivolume understanding of human ecology has its genesis in *Man in the Landscape*.

Any book that covers concepts of evolution, art history, sense of place, landscape appreciation, tourism, wilderness, hunting/gathering societies, and environmental degradation is going to be difficult but very rewarding. Shepard's ideas were ahead of their time when published in 1967. Even today, when holism is accepted, his breadth of coverage is profound. As example (From chapter two, "A Sense of Place," p. 28):

> Given a choice of temperatures, humidities, pressures, odors, vibrations, light intensities, wind velocities, and spatial structures, an animal moves to or builds what

amounts to a combination satisfying for him. To man paradise is the desired ultimate unity of these conditions, but the daily business of living deflects the searcher and routes him out. Environments change. The quest continues as long as life.

(From chapter three, "The Image of the Garden," p. 118):

Since the garden is an abstraction of the natural organic world, it is not surprising that it is depreciated or perverted in our machine-oriented society. Perhaps the same set of values cheapens the place of women, whose organic creativity is both materialized and etherealized as the garden. The garden has not ceased to be important as an art form, but its present destitution marks our "conquest" of the natural world.

(From chapter six, "Fellow Creatures," p. 211):

What do the hunt and kill actually do for the hunter? They confirm his continuity with the dynamic life of animal populations, his role in the complicated cycles of elements, his sharing in the sweep of evolution, and his place in the paterns of the flow of energy and in the web of his own society.

(From chapter seven, "Varieties of Nature Hating," pp. 214, 215):

The machinery for pigeon-holing the ravagement of nature is itself part of the process. We treat nature as though it were something out there, separate from ourselves, which we can turn over to a bureaucracy. It is convenient to blame the destruction of nature on impersonal, inexorable, collective forces incidental to progress, technology, or civilization. . . . We are like blind men exploring, not parts of an elephant, but the root system of a forest, the eddies of an estuary. The only certainty we have is that it is *our* monster; it is us.

Paul Shepard's books taught me that we could live better, see more, sense more, enjoy life more when we are attuned to biological cycles, when we are aware of phenological richness.[8] We spent a very long time evolving in an environment in which our health and our sanity were conditioned by an awareness of changes in biological patterns. Our ancestors knew when it was time to harvest or hunt or forage by a sensitivity that is almost lost to us now. Not being attuned to natural cycles has left us the poorer, the more deprived. It is awareness of how we fit in the cycles that is now lost.[9] As a concept it should receive more consideration in the planning of our cities, our towns, and in our own personal development.

With such beliefs, it is not surprising that chapter six of *Man in the Landscape*, entitled "Fellow Creatures," is of special interest to me. In this section Shepard explores concepts about the environment as they have been affected by our hunting and gathering traditions. By traditions he means both evolutionary imprinting and more recent hunting behavior. Shepard argues that hunting "may be regarded as a form of behavior that unites men with nature rather than alienating them." For some, this view will seem out of context in 1990. As Vance Bourjally has argued, for those of us who are in middle age or beyond, it is strange to know that a large fraction of society which once accepted hunting now considers it repugnant. I have come to believe that Shepard's position reflects a very thoughtful and sophisticated understanding of human ecology.

In 1972 Paul Shepard helped arrange for the translation of philosopher José Ortega y Gasset's *Meditations on Hunting*, originally published in 1942. This book remains the most lyrical and poignant statement about the consciousness of hunters and gatherers.[10] It was Paul Shepard who raised the question about what was the importance of this hunting activity which dominated our evolution and José Ortega y Gasset who described a kind of participation with and attention to nature that is now foreign to us.

The chapter "Fellow Creatures" is typical of the other chapters in *Man in the Landscape* and Shepard's other books. It is provocative, it makes one think about another set of questions that are peripheral to the central ideas of the book. These questions can transform one's professional and personal life because they are concerned with human ecology. From this point new questions from other perspectives affect our growth.

Consider the implications of the chapter on fellow creatures. The essential argument is that hunting and gathering activities dominated a considerable majority of our evolution. They do not occupy a significant part of our life today. What is lost? Hunting itself is not the answer or the question. In a world of ever-increasing population and resource depletion, hunting is not even a viable alternative for the many. Shepard challenges us to think about what is lost from a mature understanding of human ecology and the determinism of our evolution.

Many years ago, as a young boy, I was initiated into a special place that was described as the Old Shack. Memories of those times come easily—it's autumn, the sky is bright blue, and the rushes are gold. All those people are alive again. I am eleven years old. I am lying in a big brass bed, in the dark, and smelling kerosene from the other room. In the next room, my father's friends laugh good, deep laughs. I can remember the glasses tinkling and the sound of hearty appetites for good life. I cannot visit it in actuality, but it is not impossible to get back to it in my mind. It was the magical quality about the trips, between my own imagination as a child and the real excitement of what we were doing, that made those "shack times" such an experience for me. And it is these types of experiences that are becoming more lost to us all.

That old shack taught me *how to learn to see*, it taught me about *perceptual richness*. How did it do that?

Through successive visits: which revealed similar areas but different events: today a golden reflection on the water, with silk-like spider webs floating off to nowhere; tomorrow a change to choppy cold gray waves and fingers that cannot bend.

Through "rites of passage": most importantly, to see my own changing over the years in the context of everything else being stable, yet slightly changing. The importance of growing up and experiencing hunting traditions day by day with fathers, uncles, and friends—side by side.

Through foraging: to understand the natural world and

be able to gather from it means that your perceptions are honed to its changes. Your knowledge is a way of understanding change and learning the cycles of nature.

Through a chronology of explorable spaces: of course, a marsh with a canoe as one's transport is particularly good for this, but the lesson of learning to see *sequential* change has been one of design's most important lessons: "travel not arrival."

Through association with people and events: to learn the continuity of association with people or things one has never actually seen. It does make a difference to us if someone we revere or treasure also slept, walked, or thought about life here at this place. And this association continues as memories from our past are linked with physical connections to the present.

Through imagination about changes: those to come, and later to remember about things that were. As Edith Cobb tells us: "wonder and imagination are the genesis of knowledge."[11]

In *Man in the Landscape*, and in Shepard's other books, you are forced to ask about a concept like hunting and its role in human development, in an ecology of man. Similar questions are asked about all forms of alienation from nature. The specifics are not as important as our need to understand what we must hold on to for our own development, to reunite the perception of the spirit with nature and natural beauty.

A relationship with the natural world can lead to knowing its perceptual richness and eventually understanding ourselves. Once this is understood, then we embark on an *entirely different way of seeing*.

T. H. White in the *Book of Merlyn* writes of an old King Arthur on the evening before the final battle: "He suddenly felt the intense sad loveliness of being as being, apart from right or wrong: that, indeed the mere fact of being was the ultimate right. He began to love the land under him with a fierce longing, not because it was good or bad, but because it was: because of the shadow of the cornstalks on a golden evening, . . . because the clouds in the daylight would surge it into light and shade, because the squadrons of green and golden plovers, worming in pasture fields would advance in short, unanimous charges, head to the wind. . . ."[12]

Michael Martin McCarthy

NOTES

1. Disagreements exist about the actual time frame; however, archaeologists are in general agreement that people lived in Tasmania for over twenty thousand years. About twelve thousand years ago total inundation of Bass Strait occurred as the climate became warmer during the last ice age. See R. Jones, "Tasmania's Ice-Age Hunters," *Australian Geographic* 8 (Oct./Dec., 1987): 26–42.

2. There are various interpretations about the extinction of Tasmanian Aboriginals, who probably numbered four thousand and comprised nine to twelve distinct nomadic communities prior to settlement. While all the original native people were exterminated and dispossessed, descendants exist as a result of interbreeding with European sealers and settlers. These people of mixed heritage lost most of the aboriginal culture. See L. Ryan, *The Aboriginal Tasmanians* (St. Lucia, Australia: University of Queensland Press, 1982).

3. A thoughtful summary of the Tasmanian Aborigines can be found in the last chapter of N. J. B. Plomley, *The Baudin Expedition and the Tasmanian Aborigines, 1802.* (Tasmania, Australia: Blubber Head Press, 1983), pp. 160–213.

4. Ibid., pp. 56–57.

5. Ibid., p. 58. On the next day, in an equally beautiful site with an impressive vista, Peron found a second monument and in his text he presents a convincing argument that these structures would soon be destroyed by the weather, and feels fortunate to have discovered two.

6. Ibid., p. 60.

7. *The Sacred Paw*, with Barry Sanders (New York: Viking, 1985); *Nature and Madness* (San Francisco: Sierra Club, 1982); *Thinking Animals* (New York: Viking, 1978); *The Tender Carnivore and the Sacred Game* (New York: Scribners, 1973); *Environ/mental: Essays on the Planet as a Home*, with Daniel McKinley (Boston: Houghton Mifflin, 1971); *The Subversive Science, Essays Toward an Ecology of Man*, with Daniel McKinley (Boston: Houghton Mifflin, 1969); *English Attitudes towards the New Zealand Landscape before 1850*, Pacific Viewpoint Monographs #4, (Wellington, New Zealand, 1969); *Man in the Landscape: An Historic View of the Esthetics of Nature*, (New York: Knopf, 1967; College Station: Texas A&M University Press, 1991).

8. Some of these ideas were first published in *Landscape Aus-*

tralia in an article entitled: "What Would Be the Form of Our Cities and Towns If Living Well Really Mattered?" (1987): 237–41.

9. The importance of natural cycles is presented in a new work by Michael Young entitled *The Metronimic Society: Natural Rhythms and Human Timetables* (Cambridge: Harvard University Press, 1988). Some of the most widely read environmental books are about natural cycles. Henry David Thoreau's *Walden*, ed. J. L. Stanley (Princeton: Princeton University Press, 1971), and Aldo Leopold's *Sand County Almanac* (New York: Oxford University Press, 1949). Leopold's interest in phenological phenomena extended to his scientific papers, e.g., A. Leopold, and S. E. Jones, "A Phenological Record for Sauk and Dane Counties, Wisconsin 1935–1945," *Ecological Monographs* 17 (1946) 1:82–122. This "Walden/Sand County Almanac" theme of the cycles of nature and human interaction is continued in many other writings: R. Adams, and M. Hooper, *Nature through the Seasons* (New York: Simon and Schuster, 1975); R. Adams and M. Hooper, *Nature Day and Night* (London: Penguin Books, 1980); G. Firth, *A Natural Year* (New York: Simon and Schuster, 1980); S. Hill, *The Magic Apple Tree: A Country Year* (London: Penguin Books, 1982); B. Logan, *The Land Remembers* (Madison: Stanton and Lee, 1985).

10. José Ortega y Gasset, *Meditations on Hunting* (New York: Charles Scribner's Sons, 1985). Another writer who beautifully describes the level of participation of hunter/gatherers is Laurens Van der Post. See *A Story Like the Wind* (New York: William Morrow and Company, 1972) or *Testament to the Bushmen*, with Jane Taylor (New York: Viking, 1984).

11. E. M. Cobb, *The Ecology of Imagination in Children* (London: Routledge and Kegan Paul Ltd., 1977).

12. T. H. White, *The Book of Merlyn: The Unpublished Conclusion to the Once and Future King* (Austin: University of Texas Press, 1977), p. 151.

Preface

THE PROSPECT OF this new printing of *Man in the Landscape* seemed at first a chance to make the big revisions and little touches that had come to mind over the years since its publication. I had wished, for example, that my language and thought (even the title) had not been so sexist, that the material on the diaries from the Oregon Trail had been fleshed out, that I had given more to the history of Christianity's ideas of nature, that there were more illustrations. Now it seemed that the opportunity of a new edition might bring those topics to a kind of glorious maturity. Then I realized that it would be a mistake.

In 1967 one reviewer wrote that Paul Shepard "has parlayed his doctoral thesis into a book," and I was stung by his image of me hunched at the gaming table of Literature, pushing my one chip here and there with cunning or luck, squeezing a windfall from work that had already served its purpose, the perfect example of the academic drudge compelled by his trade to publish or else. The thirteen years between the thesis and the book's publication were invisible to the reviewer. He could feel nothing of the effort of seemingly endless rewriting, dragging the manuscript here and there summers where I worked between academic seasons. I wrestled both with the devils who disintegrated the book's diverse topics and with my inner demons who thwarted the writing of lucid English.

It is the scope of those years that now deters me from rewriting a new edition. The book was part of a period both for me personally and for the meaning of nature in America. That time seems volcanic to me now, extending from 1950— when I left the employment of a sportsman's organization, the Missouri Conservation Federation, to go to graduate school— to 1967, when the book was published. At its beginning I was an organizer of "conservation" clubs in order to influence the state legislature, at its end a professor, a hunter awakening surprised, in academia.

Of course, much else was at work outside myself. Between 1954 when the thesis was written and 1967 when the book came out, life in America changed. Ideas of gender, race, and nature were radically shifting. The era started with Eisenhower and ended with Johnson; began with our government's effort to dismantle American Indian lands and ended with that effort blocked by a burgeoning general sensitivity to the earth wisdom of native Americans; began with nature as "natural resources" and moved into the era of "land ethics." The modern environmental movement came into existence. I was being educated, and the manuscript could barely keep up.

The reviewer could not have known either, or perhaps understood, how I felt and still do feel about the kindly patience of my editors, the late Phil Vaudrin and then Angus Cameron at Knopf Inc., or of Alfred A. Knopf's own doubts that the book had a clear audience, that it would "fall between two stools"—a graceless comment that did nothing for my confidence even while it hardened my determination.

It is tempting to say that by 1967 the book had finally become all of a piece, but I don't think it ever did. The notion does not do justice to the price paid, the black hole of perpetual revisions in which frustration contributed to acts of personal and professional desperation. In the end I knew the thing had become an obsession. Perhaps that overwrought and overlong passion for coherence is why I wrote the throw-away chapter descriptions in the table of contents, an effort to recover some irony in an otherwise dogged project, subtitles which brought a snort from one of my former teachers who saw my effort at whimsy as trivializing.

In spite of a nomination for a National Book Award and

a Ballantine edition in 1970, *Man in the Landscape* was not widely read. Perhaps, as Knopf predicted, it had no identifiable audience. It also offered few solutions to problems. As Ivan Illich says of his own work, I find identifying and understanding the issues wholly demanding. Cadres of experts are needed for solutions. I also think the book's obscurity may have been a result in part of my failure to cultivate the literary establishment. I have always thought of myself as a naturalist, reading as my means, not much interested in literature, in professional literary journals and organizations, or in reviewing and editing. I now know that, unless one is especially gifted—an Aldous Huxley or Loren Eiseley—one's books may be invisible to those whose favor may make a difference. This unhappy fact produces a pain in the ego, against which one creates such solaces as a fantasy fellowship with Thoreau, whose *Walden* also got stuck between pen and print for thirteen years and made no great waves when it did appear.

Over the years I have found who the book's readers were. They wrote me letters. They were an idiosyncratic mix of visionaries, young geographers and landscape architects, ecology-minded proto-philosophers and historians, even a skein of biologists interested in the margins of their field. I now see that we were trying to reinvent "landscape," to see it as a middle ground if you will, where visual perception, nature esthetics, and ecological order might meet, to find an area of understanding released from the opposition between Art and Science, even from the tyranny of the disciplines.

A virtual embodiment of this congress of perspectives had already been represented by my mentors at Yale. I can still see them seated together at a folding (not a conference) table, discussing what such a thesis as mine might attempt: Paul B. Sears, the ecological conservationist; G. Evelyn Hutchinson, the erudite zoologist; William Jordy, then a keen young art historian; the eminent architect Christopher Tunnard; and sometimes Ralph Henry Gabriel, the historian of distinction. No student could have been more fortunate in the array of elders during those mid-century years when "interdisciplinary" study was considered in bad taste.

If this book is in any way prescient, it is because of the generous venture of those five onto turf at the edges of their fields. Since its publication every topic in this book has been enlarged by more knowledgeable students than myself, working on outdoor sensory psychology, the natural philosophy of gardens and landscape painting, the phenomenology of travel, gender issues in nature attitudes, human ethology in territory and domain, the significance of place, the intrinsic ecological morality of foraging peoples, the history of the national parks, and the cultural baggage of immigrants in the American West.

Looking back, I now realize that I was attempting to apply an old question to new material. To what extent can ideas be regarded as causes of our actions? At mid-century Aldo Leopold coined the phrase, "land ethic." In 1967 Lynn White's essay "The Cultural Roots of Our Ecological Crisis" set off a debate that continues today on whether Christianity is responsible for our environmental despoliation. It first appeared in print several months after I had attempted the same theme in the "Nature-Hating" chapter here. My less authoritative and much less magisterial effort was also qualified by pointing to the positive themes of responsibility and compassion in both Judaism and Christianity. Although the history of ideas does still seem to me to have been a neglected facet of our ecological debacle, I suspect that there is a prior impact of place on mind-set, that desert-edge conditions and catastrophic deforestation and erosion of Mediterranean and Near Eastern soils into the sea, for example, are essential to understanding Western world views.

The subtitle of this book, "An Historic View of the Esthetics of Nature," indicates that I had wandered, ecologically, into the history of art. In the years following its publication the idea of landscape as a magic concept was dealt a terrible blow for me by Marshal McLuhan. By terrible I mean that the assumptions on which I was working were crushed by his insight that the pictorial image and the mathematical vision with which it is synonymous were alienating rather than unifying. I have never been or wanted to be a neutral observer. Before my academic career I had twice been a whistle-blower in state and national park services. My vocation is the advocacy of the natural world and a human harmony with it. McLuhan, contradicting generations of historians, made it clear that the sixteenth-century invention of *landskip*, ostensibly sympathetic to nature, was in fact the mask behind which Francis Bacon's and Rene Descartes's agenda for the domination of nature coopted a rising sentiment. Linear perspective, that reflex within which our modern delineation arises, was not a loving means of verification, but of distancing, detaching, and disintegrating—the means of stepping out of the picture.

In my own redaction of McLuhan, I have come gradually to realize that landscape became a kind of cultural icon, a wedge by which the ideology of exploitation of the environment and of the philosophy of human exception from the natural realm thwarted an impulse which all of us share deep in the bone as a human endowment. If, basically, the landscape meant the wonder and mystery of the natural world, those feelings of an intuitive sense of shared existence and a common ground of being, it was used to subvert and capture that impulse by transforming it into scenery. Thus it served corporate greed and the industrialization of the world. The landscape provided a facade of conventional appearances that denied our real work, turning us all into voyeurs and tourists.

Calendar pictures, tours in protected and contrived places, media-selected "nature," and all the forms of the industrial park offered escape from the real world of biospheric and ecosystem devastation around us. The relativism that emerged in early-twentieth-century art theory siphoned through the landscape concept to nature itself. For example, in a double-page advertisement in the *Saturday Review* a logging company in the mid-1960s proclaimed, "If you think it's beautiful now, wait until we chop it all down." Posturing as an art critic, the company knew that the public had absorbed the notion that "beauty is in the eye of the beholder" and that landscape beauty, that is, the quality of nature, was subject to shifts in taste and personal preference. No tree falls, the psychologists told their freshmen, where no human ear hears the crash.

The idea was adroitly argued by one of its proponents,

the geographer David Lowenthal, to whom I owe the horrifying realization that this thesis—that the value and beauty of nature is but a form of taste—had a strong appeal to intellectuals and educated people in general. I suddenly saw that the arrogance of humanism was not only the moral basis of a utilitarian culture and popular self-indulgence, but was also thriving where it had first been nurtured, in the arena of arts and letters. When Lowenthal attacked the meaning of the buffalo and the esthetic of wilderness as "merely a congeries of feelings" I could see that the new criticism had been applied to nature. As a creed of the "new critics" it was craft, not content, that was important, and the esthetics of nature could be judged like any work of art. This was the landscape, which I had taken as an appropriate vehicle for the integration of "intangible" and utilitarian values and as the means of reconciling both with ecological ideas.

And so the landscape was stood on its ear, serving ends to which I, as a naturalist, was opposed. A certain part of me was paralyzed. Over the years after, I took a long turn away from the concept, seeking in anthropology, psychology, and history for a new instrument.

But the turn away was an arc, ultimately permitting a circling back from the other side. The "portraits of place" by which the Dutch and Italian painters translated the new idea of portraits of persons into the subject of the broad-scale environment, implied a new scrutiny and a renewed sensitivity. The representation of what Ortega calls "our circumstances" does not have to be ruled by linear rationality, though that is its history. I still believe that a concept such as the landscape offers a wonderful potential for reuniting our fragmented experience and understanding. Such a device is necessary to help free us from three millennia of the despiritualizing of a world ultimately whole and sacred, and the splintering of ideas conferred on modern thought by three centuries of materialist greed and waste.

What such a concept might be other than the landscape I do not know. Ecosystems and biomes remain too theoretical and abstract. In the chapter on the image of the garden I have expressed doubts that "Mother Earth" (now popularly referred to as "the Gaia hypothesis") is the figure we seek, although an organic metaphor is surely better than the vitiated notion of a world machine.

Today I have no doubt that in eighteenth- and nineteenth-century landscape pictures, garden imagery and language were diversions from real destruction, lending themselves to that education of the eye in which popular judgment about the visual world found its criteria. But, having recovered from my McLuhan/Lowenthal trauma, I can glimpse the surviving virtue of the idea. Those same lithographs of sublime mountains, imitations of beautiful pastorality, and all the yearning of the silly tourists with their cameras can also be seen as the bad performance of a true virtue. They were enacting the awkward indigenization of a ruling culture, like the paganizing of the Church as it absorbed new peoples; in this case a desire for wholeness subordinated to the destitution and seduction of the landscape arts by the control-growth-and-consuming mania of both Marxists and capitalists.

Even if the idea of the landscape became a tool of the destroyers, diverting our attention from the decimations and wreckage of chemical and engineering technology, it was and is even so a sign of deep yearning for a natural presence. It may have been used to misdirect that feeling, but the bent for the "romantic" ideas, that is, the natural world as an organic counterplayer, is viable and sound. In the face of the narrow motives of the masters of economic progress, the arts of the landscape—especially travel, gardening, painting, and natural history—express a healthy concern and endure. They have only to disentangle from a mission of inventory, artistic relativism, and the legacies of Renaissance humanism. Renewal is already in motion. Indications are in the many new studies of place, awakened attention to the feminine qualities of experience, the holographic parallels of the structure of the brain and the terrain, the deep psychic value of wildness, the recovery of a generic sense of the human habitation, the need for conceptual and perceptual tools in the awakening of bioregional consciousness, and the remaining tasks of articulating the sensory modes and philosophical genius of indigenous peoples in ways that will mend the landscape's overly visual and crippling literary reference.

Instead of its being one subject matter in art, we may come to see the landscape as the story of our being. It represents the idea of a context once described as the ground of a gestalt in which being alive and being human is the figure. But that metaphor relies on a static contrast or opposition. New and better metaphors are emerging. To this creativity, *Man in the Landscape* is rededicated and is in some ways, I hope, antecedent.

Preface to First Edition

§

IN THE MATTER OF indebtedness of idea and motive I find that there are so many to whom I owe so much that I have the feeling of being only a nexus of the momentum of others' thoughts and despair of claiming anything herein to be original. I am like a coral animal who stands ready to take something from every passing tidal current, and I feel not only grateful but almost guilty for turning the wisdom, money, love, and time of others into so much rock, or, as the case may be, carbon dioxide. Pre-eminent among them are my parents and my teachers. Among the latter to whom I owe a great deal are Paul B. Sears, John Collier, G. Evelyn Hutchinson, and the late Rudolf Bennitt.

Others whose aid and encouragement I wish to acknowledge are William VanDeventer, Dan McKinley, Christopher Tunnard, William Jordy, Hermann Muelder, William Matthews, Hans Huth, John B. Jackson, and Melba Shepard.

Support at one time or another in the course of this accumulation came from the National Council of State Garden Clubs, the National Wildlife Federation, and Smith College. Knox College contributed a faculty travel grant and assistance for travel from the Ely Lilly Fund, the opportunity to try these ideas on students for a decade, helpfully critical colleagues, and other institutional indulgences in a dark-horse project. No government agency had any hand whatever in this undertaking.

My wife, June Shepard, has been my best critic.

Except for Chapter VII, a primitive form of this book was accepted as a doctoral thesis at Yale University. Parts of Chapters I, II, V, and VIII have appeared in *Landscape*. Other parts of Chapter V are in the *Proceedings of the 12th North American Wildlife Conference*. Parts of Chapter I appeared in *School Science and Mathematics*, and parts of Chapter IV in the *College Art Journal*.

Paul Shepard

Introduction

🙐

"TO PUT IT BLUNTLY," said my friend, "nature is out of date." He had already enumerated the various forms of impending world disaster, the smoke everywhere of social and political conflagrations, the drift of peoples in frantic search for identity and security, the removal of geographical frontiers to outer space, and the perverted state of leisure which made lackluster the slow rhythms of organisms and landforms.

By nature's being out of date he meant that the question of its relationship to man had receded, or was accorded only despair. The sharp joy of the outdoors was blunted against new cynicism.

The natural environment had seemed pertinent to the human situation until the present century. Its relevance diminished behind concrete and steel. The confrontation of nature succumbed to a fashion of discounting the possibility of knowing anything about the "real" universe, even to doubt that it exists. Weighted with older cultural anti-nature the current agony of human isolation could be used to free man from determinism or to plunge him into a hopeless fatalism, abandoning either way the idea of happiness in the bosom of nature or reliance on a "natural order."

The existentialist division of man and nature is a reaction to the use of science on man's thinking about himself, to its generalizing and abstracting, to depersonalizing, to finding norms and averages and generally "reducing" humanity to statistical traits. The existential judgment is that these abstractions are irrelevant. It holds that therefore only what *I* experience for myself is real: events unique to me, about which no generalizations are important or any real descriptions possible. Only specific contacts with other individuals are considered significant. Every moment I face the prospect of a choice, which I am actually free to make. I am free only in this. Such is the excruciating sickness of self-consciousness.

The proponents of this fanatic individualism retreat from a hostile and absurd world to an inner life whose only values are personal and subjective. By valuing only the unique and individual they rightly oppose mass man and the treatment of human beings as replacable machines—at the price of ecological nihilism. It is the act of a screaming and demented oyster.

The apprehension of human alienation from nature is not new—nor is the isolation of the individual uniquely human —but in this situation it too easily justifies our destruction of the world and each other, ignorance of other life, insistence on the dichotomy of man and animals, and organized narcissism. Because society is a leveling agency it is to be made irrelevant. The attempt to care nothing for nature outside individual experience is a pseudo-separation from nature in a world composed only of objects, a frozen place where there are no significant events other than the flashing lights of one's own mind.

As my friend attempted to explain how intellectual nature hating had come about I thought of our immediate habitat there in Illinois. I wondered exactly how this intellectual relativity was related to the things we were doing to our world. Adolf Portmann has observed that in the past "man had to defend himself against natural catastrophes, wild animals, outside influences of every sort, and had somehow to survive despite them. Today it is we who uproot and transform, who threaten nature." Not far from us as we conversed, the world's biggest shovel was gouging a forty-foot-deep trench through the prairie soil and underlying rock to get to a layer of coal. The logic and importance of this activity was periodically explained to the public by the mining company's public-relations officers. Was it part of the imminent tragedy described by Portmann or was it, as the company claimed, a public service? Publicity would not cloak the wound in the earth; indeed the cut uncovered all those rationalizations and passions in the deep layers of the mind which would be twisted into a eulogy of destruction.

Some of the coal-company values my humanist friend would have shared, though he might have objected to such thinly veiled cupidity masquerading as service, which would change from time to time in step with "the economy." An economic system is a human fabrication. And so is perception, said my sophisticated friend. Nobody believes in "natural laws" any more. If ocean currents, whole forests, and the gaseous content of the atmosphere are to be manipulated by men it violates only natural laws, once thought to govern these systems but now recognized as human inventions or appropriate abstractions. These constructs change with the advance of science. Who could trust his pleasure or his convictions concerning nature in such an inconstant reality?

But hasn't the Darwinian revolution reached you with the message of man's continuity with nature? I asked. To be sure it has, but the sword has another edge than the containment of man in a natural order; it is a theory of change, for growing up and away, developing above and beyond the primitive, a creative emergence. What could be more evolutionary than that? Hasn't an outstanding biologist, Julian Huxley, said that man is the end-all of evolution? That in man organic evolution ends and a new evolution begins? And Teilhard de Chardin has left us the gifted vision of man as the evolutionary step toward angelhood.

So, the next step is to "control the world environment." Not long ago the director of the Minnesota Institute of Technology, Athielstan Spilhaus, writing in the *Geographical Review*, explained what this means. He spoke for the technical realization of vainglorious ideas of the exalted place of man. Control of the world is based, he says, on an "essential difference" between man and the lesser animals: his ability to modify the environment for his own benefit. Zoologists will be surprised to hear this, as there are many species of animals in every major group which do so, some by very elaborate devices. Shelter-seeking, building, herding, agriculture, and food storage Spilhaus alleges to be uniquely human, but all of these occur among the insects alone, and shelter-seeking and food storage are so common among mammals that it is difficult to think of any families in which these traits do not occur.

That part of the world unoccupied by man he calls "the presently uncomfortable empty areas." A compulsive drive toward an unlimited human population and its spread into the "empty" spaces is the underlying theme of his paper. It needs only in addition an editorial which Lawrence S. Kubie, M.D., once wrote for the *Saturday Review*, prophesying victory over human death and the attainment of physical immortality. Such is the vision of heaven on earth; the best of all possible worlds and an artifically sustained interminable life to "enjoy" it.

Spilhaus asserts that "we do not now rob Nature." Yet, in the rich soils of the Midwest where the farms are prosperous it is necessary to drive many miles to find a farm in biological equilibrium with its environment, for these "model" farms are operated by drawing on the accumulated capital of a deep till soil, force-feeding with nutrient elements, the broad-scale use of chemical herbicides and pesticides, and increasingly efficient extractive machinery.

We are on the verge, he says, of "an explosion of technology." This is appropriate terminology for describing an economy based on exploding matériel. He continues, "The aim of our learning in science, both natural and social, and in the arts and humanities should be to maximize improvement of our living conditions, including the constant raising of human values, with the minimum exhaustion of real resources." But what are the *real* resources for the good life? Even a small change in techniques may disrupt the internal structure of a society. Some societies absorb and adjust, others are refractory, but even the most resilient need to make the changes at their own tempo. In the name of progress we have served the "backward," "underdeveloped" peoples with an ultimatum, but will the biologist and anthropologist be heard on the question of pace as well as direction?

The future of nuclear power is said in his paper to be bright. We will shoot the radioactive residue off into interstellar space in "garbage scows." Out there is "truly plentiful space." That is what the pioneers and exploiters said about the American landscape when they laid down the now obsolete patterns of sewage and industrial-waste disposal in the nineteenth century. "Perhaps half of our common rock" could be converted into nuclear energy, Spilhaus exclaims. We will enclose larger spaces, putting whole towns under roof. Why put towns under roofs if we are going to control the world's environment, unless it is an exercise in the economics of his-and-her bathtubs and all the other fatuous manifestations of extravagant consumption and waste? The world, he says, will have immense new greenhouses, or "automatic food factories." Here "one would merely put plant nutrients in and take human nutrients out."

So far hydroponics produces a limited variety of very expensive and tasteless vegetables. Plant physiology, soil chemistry, and the very nature of climate have a way of withholding ultimate secrets. Complete engineering success would require the creation of a living system resembling the organization found in undisturbed nature. What the technicians are so painfully piecing together in pursuit of a stable, productive, efficient greenhouse already exists, but is disappearing beneath their feet as they destroy it to create space in which to try their relatively crude constructions.

And so we come to other aspects of engineering life and landscapes—the banishment of seasons, the abandonment of meat-eating, replacing the whole "present batch process" with a "chemical engineering process." We have for fifty years been witnessing the disappearance of agriculture as a "way of life" which Spilhaus's engineering would finish. Even apart from its process, is the older idiom and image of no value? What will happen to people without a pastoral ethos? Is it merely sentimental to observe that most of our philosophy, religion, and social form emerged in a world sustained by the "old" agriculture? Is the rural world truly a touchstone of renewal for the jading, corrosive drain of the city, or will parks and playgrounds do as well? Is the love of seasons only poetry and of the rural countryside a convention?

Spilhaus proceeds. He will condition the open spaces, master hurricanes, limit polar ice, dismiss night by manipulating sky glow. The rhythmic cyclicity of day and night is so fundamental a part of the living world that a biologist might well be speechless with premonition of disaster. Though ignoring the fate of perhaps half the world's organisms, Spilhaus does acknowledge some human problems. But these are not new: the "proper use of leisure," the need to use spare time in "contemplative and creative ways," matters of "sufficient wisdom," and so on. But there are no answers. It is enough that engineering will create heaven on earth. Overpopulation and resource depletion are pseudo-problems, obsessions of those who do not fully appreciate the convertibility of the untouched rivers of energy and materials into human protoplasm and the independence of that protoplasm from the life and landscape of the earth. Spilhaus and his ilk are not the most reckless men in history but, because of their tools, the most dangerous. The headlong race into a mechanical cornucopia conceived on the pushing and hauling of the physical foundations of our environment is worse than military brinkmanship because we have fewer moral and ethical restraints on our disposition of nature than of each other.

But the two are not disassociated; neither my humanist colleague nor Mr. Spilhaus would consider himself part of a natural field of events which was beautiful and orderly in the way I would. I do not believe that we could construct such a world without fatally disrupting interlocking systems that keep the biosphere—all of life on earth—intact. Human culture and life are inseparably locked into organic interrelations, element cycles, and energy transfers that bind many species of plants and animals to place and time and each other. This brotherhood has two dimensions: ecological, the dynamic web of the living; and evolutionary, the converging lines of antecedence. There is no freedom to be found in its denial, although it seems to me some existentialists seem to think so. The genetic coded model of the living being is a cumulative heritage of nearly infinite duration. It is the outcome of millions of embryological events in which the ego has no say. It does not deal only with the individual's embryonic life, as the processes of development never end; growth and change are inseparable within this system and are inexorably shaped by it. Time and experience continuously force new choices and irrevocable commitments in the formation and behavior of the individual. The genes are not absolute determiners, but their final expression depends on what the environment evokes. Their environment extends from the immediate nucleoplasm surrounding them in the cell to the distant stars. It ranges from the colloids and membranes upon which they float to the light from the sun and the croaking of frogs. As for the ego, it is free to learn where its freedom begins, if it will. It does not begin in the destruction of the organic world which produced it, though it may end there.

Most human experience of nature comes through a narrow window. It opens midway between molecules and the Milky Way. It is astonishing that our limited view makes any sense. Even so, the earth's surface, split by the horizon and animated by other life, is being written off as a dated trick, the food for technology or the backdrop for re-creation. It has ceased to be the way to God.

This harsh judgment on the surroundings is partly a disillusionment, a reaction to the frailty and fungible quality that we now see instead of "solid" reality. It is suggestive that science should make us cynics in nature—as science is ordinarily considered materialistic. Perhaps it is the lack of materialism in science which makes this so. We are frequently told that what ails mankind is its insatiable materialism, the glut of things in our lives. Warren Weaver has observed that we are virtually immersed in a single view, "one which many accept without realizing that they do so, and without realizing that there are alternative possibilities . . . the assumption that the whole quantitative time-space-mass-energy set of concepts which have been developed within the Greco-Judaic system is capable of capturing the variety and subtlety of nature." But it is easy to confuse time-space-mass-energy with materialism. Alan Watts has rightly pointed out that true materialists do not destroy their natural environment, that a real concern for material qualities does not permit the embrace of the shoddy, the synthetic, and the vulgar in tools, objects, clothing, and art.

Between existential despair and the utilitarian or conservative exploitation, the range of viewpoints has generated a frenzy of organization and communication. It is not in the interest of the exploiters or commercial users or professional managers to sanction a "soft" approach to nature, nor has "love of nature" the assent of those who have never seen their own lives against the loom of the wilderness.

I am not ready to interpolate a philosophy of cosmic benignancy, to mediate between the neo-humanists and the nature lovers. But I am dissatisfied with the present choices. Conservation has failed, as Joseph Krutch has so ably said, being nothing more than prudent exploitation. When it is not it does not understand itself. The attitude of despair and apathy is simply defeatist or, as an aggressive form of humanism, an intellectual and passive accessory to destruction.

That nature is out of date suggests that what we think of as a love of nature is a kind of fashionable sentiment. The difficulty is that this is both true and false. It is a sea of feelings, psychic imagery, literary and poetic insight, economic heritage, perceptual habit, and other factors interwoven with their own public and distorted manifestations. Nature is real and love of nature is part of its reality.

And so is alienation. As a biologist I believe that, given our present dominance and power, nature hatred is suicidal. Biology does not tell me whether we will hate or cherish, or even what constitutes each in our confusion. It does provide a foundation from which to examine and interrelate some ideas and social experiences as part of nature itself, a view of the natural history of man not limited to the natural.

Man in the Landscape

Chapter One

The Eye

THE HUMAN—the vertebrate—eye originated in the sea. Its basic structure is the same for all vertebrates, the most primitive of which are aquatic. When it is compared to eyes invented in the air, such as those of the insects, the differences are enormous; compared to eyes independently invented in the sea, such as those of the squids, the similarities are astonishing. An important difference between the sea eye and the land eye is the number of chambers, being multiple in the latter and single in the former. The single-chambered eye is apparently more effective in the murky, homogeneous, three-dimensional world of the sea. The flicker effect, which seems to be the advantage of the multiple ommatidia of the insect eye, is unnecessary in the sea, where, even on the bottom, light and dark are blurred in a universal penumbra, a gentle uniformity where total light gathering rather than flickering contrast is important.

With some slight additions and modifications, especially in the external protective structures and the size and shape of the lens, the vertebrates carried this eye onto the land. It was a very good eye, and was further perfected by terrestrial quadrupeds, probably both the amphibian labyrinthodonts and reptilian therapsids, before it came to the first of the mammals. But it was debased by the early mammals as excess baggage in their nocturnal lives and underground ways. Then certain of these insectivore-like creatures shifted back to daylight activity. Tree shrews have sharp eyes and may be very similar to the ancestors of the Primate order, to which lemurs, monkeys, apes, and man belong. One, the Philippine tree shrew, is diurnal, nervous, fussy, intelligent, inquisitive, omnivorous, clean, and nimble of forefoot. It has binocular vision, a round pupil, color vision, expressive eyes, and even humanlike ears. Some authorities think it is actually a primate, and it is indeed disconcerting to see these humanlike traits in a creature so much more primitive than a monkey.

Of all the mammals—some eighteen orders—the primates are almost alone in their seventy-million-year struggle to re-establish the primacy of vision. They have returned it to the daylight and built their lives around it, reinvented color vision, and made other improvements. Could this have happened with a compound eye and could it have been carried into the trees? To it the world is a mosaic with sharp partitions like the glue between hexagonal ceramic tiles. Then could it have provided the flexibility to be coordinated with the use of hands? Our thoughts are teased by the consequences of a rebuilt sea eye on the delicate ego of a grounded primate, or, more exactly, the role of a salvaged reptilian-amphibian-ichthyoform eye in making the man.

It is impossible to say whether good eyes or arboreality came first. What the "bottleneck" mammals, scrounging a living at night through the mid-Mesozoic, bequeathed to the primate ancestors was probably not much better than the dim little brown orbs of the modern ground shrews, the wasted remains of the elegant structures of the reptilian forerunners. Night eyes need not be degenerate if the animal remains eye-minded, as did the cat, owl, and tarsier; but near the ground or under it, where food is but fat grubs and crunchy roaches, there is no visual imperative. The smallness of the eye is itself a weakness, as it contains fewer sensory cells. And in the night eye these are entirely rods, the type of receptor functioning in dim light, their communication to the brain pooled by neural connections so that the message is "summated" and the ultimate picture coarse and colorless.

The first arboreal pre-primate forms may have clambered up trees at night as though following vertical trails. If so, these were "nosy" animals who rediscovered the use of vision only after electing to remain in trees. An animal heavily dependent on the sense of smell is a good candidate for the progenitor of a brainy one relying on sight, as a "braininess" specifically means elaboration of the cerebrum of the forebrain, whose enlargement was begun for the receiving, mixing, analyzing, and storing of information from the nose. The combination of ground and tree life, or even of traveling on the vertical and horizontal trails of tree trunks and branches, is a kind of re-entry of the sea eye into a three-dimensional world. In both, gravity is the principal orienting force, so that the proprioceptive sense of weight, the inner ear, and eye work together to separate experience into vertical and horizontal planes. Perhaps our esthetic feeling for symmetry and balance, our inclination to abstract the vertical and horizontal lines and to follow them with our eyes, belongs to the following of trunks and limbs, first with bodies and then by sitting and looking. When art critics talk about the "tension" or "motion" created in sculpture or painting by oblique lines, I am inclined to remember the primate preoccupation with the horizontal planes of the ground and forest canopy, the vertical trunks that connect them, and the occasional leaning tree that is neither one nor the other.

As for following those trails, very much depended on how it was done. Creatures who crawl, such as the raccoon and some of the lemurs, keep their long snouts. But these are a liability for jumpers. Not only does the nose get in the way upon landing but also it obscures the view ahead. Smell is not very important anyway in the trees, at least not for diurnal forms who depend upon seeing their enemies as well as their food. Within the broad scope of omnivorousness, emphasis shifts from insects to fruit and plant material; in its arboreal pursuit walking feet are modified into squirrel-like claws, tarsierlike pads, or fingerlike digits. Judging jumping distance is accomplished mainly by bringing both eyes to the front, as in tarsiers, cats, and monkeys. Though by no means the only approach to seeing depth, binocular stereoscopic vision is the most efficacious, depending on central fusion of unlike images from the two eyes. In man the total visual field is about 180 degrees, the zone of overlap or stereoscopy about half the total. When the slightly convergent eyes look at an object every part of it falls on corresponding parts of the two retinas and the two eyes normally move in conjunction.

Animals have become binocular for two reasons: predation and jumping, either or both. That much of the human eye is a product of life in the crown of a tropical forest is indicated by its similarity to the monkey eye. Our binocularity developed in jungle treetops where primate ancestors jumped from limb to limb. An extraordinary effect of this convergence of the lines of vision of each eye is that all objects at greater or lesser distances than the point of fixation are out of focus. Focusing is accomplished in each eye by adjustment of the tension of the fibers holding the lens and allowing the lens to change shape so as to focus the image at exactly the right distance away from the retina. The amount an object is blurred depends on the distance it is short of or beyond the point of fixation. Of course, the "point" of fixation is not a point at all, but part of a continuous curved "surface," each part of which is equidistant from the eye. All of this surface or horopter is not only in focus in each eye, but all parts of the image fall upon "corresponding points" in each eye—at least in animals whose eyes are conjugate, or moved together. All other objects and points, short of and beyond the shell-like horopter, are blurred and are seen double. Our visual life is spent in the center of a nearly hemispheric transparent shell whose distance from us we fixate. The rest of the world is a jumble of subliminal double images. These double images serve depth perception, however, because they are wider apart the farther they are from the two-dimensional screen of the horopter. Objects deliberately blurred by a landscape painter to suggest distance and nonfocus can give only weak approximations of actual distance. Our conscious awareness of this vast amount of duplication is not normally great, but its possible implications for our more basic mental events may include our widespread philosophical tendency to see the world dichotomously, as infinite antinomies. Horizontal lines are one component of the environment that are not seen double when the head is in a normal position. The practical effect of this is that jumpers in trees do not have to focus before leaping to another limb. Experimental work on visual habits shows that the eye, in a random examination of the surroundings, tends to follow flat lines and vertical lines. This contributes to our rectilinear sense of the world, a sense certified by the gyroscopic activity of the canals of the inner ear in their control over posture, motion, and equilibrium. We experience a kinesthetic relation between the sense of motion and the visual field, oblique lines giving a sense of motion as the eye moves swiftly along them in a search for the symmetry of verticals or horizontals on which to rest.

The sense of continuous distance is due to the continuous array of surfaces whose differential reflection of light is projected upon the two-dimensional surface of the retina as a gradient of ordinal stimulation. That is, a complex of perspectives is visually experienced as gradations into the distance. These are perspectives of texture, or changes in the density of patterns such as leaves, perspectives of size, convergent lines, amount of blur, the disparity gradient of double imagery, and motion perspective, or the amount of displacement of a distant object relative to a nearer one as the observer moves. Together with such clues to distance as overlapping and upward location in the visual field, these all contribute to the estimation of distance by a visual organ whose functional surface is nearly two-dimensional. The combined effect of these gradients is the visual continuum we perceive as relief or terrain. The diminishment of texture creates not only the impression of continuous distance by a regular gradient, but represents contours by breaks in the gradation. The same is true of grades of illumination, gradual transitions indicating curved surfaces, and abrupt changes showing protuberances and indentations in the terrain. These variations in shading and textural density, functions of the orientation of surfaces to light, give relief to a surface and are more important to sight than separate points of light.

As white light passes through the lens its colors refract at slightly different angles. The two ends of the color spectrum, at the limits of the frequencies which we see, cannot both be focused at once. For example, when we fixate adjacent red and blue patches the red seems close and the blue far away. It is also possible that we have a proprioceptive awareness of the ciliary muscle in the eye, whose contraction permits distension or focusing of the lens at points within about twenty feet, and also that we are clued to distance by the degree of convergence of the two eyes as the external eye muscles contract to keep them each directed at an approaching object.

That there are so many sources of distance information confirms the simple crucial necessity of accuracy and quick adjustment by a rapidly moving creature. The well-camouflaged sloth adopted one way of avoiding eagles and predatory cats, the squirrels another, and the ape ancestors still another. I doubt that the sloth cares much about judging distance or could very easily produce descendants who would make good test pilots or polo players.

Both monkeys and squirrels are concerned with spotting food that holds still and enemies that move. But it is not only the movement of an object that causes its image to shift on the retina. When the object is fixated, or looked at, its image is focused on the area of sharpest vision, the central area, and on a pit-like depression, the fovea, whose visual cells and geometry combine to produce the extreme resolution and visual acuity of which the eye is capable. The eye roves or scans just sufficiently for the image of the object to wander somewhat on the fovea. So, even when the object sits still, the set of gradients composing the image do not simply sit on the retina but shift constantly, producing an adjacent order of excitation of the visual cells called "ordinal stimulation." The image flows across the retina in a patterned arrangement of focused light. There is a constant ordered relation in this transposed image, somewhat like the shifting of light flashes on an animated electric sign.

Eye movement is also affected by body motion, turning of the head, and rolling of the eyes, all of which tend to displace the image. In addition, there is an extremely rapid vibratory scanning of only about half a second of arc, oscillating about one hundred times per second. This produces a flux in the input of any given visual cell producing the patterns of ordinal contrast which add the ultimate touch of keenness, so that lines and points are discriminated more finely than would otherwise be possible. The system cannot deal with a steady input; blindness to an object occurs if the object is vibrated so that its image holds a set position on the retina. Motion produces a necessary fluctuation of an image across the visual cells.

Scanning constantly tests the similarity or congruence of the sets of stimulae. The straight line exists by virtue of its congruence or repeatable pattern of signals. This mosaic system of vision selects certain of these congruent pattern systems which are frequently repeated in everyday life as unique. Such self-congruent forms as straight lines, parallels, equidistances are sought out, providing the most fundamental order of visual experience, the instinctive abstraction from the environment of geometric forms. Perhaps the bilateral symmetry of animals is one such pattern, the radial symmetry of some plants and animals another. In addition to being a pattern-locating system the eye is attracted by movement or motion of an object in the field of vision. Good-eyed animals are "interested in" moving objects.

A headlong dash through the treetops, the pursuit on foot of a woolly mammoth, and the broken-field running of a football player are part of the catalyst of motion in the development of the vertebrate eye, as it was carried from flight to pursuit, from tree to ground. Travel produces apparent displacement and skewing of the whole visual picture. If the traveler looks ahead, the point of fixation on the horizon becomes a germinating bud of landscape, from which the world dilates as he approaches. It flows on either side and above him in gradients of velocity and direction, finally diminishing and contracting toward a vanishing point behind which whole visual fields are swallowed up as new ones are born in front. To the side, nearby points pass rapidly, distant objects slowly, in a graceful, parallactic shearing. Every object in this fantastic deformation grows exponentially as we approach and shrinks as we depart. Only the clear sky is free of this deformation, its great vault serenely substantial because it has no surface. The impression of space does include the sky, the apparent distance of which varies according to illumination, weather, clouds, and its figure-ground relationship to terrestrial objects. Objects seen against the sky or against the terrain seem to contract as the field of view expands; that is, objects seem smaller when seen by an observer in the open than by one looking through a window. Life in the treetops is almost entirely one of looking through the windows, and so is the terrestrial visual effect of stalking.

As we pass through a forest, the graded motion of vegetation overhead does not seem a jumble of branches and leaves; on the contrary, the elaborate mesh and interlacing seems to untangle and each twig to take its proper place in space. Here too the visual world is different from a painting. A stationary observer tends to presume that all objects extend at right angles from his line of sight, as they do in a painting. But as he moves through an actual terrain the sense of being at the center of a three-dimensional world falls upon him with the delight of a continuous unfolding revelation. Perhaps this suggests to him that he is the center and therefore the master of all the world. We might expect the eagle, lion, stag, and man to have more egocentric personalities than such creatures as mice, grouse, opossums, or even whales.

As I have already mentioned, the curved surface of the retina does not deal uniformly with the image. Light entering the eye from a fixated object travels close to its geometric axis on its way to the central area. Here the retina is rich in cone cells, which maintain a high proportion of separate neural connections to the brain, so that the fovea conveys more separate bits of information to it than do other parts of the retina. The cone cells function in daylight and mediate color. The diameter of the fovea is about one degree of arc, and represents an emphatic refinement of keen vision. Most sharp-eyed forms have one or two foveae, especially if they are also intelligent. To "look at" is to bring the image of the object of attention into the fovea. The philosopher's capacity to "look at" an idea is related to the primate's recovery of the object of attention onto the fovea, and philosophers should give thanks for it. Without it they could do no better than be generally alert, their ultimate limits of philosophical speculation to isolate this or that in their world and their thinking. In view of the primate invention of the human fovea, the comic statue of the monkey meditating on Darwin's skull assumes a new, tender sense of mutuality.

The foveate retina is nonexclusive. It does not operate like a telescope or a zoom lens, blacking out the periphery. It is an area of sharpness in the visual screen of the sea eye, to which the whole visual field offers up possibilities for attention, a broad field within which the mind is directed. It partakes of the gestalt of figure and ground. Yet the peripheral portion is more even than a context, for the mind is not wholly seduced by concentration. The whole is continually perceived. The object on stage in the fovea is not separate from its environment. The surroundings give and take on meaning relative to the object. The complete abstracting of the object from its environment is one of those higher intellectual activities which can deliver new insights at new and almost unimagined risk.

The peripheral retinal image is not uniform. The relative proportion of rod to cone cells increases away from the center, so that the rim of the retina near the pupil is almost entirely rods. Here, acuity and color are minimal. Light strikes the peripheral retina at acute angles. An image in motion produces an exaggerated displacement as it sweeps across this part of the retinal surface which is oblique to the entering light. The combined effect of the diminished acuity and accentuated motion is that information from the limits of the visual field is almost entirely about motion rather than appearances. This is less true of nonfoveal animals such as tree squirrels, whose retinas are composed uniformly of cone cells; the squirrel's blander brain reflects its blander eyes.

The squirrel's eyes are set in the head in a compromising position to gain the widest possible visual field for safety against attack without losing an area of binocularity in front. Their eyes are about intermediately placed in the head between two extremes—those of the rabbit, which are set laterally for a 180-degree view, mostly monocular, and the complete frontal vision of the gorilla, who apparently doesn't have to worry so much about who might be coming up behind him, or who has other ways of finding out. The differentiation of parts of the retina is a concomitant of primate frontality and binocularity.

Man could not have been produced by any other than a diurnal arboreal ancestor. Of all the possible candidates for the honor of being the human ancestor, it is noteworthy that squirrels did not become monkeys and produce bipedal forms and terrestrial descendants. Certainly the order of rodents is a potent and vigorous group; rats are capable of enough braininess to tax the ingenuity of psychologists. The answer partly lies in the temperate center of origin for the squirrels as opposed to tropical origins for the monkeys, apes, and man. The frugality of the winter fare limited the squirrel to nuts and seeds; the season exposed him by either blowing away his leafy cover and driving him into the hollows of trees, thus keeping him small to fit holes, or, if we mean squirrels in coniferous forests, keeping him small enough to climb to the tips of the branches for cones. In either case the vicissitudes of living in a cold climate depleted his numbers so rapidly that a half-dozen young were necessary for replacement each year, in contrast to the higher primates.

In spite of the squirrel's genuine horticultural contribution of planting whole forests, there has not been as much mutual evolution between nuts and squirrels as between fruits and monkeys. Locating colored fruits may have been the making of the primate fovea, which lends itself so well to finding fleas and other sorts of mutual grooming such as we see at a cocktail party. It is possible that the lack of brightly colored nuts as much as anything else keeps squirrels from becoming human. If he knew this the squirrel might be very grateful and have an annual holiday, shouting "Hooray for the monochrome nuts!"

It is true that some monkeys eat pods and seeds and leaves and small animals as well as fruits, but not all monkeys are like the ancestors of man or ape. Colored vision is a great help in finding brightly colored durian fruits in the tropical sea of green—and possibly in spotting some kinds of dangerous snakes. It helps in differentiating all sorts of things in a world much fuller of things than the relatively sparse environments where squirrels coldly eke out their existence. Color vision, binocularity, and retinal acuity are a powerful combination in a diurnal eye, but why should the monkey sort things out? Sorting things out visually, at a distance, helps one to know before coming close to them whether to eat them, run from them, or signal to them (and the brilliant posteriors of some baboons clearly show a mating esthetic based on color). Sorting out has to do with leisure time and intelligence. It has to do with time for working out subtle visual communications in a society and in addition to grooming each other a general plucking, picking, poking, and manipulating. If curiosity killed the cat it was because the cat extended it beyond the question of whether yonder moving spot was edible. It occasionally kills the monkey, as when a baboon cannot resist approaching and teasing a leopard feigning sleep. But to his advantage, curiosity put the monkey in touch with the extraordinary richness of the tropical world and excited him intellectually, just as it aroused the imagination of Charles Darwin during the voyage of the *Beagle*.

The braininess of the primates is a complex coincidence of luck, environment, physiological and anatomical inventions, habits, and opportunities. The visually acute, diurnal, binocular eyes seeing color and having a fovea are inextricably a part of the human evolution—not a result or a cause, but an essential ingredient.

The monkey was prepared to examine objects which

seemed to be nonessential. Perhaps for the first time foveal vision was not merely a searching for a specific signal or sign to which the animal was internally ready to respond in a stereotyped manner, but a searching at once aimless and more fertile. Freedom from a life governed by a limited repertoire of signs means the difference between driving on a well-regulated thruway and flying your own aircraft; there are rules in both cases but the number of choices, the opportunity, and the risk are greater above ground than on it. Built-in responses to an array of visual signals is characteristic of animal life, including man. The relative amount of this kind of behavior varies. In higher animals there is a more or less free search, when the creature is internally motivated, for such signs. The total behavioral pattern is a linkage of actions of varying degree of rigidity. Some are severely fixed; others habitual, conditioned, learned, or random. The signs which release and direct these actions vary from inherent to learned, with some in between, in which instinct predisposes the animal to learn but the exact signal depends on experience. One kind of behavior is not really higher and another lower. The innate and instinctive patterns are sometimes called lower because they are regulated in a more ancient part of the brain or because a greater proportion of the lives of the more primitive animals are regulated by them. But these unlearned behaviors are often more complex than learned ones, such as the regulation of body fluids or the movements of a falcon after its prey—much too difficult to be undertaken by learning.

Some signs are inherent, such as expressions of the human face, and others are learned unconsciously, such as the movements which indicate one's emotional status or the visual keys and clues of a migratory route over which the Eskimo navigates for long distances without getting lost. Sign signals are common in both animal and human life.

Binding ourselves to visual signs is partly inevitable in the process of attaching meaning and of going about our daily business. The danger is the habit of seeing only a world full of labels. Practically useful objects especially become so la-

beled and "invisible," so stereotyped, that they become difficult to see in any other way because we never examine them
closely; at this point we have betrayed our ape innocence and
hard-won visual naïveté. This suggests that we may see better that which has no utilitarian value, which is just what the
monkey discovered. There is another way of making things
invisible: a kind of abstract vision which generalizes, finds
species and categories and classes whose common properties
may become all we see in an individual encounter.

Useful objects may retain the demand for visual scrutiny if their fine differences are socially important. The automobile and female figure are not reduced to shorthand tokens.
Many men note their subtle variations of the most minute
morphological amounts and spare them the tag of trite invisi-
bility. They are the subject of popular connoisseurship. Similarly refined differences occur in farm equipment, trees, and
sea gulls, of which farmers, botanists, and sea gulls are
aware.

Students of natural history strive to overcome the habit
of mere labeling when they toil over the outward appearance
of a small fish in the fashion of Louis Agassiz or penetrate
with H. D. Thoreau the prosaic surface of a small pond.
Painters do similar things, even when they seem only to
abstract. Modern nonobjective painting and literature reject
the old signs; in recent decades this has meant escape from
"documentary" or "representational" forms and "scientific"
or "naturalistic" perspective. The abandonment of old visual
handles and the exploration of forms without historical reference carries its own danger, of course, like mathematical
constructions whose internal order may or may not correspond to reality. A good example of the excess to which the
striving to escape old bonds can lead is an art critic's comment that "No one who has a real understanding of the art of
painting attaches any real importance to what we call the
subject of a picture—what is represented." The natural world
is dismissed along with the old symbols of it. Judgment is
conducted, to use Rebecca West's words, in a "passion of
self-love," by turning the eyes inward, "so that they will see

nothing which compels them to admit they may be mistaken about the nature of reality." Not all artists repudiate "what is represented" though they may represent "things" that have not previously been represented and use new symbols to do so.

Of course this search was not actually begun in the last few decades but early in the Cenozoic by our ancestor monkeys. In our eagerness to identify what is uniquely human we have not been warm to the primate heritage. Man is the animal who makes symbols and through this capacity acquires culture. But culture is common among animals. The sign is a resistant, commonplace, and simplified symbol. New work in linguistics compares the language of bees, dolphins, and men, finding common underlying structure; sign and symbol are part of the same series of communicative forms.

Our spontaneous joy in the colors of crayons and delight at sunlight penetrating a dusky room are another kind of uncensored, visual innocence. "There are two sources of pleasure in the visual aspect of scenery," said Vaughn Cornish, "the association of ideas and the physical satisfactions of the eye. The latter are not experienced as a local sensation, and so, being apprehended purely as emotions, their origin is apt to escape recognition. When no association of ideas can be found to account for the ecstatic mood it is often attributed to some spiritual faculty higher than ordinary thought and thus further removed from the mere senses." That is, of course, what many painters have aimed to produce.

But it is not only the free, fresh, primitive, childlike, naïve, visual attitude which is to be preserved like a coat of arms handed down from some tree shrew or monkey. Abstracting can be creative too. It finds unexpected variations on themes: a steel bridge and a human back, a tropical mountain watershed and hot syrup on ice cream, the horns of animals and shells of snails. It is easy to criticize the "reduction" of visual experience to signs. The use of literary symbols would be impossible if the writer could never bypass the immediate visual confrontation of the world via this mental shorthand. Sign value is both efficient and stultifying, but the processes of abstracting which create them need not be.

Are visual signals inherent or learned? Is any aspect of vision inherent? Spatially the person born blind lives in a world of sequential tactile impressions and comprehends nothing of his visual experience when he is first sighted by surgery. He sees a painful blur of floating color patches, a chaos of pure sensation without localization, surfaces of shapes, only uncomfortable brightness, and senses a new insecurity. He has not lived in a spatial world; even the extension of his arm was not a movement into depth but a muscular sensation; walking, not the penetration of space but a psychophysical goal-directed posture and activity. Shapes have not been spatial but felt successive contours. The most familiar objects are strange. He can learn them only by following their contours with his fingers and counting corners with his eyes. The transition is difficult. He becomes discouraged and irritable. Deluged by an overwhelming flood of meaningless impressions, he learns with great labor to differentiate a square from a circle without touching it. He loses the serenity of blindness and may despondently and peevishly refuse to make the effort to distinguish one form from another and then to associate its name with its visual image. He learns signal sets or signs, which are abstractions of essential features, with progressively less conscious effort, until he builds a scheme of elementary form and structure. Eventually all the variations on the theme "chair" are apprehensible; he has freed vision from its tactile crutch and may then even learn to read.

How similar is his experience to the visual awakening of the infant? There are some extremely important differences, although prognosis of the newly sighted blind man suggests that there is almost nothing inherent to perception except the organs of sight. Yet the clinical record indicates that even the newly sighted starts with a sense of spatiality insofar as the objects around him are never assumed to be touching his eye but located at a distance. They are perceived immediately as solids rather than only surfaces. His unlearned visual behavior includes scanning, fixation, accommodation, and convergence. The congenitally blind person is not a native impressionist but is immediately involved in constructing a world of association from a sequence of visual fields. He does not enjoy meaningless forms. His struggle to posit significance or else to disregard the visual world implies that artistic impressionism is not a recapturing of the joy of sight either in childhood or in paradise.

In spite of the seeming absence of given meaning, built-in responses to certain visual signals are characteristic of all creatures with eyes. It has been supposed that the animal's response—such as the automatic gaping of young birds to a touch on the nest—carries no awareness, no emotion, and no intellectual content. I find this merely another form of the Cartesian argument that animals are machines without souls, hence without feeling. Some human behavior is likewise spontaneous display, such as the smiling reaction of an infant to the human face. On what grounds are we to deny the possibility that the infant experiences an emotion at the same moment? A whole panoply of visual archetypical and symbolic figures which flow through the history of human art and mythology are emotionally evocative, but their impact and significance can be translated only poorly into words, or even into consciousness. If they could be converted into words they would probably not exist.

To set what is inherent against what is learned is unnecessary. Learning is partly instinctive, which means that it is ultimately inseparable from the growth, development, and physiology of nervous systems. Some kinds of learning are strictly predisposed to occur in certain directions and times; some kinds operate from a neural complex which is very permissive, others from inherent patterns of organization which need from experience only to receive the visual or other sensory image to which a rigidly inherent response is to be united. Traits of temperament or personality may be "learned" from chemical information in the uterine environment or from tactile information in childhood or from traumatic experience in a wide variety of situations. The learning processes are profoundly affected by bodily states, not only the momentary flushes of excitement or depression but also rest and fatigue, hunger and satiation, and fundamental rhythmic changes related to birth, puberty, and senescence. Part of learning, though not rigidly instinctive, is learning to learn. This includes picking up operational patterns by analogy from the environment; learning assumes a style which may depend on whether the surroundings are a forest, a prairie, or a city, whether babies are always carried or sometimes left alone, whether food is slaughtered or picked. Conversely, visual experiences of certain types, regardless of the environment, are probably organized in narrowly inherent ways. We may learn to use some innate events and instinctive processes such as sleep in learning. There is woven throughout the unknown land of our minds a swinging between nature and nurture which riddles the boundaries of those terms—*transactions* engaging the individual with his world across infinite frontiers in which experience may mean both a confrontation of our own chromosomes and of the world.

The sea eye was first connected to a fishy brain and body. When taken on land it continued to see only the spectrum of light transmitted by water and to commutate the "coolness" of the blue depths and "warmth" of the reddish, sunlit surface in a hundred ways. Parts of the aquatic temperament may have been lost or adumbrated or transposed in amphibian and then reptilian life. The reptile added much that was new as parts of the brain expanded to receive, store, mix, and control. It had "learned" the joy of periodic return to water from an amphibious ancestor. How the joy is experienced may not be discoverable, but it remains, perhaps as the pleasure of individual cells immersed in an optimum level of body fluids.

In the treetops of our pre-apehood, a now extinct monkey expanded visual learning in a new direction: the social context. To him we trace the perception of and anthropomorphic perversion of the world as a whole. Creatures who learn from each other socially extend their learned perceptions to the world, as though saying, "Who is my teacher now, Mother or Mother Nature?" But the nature of the anthropomorphism can only be understood in terms of the nature of the society. Among higher primates, society is highly organized, its forms mostly learned by the members. Learning, associated with plasticity and growth, is most efficacious in the young. There has been a natural selection among these creatures for the extension of immaturity and a reduction in the number of young born at a time. Sociality, delayed development, and leisure have given the higher primates time to develop a fine capacity for subtle visual communication. Postures, gestures, and facial expressions are well developed in monkeys and apes. Eyes can give as well as receive information; the palpebral fissure or opening between the lids, the lids with their lashes, the nictitans or third lid, fissures and wrinkles, the brows and other bristles, the colored iris with its changing pupil, moisture and tears on the cornea, the reflection of light by retinal devices causing eyeshine, highlights on cornea and lens, and the visible part of the sclera or white have all assumed a secondary communicative nature. The monkey, dog, and parrot watch man's eye and he theirs. More than any other single factor, eye communication transcends the profound barriers of communication between species.

Few other than the higher primates can roll the eyes and expose much of the white. This ability is supposed to correlate with high intelligence. Perhaps rolling the eyes was at first a way of following the flight of an eagle without the added peril of head movement, but at the same time communicating to companions the direction of danger. Once it had become communicative, new meanings could emerge, such as rolling the eyes in concentration as though "to see" an idea clearly. The colored iris set in a white background is one of the most compelling features of the human physiognomy, part of the evolution of the face. The meaning of a face is related to the invention of esthetics by ancient apes or monkeys. Although the dogs seem to make the best of it in some of their greetings, it is difficult to imagine creatures with long snouts and lateral eyes embracing face to face. The application of esthetics to the whole body may have been a factor in the reduction of hairiness and the retention of certain patches of hair. It seems probable that the ancient pre-man *Australopithecus* was probably not so hairy as cavemen are often

pictured, but that hairlessness developed with increased sensuousness of the body surface very early among the human
family. Man has strongly emphasized the infantile trait of
diffuse eroticism of the erogenous surface of the body.

The australopithecines lived a completely terrestrial life.
But there was a long interval between the early terrestrial
monkey and the caveman, perhaps fifteen million years.
Pre-human terrestrial life probably emerged by degrees, as
pre-humans moved from the deep tropical forest to the river
margins of bottomland open places and ultimately to savannahs, temperate forests, and prairies. A great deal had happened to the sea eye in the canopy of hot forests. It had found
in the gloomy arboreal depths a home more like the sea than
the amphibians or reptiles or primitive mammals had given it.
It favored a mentality which a porpoise might understand
better than a dog or horse. Movement through the dense
crowns of trees is not at all like moving across open spaces.
There is a more emphatic streaming, a clearer before and
after. Three-dimensional travel requires more decisions and
perhaps better planning, in which past experience is critical.
Seeing ahead in space was inextricably bound with seeing
behind in time; seeing ahead in time was a metaphor of seeing
ahead in space. By translating adjacent order to successive
order, time and space became interchangeable, with an incipi-
ent cross symbolism.

When this sort of mentality was carried once again to
the ground it may have opened new vistas to thinking, a
widened capacity for tradition. In transmitting cultural information, "I see" means "I understand" when applied to events
in the past. A "seer" is one whose vision extends forward
through the unity of time and space in which the tradition-
oriented society lives.

Tradition also incorporates a new self-consciousness, increased awareness of being part of a larger context. Flexibility of head and eye and the assurance through peripheral
vision of the eternal presence of brow and nose give a sense of
"being here" and of putting us in history. The constant sight
of our noses assures us that we are not disembodied observers.

One's own body seems to have an otherness which threatens to fracture experience into three parts: the environment, our body, and our self. Or, if we lump self and body, the nose becomes the great polarizer: it is a part of all seen space and we become naïvely convinced that man always occupied space. One goes ahead thrusting one's nose into all sorts of things and places in a confident way impossible for rabbits because they cannot see much of their noses or for possums who are not visual enough to care much about what they see.

The bush apes ancestral to man gradually worked farther from the forest. They took the sea eye out of the gloaming and into the radiance of the open day, though not without some enduring nostalgia. The awareness of glare in the open air and a sense of vulnerability when in it have not been completely dispelled. An affinity for shade, trees, the nebulous glimmering of the forest interior, the tracery of branches against homogeneous surfaces, climbing, the dizzy childlike joy of looking down from a height, looking through windows and into holes, hiding, the mystery of the obscure, the bright reward of discovered fruits are all part of the woody past. Restfulness to the eyes and temperament, unspoken mythological and psychic attachments, remain part of the forest's contribution to the human personality.

It was not possible to see the forest while in it. Once out, we acknowledge the bond by remaining near its edge, cutting it back the right distance or planting forest-edge growth near us. The temperate or deciduous forest is not at all the same as the tropical, yet our attachment for it seems very great. Perhaps this has to do with its remarkable geometry when leafless and its cool half-openness, or perhaps because it happened to have just those elements in common with the jungle for which compatibility predestined us, or yet again, our affection for it may be a relatively late acquisition. The jungle forest scarcely evokes our affection, but instead the impression of a formidable and implacable foe. But perhaps our feelings are shaped and named too quickly. The confrontation is profoundly subjective and disturbing in the same way that an ape agitates us more than a dog. Our relationship with the ape is still close enough to awaken vestigial memories or emotions, perhaps once associated with survival.

It need not be supposed that a deep hereditary response to former habitats would necessarily be experienced with pleasure. The unconscious is a labyrinth of levels and processes that may or may not always surround the individual's personal experience of a natural habitat with a texture of evolutionary background. I would suppose that any part of our past, personal or evolutionary, may influence our experience at any moment. If so our feelings about nature are complex yet sometimes predictable. As we have seen, the brain seems to demand flux in the sensory input from the eyes, and the mind needs variety. Without diversity the mind creates autonomous, hallucinatory experience. The mobile animal which flits through space meets this demand for multiformity. Perhaps the changing habitats in the evolution of an animal from water to air, from day to night and back to day, from ground to trees and back to ground, created that demand.

Art also contributes sensory novelty. Art is not a thing in itself with a life of its own. It is not an improvement on or an escape from life. It is never free from the past. To suppose that because it is abstract it has detached itself from the environment is to ignore the biological role of abstractions, which is the representation of essentials. We sometimes hear that an art object has a "meaning" of its own and refers to nothing in "the world," but our experience has been not only that of humans. We and the painter chimpanzees of England share a delight in abstract color schemes, curves and vertical and horizontal lines, a mutual sentiment for the forest—a heritage from mutual ancestors. Man does not have a priority on creativity, which is a pervasive activity of life, and perhaps of the universe.

Rebecca West says that an artist works like a nervous system, selecting highly significant details of the environment and synthesizing from them an "excitatory complex." He manipulates some bits of his environment in such a way as to confirm his experience of some part of the world, washed through his nervous system as sense data. He incidentally loans this extension of his nervous system to others, some of whose circuits and processes are sufficiently similar to lock onto the object. It is a communication, in spite of highbrow reactions against any definition that seems to limit the possibilities of art, such as "communication." Taken as information, the identifications of art with communication may widen the horizons of those who think art and nature are antithetical.

The artist is not only behaving in a manner similar to but is creating an extension of the nervous system. The art object represents a critical, unified, external part of an internal model—or image, analogue of experience, construct, fantasy, or schema, whichever term you prefer, so long as that term is not limited to rational intelligence or to imagination or emotions. The model affords a set of rules for brain activity, a pattern of increasing fixity for screening and channeling sensory input. The quality of art objects varies greatly, at least as much because of the validity of particular experience as because of supposed nonbiological qualities such as materials, brushwork, design, tones, structural organization, rhythm, motion, forms, lines, etc. These abstract qualities, in contrast to the specific content or subject, are its more generalized organization at once superficial to and deep in the unconscious, the more basic elements of the natural environment. The extremely abstract escapes immediate events and species only by retreating to what is common to many. In times of social stress art retreats to such secure foundations; in times of peace and harmony it cautiously approaches the endemic and particular.

The art object is a message projected by the painter to himself and to others by a route through the external world. When the observer looks now at the forest and then at a painting of the forest a feedback is turned on, a circuit of constant comparison, discovery, and modification. The sensory input from the painting and from the trees interact so that the perception of each is affected. Recurrent cycles are initiated with the production of a succeeding painting, though this does not mean that the next picture will resemble the trees any more naturalistically or abstractly than the first.

The overall event has to do with "vision," a word connoting a sublime, sometimes traumatic, event or an extraordinary sight. The phenomena of ordinary sight begin with the penetration of our eyes by quanta of energy. The modulation of this energy in the retina activates an electrochemical code of impulses to the brain. The energy for these impulses comes from our oxidation of foods ultimately derived from light stored in green leaves. The input to the brain is shunted in a lattice of circuits. Its information value is partly due to what has come before; information of high value probably increases the orderliness of brain activity, perhaps even brain structure.

The round of energy from environment to artist and its return in his manipulation of the canvas is an aspect of a greater energy flow which binds man to his world. Even the rocks which he paints are transitory, their temporary presence an expression of the mortality of the crustal drama of the earth, the irreversible arrow of planetary evolution. The motion of rocks is rhythmic; they are fragments of the breakup of land slowly rising. This destruction and creation is marked by flexes in atmospheric and oceanic chemistry. In a still shorter pulse, transient atoms migrate in cycles like seasonal workers, now part of the body of a miner, now of a tomato picker. They slip from the dead husk of a body into the soil, water, air, or rock and back again into a series of living systems, at once part of many overlapping systems. The living cell has its foundations deep in the physical structure of the world, where boundaries between life and death are indefinite. Patterns in this incessant flow, even the most elaborate social organizations, are no more stable than an atom.

Just as the artist's eye captures a shaft of light, plants take from the rain or solar radiation enough to do the work of gathering materials to build themselves. Each has self-informing arrangements for creating order from disarray, sucking from the sea of elements and showers of rays. The orderliness so created is at once health and perception of the universe. Striving for order is sometimes manifested by creating external designs such as bird nests or paintings, and is continuous within organisms and between them. Like a cell, a forest regulates energy dispersal. In each there is a symmetry of transmission between and within levels. Transmission involves communications, sometimes accomplished by the joining of molecules to form a protein, sometimes by putting brush to canvas.

I wish to note two consequences of this. Many creatures create a large proportion of the environment in which they live. The most extreme example is the termite, but each species of termite builds a predictable form of termitarium. In no species is the exact form of the built environment less predictable and more variable than in man. There are undoubtedly underlying constants, but there has been great diversity in the humanized landscapes of the past ten thousand years. The amount of deliberateness in this diversity has also ranged widely, from the "accidental" but practical forms of the city slum or Bantu village to the design of Brasília or a Japanese garden. When the Renaissance enlarged the idea that life and the state were works of art, it simultaneously discovered modern landscape esthetics, thus linking the fortunes of the landscape arts and the exploitation of nature by man's hand. This has sometimes resulted in the manipulation of the natural world in such a way as to communicate back to us something we want to believe about nature, fitting it to our scheme of the world. Moreover, art is sometimes regarded as a kind of superfluous luxury which can be afforded as a fringe benefit by wealthy civilized societies. Where art is misunderstood in this way, this evaluation may be transferred to the natural environment, by the assumption that natural forms not created by economic man, such as forests, are merely pleasant but unnecessary amenities.

Another consequence of modern model building has to do with the ultimate abstraction of the visual process. The final quality to which an analysis of vision and landscapes leads is light. As the supreme abstraction, light has a way of bringing abstraction full circle, as it is also an immediate, natural physical event. It is not only a physical event in the environment but also is the means by which most of our information about the world reaches us and, as I have mentioned, the principal source of energy in life. If plants have theologies and herbivores can worship, light must surely be at the heart of their prayers and philosophies. Man, an omnivore-carnivore, receives his substance at somewhat further remove, insofar as he eats meat, but even he has a metaphysics of light. In Europe the Gothic cathedral, for instance, is a model of the medieval universe, representing both the order of the world and the perfection of the world to come. Its central feature is a special luminosity, as light was regarded at the time of its construction as the source and essence of all visual beauty. "To the medieval thinker," says Otto Van Simson in *The Gothic Cathedral*, "beauty was not a value independent of others, but rather the radiance of truth, the splendor of ontological perfection, and that quality of things which reflects their origin to God. Light and luminous objects, no less than musical consonance, conveyed an insight into the perfection of the cosmos, and a divination of the Creator." This was an adaptation of a Platonic idea that light was the closest approximation to pure form, and the Middle Ages raised light to the status of mediator between bodiless and bodily substances, both spiritual body and embodied spirit. As the cause of all organic growth light was conceived as the transcendental reality, engendering the universe and illuminating our intellect for the perception of truth. As the Virgin is the "temple and sanctuary of the trinity," the garden enclosed, she is the cathedral itself and her impregnation with the Holy Spirit is represented by light through the windows, beams coming down into the gentle, dusky gloom—like rays entering the sea—making the seeing eye possible and inviting it into unimagined habitats.

Chapter Two

A Sense of Place

AN EARTHWORM, flung upon the sunlit ground, does not scamper up into the bushes, lunge into a stream, or bask on a hot rock. It squeezes underground as quickly as possible, where we may suppose it is more comfortable. Not at all sharing St. John's metaphysics, it flees from light as from the devil. Given a choice of temperatures, humidities, pressures, odors, vibrations, light intensities, wind velocities, and spatial structures, an animal moves to or builds what amounts to a combination satisfying for him. To man paradise is the desired ultimate unity of these conditions, but the daily business of living deflects the searcher and routs him out. Environments change. The quest continues as long as life.

The comfort and uniqueness of the *perfect* environment create a paradox: paradises are notoriously bland. Although the human paradise is traditionally represented as topographically varied, its very perfection insinuates a cloying monotony. If it is truly diverse then no one set of circumstances is always optimum. What is the perfect diversity to which our imagination stretches and which is the model of all models in creating heaven on earth?

First there is a sequence of ancestral generative environments; not only the sea and land and trees, but also specific habitats. Our search matches our physiology to an environ-

ment in which we prosper. Anatomy also expresses this relationship: at once the outcome of a long process confronting
the present self. As the landscapes of our pedigree changed so
did we—by modification, recombination, new functions for
old parts, and some novelty. The human body is a bundle of
relicts, a ragtag, self-repairing assembly of souvenirs, new
and old.

"Sense" in "sense of place" means both receptivity by
sense organs and awareness. Narrowly speaking, the input
from sense organs excites and directs consciousness; but the
structure and activity of the central nervous system are inherent. The distinction of inside awareness from outside stimulus
is only a convention. As Alan Watts says, inside and outside
are often banal expressions of our general mode of thinking,

> Once when my children asked me what God is, I replied
> that God is the deepest inside of everything. We were
> eating grapes, and they asked whether God was inside
> the grapes. When I answered, "Yes," they said, "Let's
> cut one open and see." Cutting the grape, I said, "That's
> funny, I don't think we have found the real inside.
> We've found just another outside. Let's try again." So
> I cut one of the halves and put the other in one of the
> children's mouths. "Oh dear," I exclaimed, "we seem
> to have just some more outsides!"

We are inclined to think of the environment as outside; our
structure, heredity, and experience, inside. But the environment in which the heredity units, the chromosomes, live and
act is a flux within the cell. This cellular environment is
continually affected by and continuous with the outer world,
receiving and giving substances carried by the blood. Like
motor impulses from the brain to the muscles, the chromosomes send out chemical messages to regulate activity. The
rest of "me" is constantly confronting my chromosomes, who
are part of my environment just as I am theirs. The natural
world around me—the forest or desert or sea—is, like my
genes, more permanent than I. Each of those habitats is like a
great chromosome which I confront and which induces me to
behave in certain ways.

Even a sense organ cannot be identified exclusively with inside or outside. The eye, for example, is a surface organ. In contrast to internal organs it is exposed to modification and adaptation to particular habitats. Its activity changes according to light conditions, but the change is delimited by perceptual habits, other personal experience, and our vertebrate history. The idea of "remembering" our life in the trees does not mean recollecting a stream of day-to-day events. The human organism *is* its own remembering. The emergence of the past into consciousness is inseparable from awareness of ourselves.

We owe more than a kind of vision to arboreality and to ancestral monkeys. Nothing resembling man has evolved anywhere else on earth. In trees the vertebrate snout yielded to a rounded head with fewer teeth and a large face with frontal eyes and binocular vision. Jumping, clinging, and hanging selected for long forelimbs and flexible joints, flattening of the chest from the tug of muscles, and reduced body dangle by shortening of the lower spine. They generated the grasping hand and foot, upright posture, the habit of sitting, a rhythmic walk and lithe movement along the limb-paths of the perforated enclosure of the forest. Among advanced primates in the trees the sense of smell lost control of habit and the seasons of mating. Primate society emerged. The gestation and postnatal development periods lengthened as learning enlarged its role in behavior. Brood size diminished to one. Sociability inspired vocal communication, coordination of hand and eye, nest-building, family life, and exploratory curiosity. No movement, no looking, no exploration, no social contact, no impress of the world on us omits the use of structures and conduct fundamentally organized by a sequence of now extinct monkeys.

Early in the Miocene epoch our ancestors quit the trees. Given some twenty million years of subsequent terrestrial evolution, the arboreal world claims us only distantly, though its claim is fundamental. Previous as well as later worlds had a part in our shaping. Before the monkeys the terrestrial reptiles of the Mesozoic and their amphibian precursors and aquatic ancestors of the Paleozoic contributed to what we are, endowed us with metabolism and form adapted to particular environments. In some ways this older heritage is easier to identify, as it is shared by all common descendants. We may see it in other vertebrates and other mammals. But the very otherness of those creatures is an obstacle. We are dumbly unable to cross the gulf in our groping to know what their lives are like. The mutual heritage is general and visible, yet evasive, less accessible to our peculiar kind of consciousness.

It is important that we do not correlate the "merely physical" with the past. No one can say what elements of our humanity or what profundity of the human spirit are the fortuitous union of a fishy psyche and an arboreal-terrestrial cycle. Delayed development and deferred maturity by the primates probably makes ethics possible, just as following limbs above the ground with feet and eyes may be the behavioral rudiment of esthetic abstraction. There is no clean division of the "animal" from our higher estate.

If our deep mute affinity for tree and forest, the covered path, the polychromatic and symbolic dimensions of vision are essentially arboreal in origin, other adaptations mark terrestrial life after the descent from trees. At the edges of forests and in volcanic clearings and savannahs we learned to run. This was achieved by a partly rotated pelvis, realignment of the big toe parallel to the other toes, extension of the heel for attaching muscles of the calf, elongation of the leg, improvement of the arch, thickening of the chest, an additional curve to the spine, bigger buttocks, a reduced number of ribs, and the balancing of the skull on the atlas. The body hair was much reduced (in size primarily; man is covered with vestigial hair). With the reduction of hair the skin was exposed as a strong yet delicate organ, linking the world to a bigger, more demanding brain through a proliferation of sensory nerves. The body was larger and heavier than its antecedents, a liability among high branches but an advantage on the ground. The foot and ankle were modified, though our aching feet signify something more than the rigors of pavement life; they are like a number of other lagging organs—incompletely adapted. Yet, a short walk on one's hands will demonstrate how well specialized feet have become.

All of these added to mobility and a certain sensitivity, for they are the anatomical dimension of the kinesthetic joy of fleetness. The sweep of distance means nothing to a tree or to a tapeworm; even to a monkey it is limited to nearby space in the fenestrated canopy.

The runner is the hunter or the prey. First in the drier openings of the tropics and subtropical savannahs, then in prairie and steppe, woodland glade, on the shores of river, fen, and sea, along the fringes of the boreal wilderness, advancing and retreating with the climatic pulsation of the ice ages, shambling into the tundra and the Arctic coasts. With tools and fire came further refinements of brain, skeleton, skin, social and cultural organization. The shift toward meat eating affected mobility in other ways than the chase itself. Predators must be mobile to find their meal as well as to catch it. Even among great herds there is not much meat in pounds per acre. In the steppe one human hunter per square mile is a dense population.

Hunters are high in the biotic pyramid of life. Except for decay organisms they are ultimate links in the food chains which begin with green leaves and end with the return to earth. Their combined weight per acre is small compared to plant eaters. Their numbers are few, especially if they are large. The larger they are the more ground they cover in harvesting the flesh of their prey. Large hunters are either solitary and antagonistic, like tigers, or social and cooperative, like wolves. Though omnivorous in food habits, man is a social hunter whose clans are scattered sparsely over their range. This scattering in all social as well as solitary man and animal hunters is necessary for efficient harvest and keeping their own numbers down to an optimum level. Scattering is brought about and sustained by the division of occupied space into territories. The territory is defended against invasion by other individuals or other groups of the same species, who are intimidated or attacked and driven out. Territorial boundaries are determined in scale by an innate tolerance distance and in precise delineation by neighborly conflict. Skirmishes occur thereafter at the boundaries but are not usually so pugnacious as ritualized. The ferocity of the territorial creature depends on his hormonal state—the internal chemistry to which his nervous system is attuned—and where he happens to be—in the heart of his territory, at its fringes, or in the neighbor's domain, diminishing in that order. All creatures limit the amount of actual injury to their own kind by various conventions. Territorial competition compels some to emigrate and to "marry" out of the clan. A dynamic balance between cooperation and aggression mediates between territoriality and sociality. There is a truce in public places where water and minerals are found.

In man territoriality is an intricate association of tenderness and antipathy, in which both are closely related to the terrain. In him too the territorial instinct varies greatly according to circumstances. It is the household, property in land, the tribal range. Perhaps even the city, state, and nation are metaterritories. The attention which the individual gives to the territory is related to his age and perhaps the season. Alaskan wolves do not seem to recognize territorial bounds or even the context of territorialism, until they reach breeding age, whereupon they mate for life, learn the territorial bounds, and join in to defend it. In some primitive human groups ties between puberty and the right to hunt hint at a similar relation between age and perception of the landscape; indeed, the major role of the territory is perpetuation of a reproductive unit. Territorial establishment and maintenance is closely related to sexuality and to other socializing processes. Love of one another is linked to love of place.

This awareness of the territory at mating suggests imprinting, an irreversible learning at a critical period in the individual's life, attaching significant and inherent meaning to an appropriate yet fortuitous object. It is part of the normal development of all young animals, a predisposition at a certain age to learn certain things which cannot thereafter be easily unlearned. It is the ultimate *idée fixe*. Young crows, for example, fixate on their parent crows or whoever is tending

them at an age of seventeen days. If they fixate on people
instead of crows at that time they became much tamer and
more docile. In men such processes probably involve the
indelible memories of childhood. There may be types of
human imprinting which we do not know to occur among
other creatures, such as fixation on dream images, on art
forms, or on architecture. Even the individual's experience of
his own weight, his awareness of occupying space, or the
feeling of sunshine may be imprinted as realities of being.

Much of what is seen and felt about the natural environment is already fixed by the time the individual is twelve, but
imprinting may be only a part of the process. The organizing
of thinking, perception, and meaning is intimately related to
specific places. The child seeks "to make a world in which to
find a place to discover a self," says Edith Cobb.

> There is a special period, the little-understood prepu-
> bertal, halcyon middle-age of childhood, approximately
> from five or six to eleven or twelve—between the striv-
> ings of animal infancy and the storms of adoles-
> cence—when the natural world is experienced in
> some highly evocative way, producing in the child a
> sense of some profound continuity with natural proc-
> esses and presenting overt evidence of a biological basis
> of intuition. . . . In these memories the child appears to
> experience both a sense of discontinuity, an awareness of
> his own unique separateness and identity, and also a
> continuity, a renewal of relationship with nature as proc-
> ess. This apprehension is certainly not intellectual; I
> believe it is rational at least in a limited sense, a prever-
> bal experience of an "esthetic logic" both in nature's
> formative processes and in the gestalt-making powers of
> the child's own developing nervous system, esthetic
> powers that overlap meaningfully in these moments of
> form-creating expansion and self-consciousness.

The environment is encountered in a way in which self
and place are related. The spatial arrangements and forms
and animation are used in learning to think. This is also
possible in the rooms of a house, though they lack the sensory
richness of the outdoors. "The child's early perceptual conti-

nuity with nature, the innate gestalt-making process of the nervous system, then remain the biological basis of intuition." Genius is an enduring measure of the intensity of this relationship. Something of this process remains in the adult memory, bathing parts of the environment with the colors of paradise.

In these special places which he will always remember with peculiar reverence, the child's play is at once monkey- and cat-like. It is hiding, stalking, and capture. Pursuit, flight, scuffling, and organizing are woven through secret hides, cherished trees or thickets, rock piles or dumps, basements and alleys. Venturing, concealment, and retreat are intensely suspenseful and emotional. The single-mindedness and delight with which children take to cover is a distinctive element of socializing. That hiding is essentially socializing seems contradictory, but only later in the adult mind do retreat and hiding suggest the hermit. The landscape to the child is animated. Loneliness is to be without a place to hide. The rhythm of being with and being apart from, coming and going, joining and separation in games is a dynamic recognition of the livingness of nature.

The nineteenth-century idea that children went through stages recapitulating the evolution of man has been criticized by modern anthropologists for the same reasons that biologists no longer subscribe uncritically to the cliché "ontogeny repeats phylogeny." The past is not encapsulated. Play in children is not a dramatic enactment of the prehistoric daily struggles. However, just as human and fish embryos are limbs upon the same tree, children probably play much as did the children of ancient men; indeed, like the young of other mammals. Play in animals is a unique combination of gamboling exercise and adaptive practice. It develops the nervous system and muscles. It is not "excess energy." To tiger, wolf, and man, games of pursuit, stalking, and coordination, skill and daring are the neuromuscular advent of the hunters' life. Given health, place, and social sanction, play emerges. Instinct inclines but does not force children to play.

This brings us back for a moment to the worm who prefers not to stay on a rock. With Cobb we may say that there is a "principle of expectancy within the animal's neural tissue" which unites perception and the exploration of the environment as an innate appetite. "For the animal as for man, the ultimate satisfaction of perceptual expectancy and perceptual exploration is the organization of the perceptual world into the 'good gestalt,' into environmental shapes that 'hold,' that are populated with forms and are rich in perceptual meaning. In bird, fish, beast, or man, the need to make a world is intricately related to the sense of identity."

In play, children often designate a place as segregated and special, much as the cult space is segregated as a place of ritual, homage, or for representation of a god. Both cult and play are related to religious experience in that both grow from leisure. Josef Pieper in his book *Leisure, the Basis of Culture* connects leisure with *intellectus*, "the capacity of *simplex intuitus* or that simple vision to which truth offers itself like a landscape to the eye." *Intellectus* is the spiritual state in which man "participates in the angelic faculty of nondiscursive vision." *Ratio* or intellectual work, the deliberate human effort, complements *intellectus*, for the latter is not a product of work but is spontaneous and given, a playful contemplation. Leisure is not idleness nor spare time. It is "listening to the essence of things." It is a way of letting things happen, a form of silence prerequisite to the apprehension of reality, an occasion and capacity for "steeping oneself in the whole of creation," a "happiness of our recognition of the mysteriousness of the universe."

We erroneously think of leisure as opposite to work—a separation unknown to children or to prehistoric man to whom the round of daily life was intricately woven of ritualized and routine events. Thought to the primitive man is not autonomous and detached "work," and it always involves a confrontation revealing a "thou," not an "it," for the "whole of creation" is a being. To our perceptions, space is not infinite, nor homogenous, nor abstract. It is bounded, and emotionally and spiritually diverse: familiar, alien, colored, hostile, friendly. The sorting out of places requires the leisurely, childlike, scientific or artistic vision—a perception of otherness, a glimmer of the utter mystery of natural beings. This awe is seldom inspired by visual middle distance, but by the great panorama of the desert, or by the very close, such as crystals in a stone or lichens on the bark of a tree.

The "founding" of a world in childhood and the special mystical experience relate play and the ritual space. They are part of a continuous process initiated in play. Play is at once a sorting out and a creation and a discovery—games, special places, and nonabstract directions or spatial organization based on place names. Play is not only a kind of precursor to the cult ritual but is in turn influenced by mythology. In this circular relationship the mature mythology guides games in a broad way, and the spatial, rhythmic, imaginative forms of play create an ethos for the adult mythology.

The special places of childhood are not sacred but the memory of them is necessary for attaching sacredness to place. "For the religious man," says Mircea Eliade, "space is not homogeneous." Holy ground is seen as distinct from the rest of space, and this is an inherent, primordial distinction. But its genetics do not specify what places. Part of the energy of this fixation expends itself on the territory and part is reserved for subdivisions of it. The territory and the sacred places within it orient the individual to topography, position him in the land and in the cosmos, an environmental gestalt of figure and ground.

The sacred place is associated with events important to the mythos—to the legend and the ritual of the people; it consecrates and makes cosmic the territory, which then becomes the center of the world. The building of habitations ritually recreates the growth of the individual, and the temple recreates the universe as a microcosm. The place is named and often associated with a hero or god. It is approached by a certain route or passage which is "the way." Sacred places may be "found" or created by ritual. They may be accessible to anyone or only to a priest or shaman. They can be represented by a symbol and their efficacy evoked by use of the symbol. The sacred place, says Erich Isaac, is not etiological; it is not a supernatural explanation of a natural phenomenon

such as a volcano. It is, rather, a realization of the sacred
potential of all places. The mythos which endows it with a
spiritual presence may incorporate an explanation, but only as
part of an elaboration. Isaac says that for this reason "there is
no uniformity in man's religious reaction to landscape features." But he may be correct only insofar as the details of
such places differ.

If, on the contrary, there is inherent human attention to
certain kinds of landforms preceding their symbolic transformation, the basis would be a common natural history and
biology. Men have always sought order and comfort in their
environment. Myth making and religious activities are expressions of the creation of a world, or, as J. Z. Young calls
it, the "establishment of certainty": rules for dealing with
sensory input, perceptual dampening or channeling; the invention of concepts and history and patterns which then direct the seeing eye. In such model building the individual
feels that he is discovering rather than making a world.

There are several basic models for creating a world—or,
more precisely, endowing the world with order. One is a
bio-transformative cluster, an anthropomorphic extension of
birth, growth, puberty, coition, death, sleeping, waking, menstruation, eating, defecating, urinating, vomiting. Most mythologies of the world draw heavily if not exclusively on
these. Such figures are in fact the fundamental perceptual
device. The awareness of bodily change is creatively adapted
to elaborate metaphors in the landscape. By contrast, historical, revealed religion is likely to discover in this world another kind of order: political, hierarchical structure derived
ultimately from order observed in the sky or projected from a
human familial or social-economic system. These are then
symbolized in terrestrial space either by discovering their ex-
tensions and correlations or by manipulating the terrain so that
it conforms to the schema. Modern science derives models
"of nature" which are celestial, geometrical, and mathematical. It is quite possible that "purely abstract" mathematical scientific models which sometimes seem to be capricious
may be the most anthropomorphic of all models; by this I

mean that they may come closer to representing an externalization of patterns of workings of the brain than any objects men make outside of art. Still another universal schema for structuring is the fitting of paradisical and hellish models onto the world. These "archetypes" are part of a "collective unconscious." Visual imagery is not itself inherited, but a pattern for brain function is given by which certain qualities and forms of visual experiences are abstracted in the normal course of perception and utilized later to ornament a skeleton of autonomous, hallucinatory imagery. The details of the archetype of the hero, the lost paradise, the mother, or the temple vary with personal and cultural exposure. But hallucinatory visual experience of these essential ideas is found in all cultures.

The rise to consciousness of archetypical forms with details furnished from experience occurs in visions and dreams. Hallucinations are apparitions whose immediate sensory stimulus is "interior" rather than environmental. Hallucinations and visions are essentially the same; one has the stigma of the induced and clinical, the taint of illusion; the other is numinous, religious, and myth-forming. Whether one has a vision or a hallucination may simply depend on whether he and his peers regard it as revelatory of the universe or merely as a phenomenon of the nervous system. Everyone lives in a visual world which to some extent is influenced by these forms. Everyone is to a degree visionary. Some experience "pure" visions, some people live in the preternatural world in which normal perception of everyday objects is illuminated from the "other world." Some have only the dimmest intimations of it. In a visionary trance the imagery is completely autonomous, but the trance is by no means the only experience of visions, as they are continuously subliminally present. Hallucinations may be induced by hypnosis, pulsating lights, drugs, the stress of malnutrition, infection, fatigue, asphyxiation, and even solitude.

The complete visionary drama, profoundly important mythologically, is less common than the "suggestive" effects of normal vision. Certain lights, objects, and places are "reminiscent," such as the brilliantly colored or glittering forms, having in Aldous Huxley's term "transporting" qualities. They open to us some inner region whose geography we know below awareness. The natural world contributes these details to the synthesis of visions erected on the bare outline of the archetype. They also transport us to that paradisical or to that hellish other world whose fantastic architecture or animals may delight or terrify. There are monolithic, intricate landforms and buildings shining with the radiance of gems or fire. The visionary landscape is either distant and panoramic or intimately close and detailed—seldom the middle ground of the human scale. Whole landscapes or paintings may be reminiscent of vision, or our perception may be transfigured by a previous trance, or by paintings or legends communicated to us by visionaries. The everyday world is an attenuated other place, parts of it reminiscent of paradise with its limpid streams, birds, flowers, meadows; or of hell, with its hideous animals, writhing movement, menace or terrifying confinement. Reminiscent objects are jewelry, flowers, birds, stained glass, ceramics, costumes, polished stone, feathers, flames, fireworks, clear water, the sunset, and so on. These evoke the paradoxical effect of remembering and discovering.

In myth there is a mixture of visions, dreams, speculation, and concentrated history—not a mixture like marbles in a bag, but a unity of perception and belief. The whole is the legend and its setting in the natural world. Cultural lore and esoteric teaching transform the world in individual consciousness so that as the brain builds its models of reality it uses older foundations. These models seem to displace earlier organizing experience, but they do not. The sensual phases of infancy and the special memory of play are regenerated and embodied in model making and myth learning. Psychic experience is portrayed to consciousness as natural forms and places. Conversely, the natural forms excite intimations of the underlying myth. The link between vision, myth, and childhood is that the imagery of the hallucination is the principal furniture of the myth while the paradisical aura of childhood furnishes it with the raw material of its details and predisposes the mythic concern with origins and generation.

The myth confers orientation on the primitive man by a set of fixed points. Some are topographical, others conceptual. Words are attached to units of experience and places named in every society. Language breaks nature down into words and reconstructs it as sentences. Language is not an inventory of nature, but a creative symbolic organization, defining experience and expectation. The retinal and perceptual experience of color, form, texture, and motion are arranged by names. Language imposes meaning and orientation and is necessary to the synthesis of ideas and man's control of his environment. The world becomes to him a more or less unified family of entities and events corresponding to words.

> The landscape and the language are the same
> For we ourselves are landscape and are land.
> —*Conrad Aiken*

Insofar as thinking itself is prescribed by language, all information about the world which is communicated with words is, to use again the analogy of the chromosomes, genetic bits socially transmitted. The words mediate between the otherness, the incredible and seemingly chaotic diversity, the existential solitude, and our necessary construct of the world. We have a primordial, syncretic level of confrontation of nature; and to it we add a cultural screening in which the perpetual flow of events is cut up, reorganized, and named. There is nothing particularly deterministic about how this segmentation is done, so long as it produces a workable and coherent world.

An environment without place names is fearful. When men land on other planets in our solar system they will come with place names. Some of the named places of the human territory are sacred. The name as well as the place is an evocation of mutually recognized reality. In addition to the naming of particular places, which is an essential part of human territoriality, there is a naming of classes and species of things. In the modern world this kind of naming predominates over the older sort of naming in which places embodied special significance: the personality of a god, the place of passage, or a mythological event. In contrast such general categories as swamp, mountain, forest, meadow, glade, plain break across uniqueness and territorial boundaries. Veneration of a fen does not extend to all fens. One naming is centripetal, in a context of an indigenous world; the other establishes a rubric of stereotyping and carves the universe into duplicable sets of units. The pioneer brings to a new land his fixed categories. The identification of part of the environment as woodland may be very useful to men moving from one temperate forest to another, but it may miscarry badly when they move to a palm grove or a fir thicket. The values, utility, inhabitants, significance of "woodland"—in short, the word's orienting or mythological role—breaks down. Such classifying frees the mind from the confined world of locality but exposes it to the disorder of rootless mythology, the empty surface forms of meaningless art.

The balance between universalizing and particularizing shifted with the growth of Christianity. The Christians took over Greek and Roman shrines, each peculiar to a tradition in its own setting, and made them temples of a religion whose god and prophets were elsewhere. Conversely, Christianity created a few new sacred places, but not many were intimately related to site in the way of the Greek shrine. Deriving its mythos from the sky, celestial order, and urban thought patterns, Christianity has diminished the Western world's diversity of special places.

Yet temples are temples, and they sanctify a site, even though they are standardized. There the myth is dispensed. Temples are assembly places, solidly symbolizing the durability of the myth, demonstrating that the belief transcends mortality. The temple contains and sanctifies the world; the altar is paradise. The temple began as a cave and evolved to the mountain, to the ziggurat or built mountain, and to the building of worship. The entry to a temple has always had a special significance. Such a passage, "the way," crosses a threshold. Its archaic form is simply an opening. Ceremonial procession may be derived from ancient dances intended to represent the labyrinthine turnings of a sacred cave.

Landscapes without place names are disorienting; without categorical forms, awful. We think of heaven and hell as places; cling to the idea of an earthly paradise, even though only in a poetic sense; venerate historical sites; and imagine sacred places in terms of habitats. The colors, architecture, and landscapes of visions do not fit our name categories. This quality astonishes the beholder. In spite of the threat of the unknown he is fascinated, freed momentarily from the name bonds and the web of intellectual and emotional associations signaled by them. He escapes, a traveler in the highest sense, awakened and inspired. He does not return entirely to the old vision of the old words. He has crossed a threshold to that world where silence reigns. He sees more clearly in this world the vividness of color and form, its "meaning," and the mystical importance of wordlessness and namelessness.

Temple and mountain are the sacred centers for communication of the core of belief. Here the society enfolds and orients the individual with ceremonies incorporating motion, sound, smell, space. Recognition of ineffable otherness has, in contrast, no fixed signals in the confrontation. Silence and emptiness convey divine immanence by their lack of prosaic forms. The desert is the environment of revelation, genetically and physiologically alien, sensorily austere, esthetically abstract, historically inimical. It is always described as boundless and empty, but the human experience there is never merely existential. Its solitude is a not-empty void, a not-quiet silence. Its forms are bold and suggestive. The mind is beset by light and space, the kinesthetic novelty of aridity, high temperature, and wind. The desert sky is encircling, majestic, terrible. In other habitats, the rim of sky above the horizontal is broken or obscured; here, together with the overhead portion, it is infinitely vaster than that of rolling countryside and forest lands. The moon, sun, and stars are perceptually exaggerated lower in the sky. Apparent motion in the horizontal plane is always greater. In an unobstructed sky the clouds seem more massive, sometimes grandly reflecting the earth's curvature on their concave undersides. The angularity of desert landforms imparts a monumental architecture to the clouds as well as to the land. The clouds seem to measure the enormous distances by a stately progression toward the horizon. In the Mediterranean regions the lower summer humidity and reduced absorption of the light enhance the radiance of surfaces. The dazzle of light in these areas is heightened by the scarcity of cloud, water, shadow, haze, mist, smoke, and fumes.

The constancy of sensory experience in the desert—or in a cave in the desert—is in effect sensory deprivation. This is the saturation of solitude, the ultimate draft of emptiness, needing courage and sanity to face. It brings introversion, contemplation, hallucination. Space and time and silence are metaphors of the eternal and infinite. To the desert go prophets and hermits; through deserts go pilgrims and exiles. Here the leaders of the great religions have sought the therapeutic and spiritual values of retreat, not to escape but to find reality.

Ernst Cassirer has said that travel for the primitive man is fundamentally different than for modern man. To the primitive man space and time are not linear. The world beyond the known world blends into the other world. Epic journeys of men have some of the same mystery as the migration of birds, uniting celestial events with the seasons and the land, a departure at the season's end like the departure of the soul from a dying person. Primitive men sometimes use the stars or the wind for navigation, but mainly they travel by landmarks. The modern urbanite is astonished at the ability of the native hunter to move long distances in his territory without getting lost, though he may go about in his own city unconsciously observing clues of location in the same way, from one reference point to another. To the primitive each important place in the terrain is named. Travel orientation is a sequence of known places, just as form to the blind man is a sequence of tactile impressions. The dead and the heroes move across the outer boundaries, making momentous journeys, searching, each step containing a clue to the next. The shaman's trance, the heroic quest, the monk's peregrination, the Dantean venture—all have in common a ceremonial departure and return. They move through a visionary world. The inner world is coextensive with the outer, the natural habitat a middle ground, lacing into each other like the fingers of clasped hands. The sacred places and passages unite this and the other world. They characteristically resemble hallucinatory forms or places.

Dreams also play a role in the morphogenesis of visionary landscapes. The dream is more distinctly visceral, a more direct externalization of our interiorness. The basic experience of a passage, and the prototype for all passages, may be the memory of being born, perpetuated in the transition from sleep to waking. Sleep is a withdrawal of sensory desire from the environment, a shifting to interior receptors and the blended colors of the kinesthetic awareness of moving muscles, of weight and metabolism. Passage also means the movement of the breath, food, urine, feces, semen, of penis into vagina. None of these has any inherent visual imagery. It must be created from experience to be manifested directly or symbolically in dreams.

Falling asleep and waking are dying and being born, and crossing from one world to another. They are the creation and destruction, the life cycle, the seasons. They are the alternation from the bright verbal world of the ego to the dim intuitive world of the unconscious. Dreaming is neither lower nor higher than rational thought, but a highly evolved and specialized human activity. The infant probably does not distinguish clearly between a sensory event whose origin is inside—say, the contraction of the smooth muscle of the stomach wall—and the outside—as when his stomach is tickled. Particularly if he is swaddled and otherwise protected from an external flux, his attention is initially focused on "feeling" his inner space. We may wonder what role in adult perceptions this experience engenders, as we characteristically are unable ever to grow out of our infantile world. That peculiar adaptation in which man prolongs infantile traits into adolescence and adulthood carries with it some incidental effects

which are also peculiarly human. I am speaking of the pleio-
tropic baggage of delayed maturity linked as parts of infantilism. When the interiorness of infantilism is combined with
sexual development in a hypersexual creature, the effect is to
interpret experience libidinously. The inner awareness to
which we shift in falling asleep casts its dream imagery
sexually. A full bladder manifests itself in dreams of water,
the warm genital lake of desire. Falling asleep is at once
dying, rediscovering the uterine paradise, and coition by entering one's own body. There is a perpetual antinomy in our
lives between contact with the world, which is oral, verbal,
and trophic, and "regression" to the inner world, which is
genital and libidinous. Life moves to and fro between them.
Sex is supremely ambivalent and mysterious, for coition is a
reentry in a state of exalted wakefulness, initially object-
directed but object-cathected in climax.

The dream is typically euphoric; the dreamer, weightless, having a buoyancy like that of a fish—ourselves the fish-
like embryo in the hot pond of the amnion or like our lobe-
finned fishy ancestor in the sea. In sleep, too, we are always
concerned with beginnings, though in a slightly different way
than in the memory of play. Mythology finds universal experience in dreams to which it supplies a particular imagery. This
imagery is partly acquired in childhood, especially during
play. Play stylizes the to and fro. Animals are people to the
child. The dream world and dream narrative is a surrealist,
totemic country of ancestral beings. Children love to play in
water. In running there is a buoyant flight and in crouching
down to hide a special touch of the earth as a place to discover
a self. The dream landscapes are composed of pools, caves,
hollows, animals. The dreamer withdraws into himself,
touching the earth of his own substance, a phallus entering
female space, himself the womb. He creates a world. Just so
the mythological hero-king descends, copulates, and re-
emerges a new king.

Because the environment echoes dream and visionary
forms, is dotted with named, sacred, anthropomorphic and
specially remembered places, and comprises a ground of in-

termediate space arrayed with plant and rock entities to
which our apehood responds in entangled and impulsive
ways, we are always on the threshold of legendary places.
The topography is always "trying" to match an image. This
meshing brings order out of the natural world without homog-
enizing it. The history of geographic exploration is rich with
efforts to match the terrain to mythical topography. For example, in a ferment of this mixture, molded in Christianity,
the exploration and imperialistic invasion of the New World
in the sixteenth century issued from two thousand years of a
fabulous cosmography. Contorted by its interlocking cupidity
and missionary zeal, it coincided with the Renaissance pen-
chant for exploring the tangible inferences of theory. It was
generated by improved communication and navigation, especially the "rediscovery" of ancient Classical geographical literature, compounded with a millennium of Christian visionary
lore. Its basic cosmography was Ptolemaic. The Alexandrine legends had become inseparable from journey mythology, and the search for the earthly paradise. Paradise was
located variously on a mountain and on an island.

Much travel in the years 300 to 500 was religious
pilgrimage and monkish peregrination. Among the most famous of the travelers was the legendary St. Brandan, the Irish
monk whose marvelous voyages in the Atlantic and visits to
fabulous islands were retold and embellished for a millennium. His "lost isle" appeared on maps as late as the nineteenth century. By the year 1000 the vast lore of twilight
geography had come to focus on the paradise, and for another
500 years "the garden" continued to have a terrestrial location. In his compendium of medieval descriptions of the Other
World, H. R. Patch says,

> With all due variations, the constant features of all
> this mass of writing of the early authors and the later
> ones, the encyclopedists, and makers of maps, are the
> following: Paradise is in the east (India or Asia, or
> perhaps so far as to be at the side of the world); it is cut
> off from man because it is located on a high mountain or
> by the ocean or by a fiery wall, or by more than one of

these, making it an island; it contains a garden with an abundance of trees, and fruit and flowers which, in some accounts, are unfading, in some have a medicinal value; the fragrance of the fruit or the flowers is sometimes emphasized; the Tree of Life, the fountain, and the four streams with their names, and the jewels, all as in Genesis, are mentioned almost everywhere; and sometimes there is reference to the birds and even the animals of the garden.

The counterfeit Prester John letters of a marvelous eastern kingdom and the spurious travel tales of Sir John Maundeville were false only in our restricted sense of geography, certainly not as descriptions of human experience.

The full extent to which this body of geographical myth nourished the roots of exploration and tourism is impossible to estimate. Marco Polo's expectations and perceptions were filtered through myth. Christopher Columbus wrote of his third voyage, on which continental land was discovered,

> I have come to the conclusion respecting the earth, that it is not round as they describe, but of the form of a pear, which is very round except where the stalk grows, at which part it is most prominent, or like a round ball, upon one part of which is a prominence like a woman's nipple, the protrusion being the highest and nearest the sky, situated under the equinoctial line, and at the eastern extremity of the sea. . . . I do not suppose that the earthly paradise is in the form of a rugged mountain, as the descriptions of it have made it appear, but that it is on the summit of the spot, which I have described. . . . From the gulf to which I gave the name of the Gulf of Pearls the water runs constantly with great impetuosity towards the east, and this is the cause why there is so fierce a turmoil from the fresh water encountering the water of the sea. . . . I think that the water may proceed from the paradise, though it be far off, and that stopping at the place which I have just left, it forms a lake. There are great indications of this being the terrestrial paradise, for its site coincides with the opinion of the holy and wise theologians St. Isidore, Bede, Strabus,

the master of scholastic history, St. Ambrose and Sco-
tus, all of whom agree that the earthly paradise is in the
east.

The extension of this mythology into political policy is
part of the tragedy and drama of the Portuguese and Spanish
dream conquests in the sixteenth century. The frantic ran-
sacking from Patagonia to Kansas drew heavily on the features of the fabulous lands, united by the Biblical image of
Eden, sanctioned by a corrupt church. Although the brutal
pursuit of wealth and power and the scramble for the ambro-
sial fountain did not directly alter the new world environment, changes in the land under the Spanish followed as a
result of the sanction of a pastoral imagery, imposed by a
political-economic-religious attitude, epitomized by the Spanish Mesta. This was a privileged class of stockmen whose
sheep had wrecked the interior plateaus of Spain even as the
Inquisition wrecked the nation's intellectual spirit. The
transplantation of Spanish sheep, goats, and pastoral customs
to Mexico and the Rio Grande initiated a destruction of the
habitat which continues today. These grasslands had persisted because of the accumulation of organic material and a
network of interlocking roots which held against drought and
desert. Heavy grazing opened the range to desiccation, to
invasion by shrubs or annual plants associated with aridity,
and erosion. The damage may not have been conspicuous to
any single Spanish landlord. It permitted the advance of
desert and shrub associations into the grass at a rate slightly
too slow for easy detection by an individual but catastrophi-
cally rapid for natural change. The relationship between the
looting of the Inca empire and the destruction of the watersheds dramatically combined the search for a certain paradise of gold and youth with an omniscient attempt to create
another pastoral empire.

The English colonies in Virginia were established in
similar visionary idiom. The imagery of Prester John's empire was employed to reify a dream. Captain Smith secured
privileges and funds more easily because he described the
new land as a paradise. In spite of persistent disillusion, the

European has never wholly lost this image of milk and honey in his vision of America. In recent centuries these myths have become part of folk history and literary ornamentation; they have became esthetic and intellectual rather than vital. Paradisaical allusion has, for instance, become the conventional criterion for "scenery," so that the dream landscape continued to serve the American in somewhat different ways.

Ecologically the Spanish quests produced mundane pastoral societies, a transfer of Spain's principal agricultural economy. This was a special case of the greater Western pastoral mythos shaped originally in the engendering of civilization in landscapes created by domestic animals. Pastoralism is more than an economy or even a way of life. Like hunting, it is a collection of images about the world which need not be practical in the usual sense to be valid. Urban men, who want nothing to do with the smell of sheep dung, but whose youth was spent at shepherding and who believe retrospectively in the virtue of the simple life, incorporate appropriate elements of pastoral mythology in their philosophy.

I would like to characterize pastorality in a few paragraphs, to identify it with an attitude toward the landscape, though certainly there were hundreds of variations in the keeping of hoofed animals, many cultural differences among pastoralists, and many intergradations with other ways of life.

Pastoralism came into existence with the domestication of large social mammals: goats, cattle, sheep, camels, horses, and reindeer. It is a kind of domesticated hunting, grading into parasitism where the animal products rather than the animals are consumed. Like hunting, the number of people it can support is low relative to the space it requires. It does not support cities.

The fierce, hierarchic society of nomadic pastoralism is partly a result of grappling with the hazards and problems of a fringe environment: the world between desert and forest, low in productivity, where herds of grass-eating mammals exist by eating their way across a very large surface. Pastorality is often mixed with crop culture and has varying degrees of mobility from a main residence. Even Bedouin nomadism is not random wandering but a deliberate migration within a territory.

The habitat of arid pastoralism is one of clean delineations: there is no soft interlacing of sky and tree or marshy transitions. Day and night come suddenly. Earth and heaven are as distinct from one another as the fruitful valley from the wilderness. The land gives little directly. A careless move or a confusion of authority can mean disaster. The otherness of the desert is at hand, rustling with invisible demons.

The Near Eastern pastoralist is dependent on an animal herd, as the farmer upon perennial plants, yet with the personality of a carnivore rather than an herbivore. Where milk is used there is a softening of this temperament; the fiercest use only the blood and the meat, slipping from parasitism to predation, from systematic predation on their own flocks to occasional hunting, from hunting to territorial conflict and aggression and feuding. The domestic animals are products and creations of human technology and their survival remains utterly in human hands. The pastoralists' watch over and breeding of a stock is a continuing lesson in the relationship between authority and lineage, a confirmation of the extension of paternity, of a creative patriarchate. Seasonal and climatic factors are important. Seasons are primarily celestial in origin, and therefore predictable; but they are manifested in the behavior of the wind—that invisible, bodiless presence. Flock protection requires watch under a cloudless sky, filled, night upon night, with the procession of stars and planets. The mathematical precision of their orbits and phases and nightly progression is an overwhelming sign of an orderly universe, like that of the pastoral clan, ruled as though it were a hierarchical system. Where landforms are unreliable or shifting, the sky is a safe means of orientation.

The pastoral milieu is characterized by the occasional rush and clatter of migration, interspersed with intervals of leisure and patient waiting. Art and hedonism are cultivated; conversation is subtle and thought deep and abstract. It is not directed toward the exploration of immediate terrestrial nature, but toward etherealized nature, religion, philosophy, mathematics, and art. As in all leisurely societies, sport is important. Commerce and the merchant caravans of the ancient East are products of this mobile life. From commerce also emerged organized banditry, slavetrading, and war. Survival in this fluid environment requires intelligence, planning, and social cohesion. Women have low status. The gods are omniscient, arbitrary, and manlike. This stern sophisticated view is ameliorated when pastoralism is mixed with farming and town life. But its homocentric, patriarchal, dualistic, abstract view of nature is the background of a hierarchical and divided universe. The New Testament carried forward this pastoral mind from its Persian, North African, and Southwest Asian origins. The medieval orthodox Christian attitude toward nature corresponds essentially with the conceits and apprehensions, prejudices and insights of animal-keeping people in the Old World subtropical semiarid lands, where the control of livestock, like that of irrigation ditches, marks the productive from the sterile, the humanized from the wild, and perhaps the good from the evil. In pastoralism the earlier inventions by the hunting society, emerging from the dim recesses of the Pleistocene, were preserved and reconciled with civilization: intense sociality and sexuality, the male-dominated cooperative clan, aggressivity coupled with a profound capacity for love, and art forms oriented toward animal life and the celestial cosmos. Leisure, tribal war, hedonism, polygamy, aristocracy—these they perfected beyond anything realized by primitive hunters. These tend to turn the attention away from the natural environment toward elaborate subtleties of communication, hospitality, trade, negotiation, philosophical discussion, and games of the intellect. To these people, as to those navigating on the open sea, the sky is a promise of order and orientation. The unseen demons of the wind move more easily into the sky than those of tree or cave or swamp. Pastorality shares profoundly with hunting the consciousness of a world not made by man, where the fragile tent and footprint in the sand are gone tomorrow, where the sky dominates the topography.

It would be easy for a modern reader to misunderstand what is meant here by activities that "tend to turn the attention away from the natural environment." The nomadic Bedouin does not dote on scenery, paint landscapes, or compile a nonutilitarian natural history. It is easy to think of him, as some historians supposed wrongly of the ancient Greek, that he is homocentric and has no interest in nature. The truth is more nearly that his life is so profoundly in transaction with nature that there is no place for abstractions or esthetics or a "nature philosophy" which can be separated from the rest of his life. Parts of his environment are truly intrinsic to religion; his mythos is in a landscape. Nature and his relationship to it are a deadly-serious matter, prescribed by convention, mystery, and danger. His personal leisure is aimed away from idle amusement or detached tampering with nature's processes. But built into his life is awareness of that presence, of the terrain, of the unpredictable weather, of the narrow margin by which he is sustained.

The struggle to protect and enlarge the grazing flock carries in its success the seeds of destruction. Possibly the warlike nature of the nomadic pastoralist and the territorial spacing brought about by tribal feuding and skirmishing have an adaptive value other than sharpening the wits and mobility of men. It may keep territories large enough to reduce grazing pressure and minimize the injury to plants and soil. Except for such possible effects of territoriality or land ownership or deliberate control of grazing pressure, the grazing herd would cut back the environment to the bone. Grazing is like sandpaper on the skin of the earth. It first opens and then kills forests, at first converts grasslands to wealth and then gradually reduces them to an indigence which is reflected in the animals and people they contain. Everywhere in the equatorial grasslands of the world, particularly in North Africa, the Near East, and Latin Europe, where Western civilization took shape, the pessimistic, dualistic outlook of the pastoralist is imprinted on all of human society. The desiccated impoverishment of the lands themselves is partly due to the deadly downward spiral of ecological degradation brought about and perpetuated by cattle, sheep, and goats. At its worst man-and-animal-made deserts remain, supporting only goats and the ragtag society of goatkeepers. The wealth in such a world is centered on oases and irrigated lands and alluvial valleys and in the cities; but these places have never been independent of the pastoral imprint, as destruction of the watershed by the trampling of ungulates exaggerates the alternation of flood and aridity.

The irony at the roots of our civilization is that the first agency by which man gained control of and radically changed his environment has destroyed his paradise. Possibly the climate contributed to this; as the last of the Pleistocene glaciers waned, the physical conditions of the Mediterranean world shifted from cool and wet toward warm and dry. Within this broad shift from the last ice age there have been fluctuations. Each dry and warm period reduced the soil and its plants and animals. A healthy biota resists these climatic surges by controlling its own immediate surroundings. It always lags behind the changing climatic environment. Natural grassland, swamp, forest, or savannah is never in perfect harmony with the climate. Its mass and composition are usually a relict. But when herds of hoofed animals break its resistance, there follows a succession of plants which are less productive, more hardy than the preceding, until an enduring and weedy vegetation emerges which is adapted to the pauperized conditions of life. Often this includes certain plants so intimately associated with domestic grazing animals that they grow only where those animals graze. In this way, pastorality—though it has many forms and mixtures with crop agriculture and varies its effect according to the climate—creates a kind of environment or habitat which is domestic. The closest wild approximation of it are savannahs, steppes, and scrublands, which are associated with wild herds of hoofed animals. These lands are precisely the type thought to be occupied by the human and pre-human hunters of the Paleolithic. To a degree the pastoralist perpetuates and creates environments resembling those of the dim beginnings, of the paradisaical origins, yet always on the verge of collapse into desert.

Fire is not part of that static image. Yet it is an intrinsic part of the grassland environment, which it perpetuates by destroying young shrubs and trees. It parallels and abets the control of the landscape by man through the agency of cattle, and in some societies it has come to symbolize that control. There the building of a fire altar constitutes legal or territorial establishment; like a small sun it consecrates that sacred space, making it microcosmic. Such was the hearth to the household.

Apart from its practical or symbolic values, it has more directly emotional, inexplicable meanings. For millennia men squatted around the warming, infrared, dancing fire, fascinated, comforted, transported, mesmerized by light in the dark, the colors, odors, sounds. Before a small fire the hushed memory of the past, the evocation of the unknown, and the mystery of life are admitted to the communal mind. In this, though perhaps unrecognized, it has an incredible hold on the modern psyche. There is in its presence an expectancy, as though some secret were about to offer itself as a clue to a greater reality. Song and poetry are employed as though something terribly important but forgotten could be summoned. Such is the heritage of an unthinkable span of Paleolithic nights and of torchlit celebrations in caves. Even now the campfire unites Boy Scouts more forcefully than any activity invented by Scoutmasters, and the wise Scoutmaster permits, at the end of the session, man and boy to urinate on the fire, whimsically, mimetically, sharing a participation mystique.

It is curious that the campfire is like a teasing thought, while the bonfire excites action. It suggests a feast instead of a communion, dancing instead of storytelling. Bigger fires evoke contagious hysteria. All over the world men continue to have seasonal burns. As *milpa*, *ladang*, and *brandwirtshaft*, fire is a tool for clearing land to plant or to graze; in the Ozarks the woodlands are burned to "kill the varmints," and in Scotland the rationalizations are even less rational. Generally, soil and land decline under fire except in prairie, savannah, and shrub asociations which are expressions of an equilibrium with fire. Technicians managing certain kinds of open forests, grazing range, or wildlife habitat employ fire as a tool—which is to say that they tend to limit its use to a productive enterprise and they try not to reveal, or perhaps even to feel, any emotional satisfaction. Where fire is said to control pests, which in fact are abundant and evident in a deteriorating environment, the two may be part of a larger pattern of ecological disharmony. Fire may be an emotional catharsis of desperate and frustrated people in wasting lands.

The legend that the gift of fire made civilization possible is associated with metal technology and the tools of war, which figure in our own image of the history of Western greatness. Lucretius and Vitruvius enunciated a Classical evolutionary philosophy centering on the acquisition of fire. They proposed a human history of "hard primitivism" as opposed to a "golden age," the emergence of man from a wilderness instead of a paradise. Boccaccio took up the matter in the fourteenth century and, following the Greeks, speculated that rampaging forest fires gave ancient man a chance to taste cooked meat and to collect embers for his hearth. Erwin Panofsky has pointed out that the idea of a wild beginning for man instead of a soft life in the garden of paradise conflicts with the classical ideas embodied in the Christian myth of Adam and Eve. Like other Near Eastern religions, and following Hesiod instead of Lucretius, Christianity contrasts the desert to the fruitful valley, emphasizing ascetic withdrawal and renunciation of pleasure and luxury for the steep rocky trail of virtue. This view emphasized the wilderness as an alien place to which man removed himself at great risk for inspiration, or to which he is driven as an exile. This and the evolutionary view are not really so different in certain ways, for the evolutionary concept, holding that the wilderness was man's original though brutish home, also postulated that the terrain contained clues into the purpose and meaning and origin of human life. A major difference is that the Christian wilderness is composed of demons, the devil, and things of this world. Hard primitivism, by contrast, stimulated a search for archaeological objects and thus endowed the terrain with

new "site value." In strange ways the pagan gods were returning, each bringing a reawakening to the uniqueness of place.
The homogeneity of the Christian wilderness was broken
up by the scavenging for historical associations and ves-
tiges to which humanism attached great significance. Moreover, to the men of the Renaissance and their successors
these remains of ancient cities and vanished empires, found
embedded in great deserts, overwhelmed by time and aridity,
could also be taken as a moral lesson or the essence of history.

In the Mediterranean world both fire and livestock contribute to the making of deserts; they are agents by which
man can bring the curse of sterility on his world. This is not
so true in northwestern Europe, where fire and livestock
helped break the great forest barriers to human settlement,
but where the more humid climate prevents these destructive
agents from damaging the habitat beyond the thresholds of
human prosperity. Groups of prehistoric men were not ran-
domly dispersed, but located in favorable places, separated
from one another by climatic and physical barriers. Such
barriers were crossed periodically and the passages through
them became important in the wandering and migrations of
people ultimately as the travel routes within and between
organized states. The opening of forests and the irrigation of
deserts gradually reduced the uninhabited space between
early settlements. Thus the fringes of habitable environment
to European man were the deserts in the south and the forests
of the north. With the diminution of the last glacial ice sheet
the Mediterranean environment probably changed from
temperate to subtropical and its forests were altered in type or
diminished. This change coincided with the northward retreat of ice and tundra from central Europe, regression of
boreal forests and invasion by deciduous forests. These events
may have ended the old hunting societies there, which depended on open country. In the second and third millennia
B.C. early farming spread slowly north from the Mediterranean, ultimately limited only by the post-glacial bounds of the
boreal evergreen forests. In central Europe, although some
natural openings existed, most of the lands had to be cleared

by hand and kept cleared by axe and hooved animals. Other
obstacles to the utilization of these fertile soils were marshes
and swamps. Many major advances in northward occupation
and civilization are correlated with clearing and draining.

Like the desert in the south, the great forest is the
wilderness of the north. It is always pressing against the
civilized world. Forest advance follows social disorder and
decadence, famine, pestilence, emigration, war, and natural
catastrophe. It does not require a fully developed forest in his
garden for the European to take heed. He is sensitive to the
first signs of landscape dilapidation. In *Henry V* Burgundy
says:

> Should not, in this best garden of the world,
> Our fertile France, put up her lovely visage?
> Alas, she hath from France too long been chas'd;
> And all her husbandry doth lie on heaps,
> Corrupting in its own fertility.
> Her vine, the merry cheerer of the heart,
> Unpruned dies; her hedges even-pleach'd,
> Like prisoners wildly overgrown with hair,
> Put forth disordered twigs; her fallow leas
> The darnel, hemlock, and rank fumitory
> Doth root upon, while that the coulter rusts,
> That should deracinate such savagery;
> The even mead, that erst brought sweetly forth
> The freckled cowslip, burnet, and green clover,
> Wanting the scythe, all uncorrected, rank,
> Conceives by idleness, and nothing teems
> But hateful docks, rough thistles, kecksies, burrs,
> Losing both beauty and utility.

The Western mode, processes, and concept of pioneering took form under two environmental extremes: the struggles against aridity and organic corpulence. The pulsations of
history have taught us the heralds of their advance: certain
species of plants for each, rockiness and thorns, wetness and
copses. These heralds have taken on symbolic roles, so that
we apprehend at once such decline in a place. A dearth of life
and an exorbitance of life; demons of paucity and turgidity;

the treetops encroaching on the sky and the burden of the sky; in one environment the human retreat is marked by an onslaught of organic forms, in the other by stone and sand. Perhaps this has been incorporated into what we mean by Gothic and Classical: two styles of art epitomizing opposite aspects of the habitat. Rather, since art is not "about" nature at all, let us say a Gothic natural history and a Classical natural history. The Classical is a broad sweep from whose general concepts the details are deduced; while northern Gothic thought laboriously pieces together generalizations from endless minute observations.

Does the environment determine the society? The old arguments about geographic determinism are as sterile as those about heredity versus environment. The key to their resolution lies not in choosing between the extremes, but in noting the recurring relationship between them. In Scandinavia the shapes of roofs are reminiscent of spruce and fir trees. In France there is clearly a similarity between the interior of the great thirteenth-century cathedrals and the hardwood forest. In England the distribution of various kinds of rock has influenced architecture, and it in turn the delicate perceptions of time, place, and the consciousness of a sensitive observer like Jacquetta Hawkes, whose lovely book *A Land* is a monument to the relationship of men and geology. In none of these situations is there a simple linear determinism unrelated to the character of the human society and matters of choice and accident. The same is true of the questions of Gothic and Classical thinking and their relationship to place.

No doubt there is a difference in north and south in the kind and scale of discernible order in the environment: the entities by which the particular place can be anthropomorphized, which correspond to mythical imagery, or which can be regularized as a reflection of a celestial schema. Good examples of the latter are the lower alluvial valleys of the great rivers in the semiarid cradles of civilization. In addition to the contrast between valley and desert, which provides a fundamental organization for Egyptian thinking, say the Frankforts,

There is another topographical feature of the Nile
Valley which finds its counterpart in the Egyptian psychology. That is the uniformity of landscape. Down the
center of the land cuts the Nile. On each bank the fertile
fields stretch away, with the west bank the counterpart
of the east. Then comes the desert, climbing up into two
mountain fringes lining the valley. Again, the western
mountain desert is the counterpart of the eastern. Those
who live on the black soil look out through the clear air
and see practically the same scene everywhere. If they
travel a day's journey to the south or two days' journey
to the north, the scene is much the same. Fields are
broad and level; trees are rare or small; there is no
exceptional break in the vista, except where some temple
has been erected by man, or except in the two mountain
ranges, which are really the outer limits of Egypt. . . .
The interesting result of uniformity is the way in which
it accentuates any exceptional bit of relief that happens
to break the monotonous regularity. Out in the desert
one is conscious of every hillock, of every spoor of an
animal, of every desert dust storm, of every bit of movement. . . . Another aspect of the uniform landscape of
Egypt was its symmetry: east bank balancing west
bank, and eastern mountain range balancing western
mountain range. Whether this bilateral symmetry of
landscape was the reason or not, the Egyptian had a
strong sense of balance, symmetry, and geometry. This
comes out clearly in his art, where the best products
show a fidelity of proportion and a careful counterposing
of elements in order to secure a harmonious balance. It
comes out in his literature, where the best products
show a deliberate and sonorous parallelism of members,
which achieve dignity and cadence, even though it
seems monotonous and repetitive to modern ears.

The Egyptian farmer whose fields make no permanent
mark on the Nile alluvium and which are obliterated by
annual floods, like the hunter and pastoralist, lives in a world
which he did not create. This is not true of the settled farmer
or the townsman. But the plow farmer did not appear over-
night. Hunters or fishermen living in a permanent domicile

may have first tended food plants and livestock. Perhaps roving bands of hunter-gatherers in the tropics and subtropics, migrating in cyclic paths, returned to harvest edible plants or their fruits from tubers or seeds discarded or planted. This may have led the way to deliberate transplanting or sowing. Plants which became adapted to this care were the first domesticated plants, dependent on man for their survival, either directly or through the agency of his livestock. Some of them may have existed fifteen thousand years ago.

Clearing for planting by fire or other means requires cooperation. The actual sowing and cultivation are, or were generally, the privilege of women. The world view of the hoe farmer and early plow farmer center on the mystery of fecundity. The seed is analogous to semen, the earth to the womb, and sowing and cultivating to impregnation, the rain and sun to paternity. The fluid similarity of semen and blood endows the blood sacrifice with fertilizing power. In the Mediterranean region the religion of the farmer included a goddess with a divine son and lover, whose death, descent, and return are a stylized form of the sacrifice, which in turn stands halfway between myth and the seasonal round, the cycle of life and elements. The idea of renewal guided the psyche of the ancient farmer. His destiny was linked to the enigmas of soil and weather, the vicissitudes of flood and frost, the invisible feeding and mating of plants, the rhythms of decay and growth. Some anthropologists regard hoe culture as marking the birth of human self-consciousness, separation from an "identity" with the environment supposedly felt by ancient hunters, a transition from unconscious unity toward conceptions of cause and effect expressed through rituals compelling nature's productivity. But the slow mystery of plant growth is so much more inexplicable, so much more pervasive of the whole environment, than the harvest of wild or domestic animals that it is difficult to understand how the roots of modern thought are any more deeply founded in farming than in hunting or pastoralism.

In a world circumscribed by the seasons, the periodism

of the living community and the life cycle of organisms furnished mytho-poetic forms for art and religion. Natural birth, growth, death, and rebirth, all synchronized with the climatic pulse, shadowed forth the legend of the divine king who is killed in the proper season and at the proper place. These ancient rites united prayer and magic. The price of the harvest and of rebirth was death and removal, making a new creation possible, and this annual slaughter and harvest mirrored nature's own seasonal fruitation and decline. Part of the crop was reserved for the gods. The sacrifice of the king or his proxy as the price of rebirth is the prototype of the emergent allegory portraying a sacrifice for the rebirth of the soul—ultimately one sacrifice for all souls.

The climatic and organic cycles are as basic to fixed-place agriculture as to primitive farming. The mythology of the divine king belongs to farming with the plow and raising domestic animals. It is difficult to characterize this myth as an attitude toward nature, for the whole of the modern world, even its cities and technology, traces from the attachment of a modified hoe to a draft animal—an animal who helped make sedentary agriculture possible by contributing fertilizer, which, along with crop rotation, achieved a productive equilibrium of surplus. The complex of animal husbandry and crops developed together with social organization and the domesticated or humanized landscape. The major features of the rural world, as we know it, a continuous realm stretching off to the wilderness and broken by towns and cities, is the outcome of more than fifty centuries of plow farming for a surplus.

Although the farmer continued to recognize the importance of the earth's fecundity, the contributions of rain and sun were analogous to his own familiar role as the fertilizer, the cultivator, the sower of seed in the furrow. Perhaps the most singular mytho-poetic and cultural manifestation of any enterprise by Western man in nature is the ritualization of the seasonal cycle in agriculture. But the power and role of man in controlling his destiny was always a delicate point. Ancient awareness of seasonal death and rebirth of the vegetation paralleled the life cycle of animals and man. The divine king who died and was reborn became fully anthropomorphized with the Greeks. His transformation was not a continuous progression in any one place. Much ancient magic and devotion to animal spirits remained. Prayer at first appeared beside older ritualistic magic. Ultimately sacrifice of the kin or his proxy for the rebirth of the year provided the motif for all sacrifices.

Much of this transpired under complex hydraulic agriculture. Irrigation required an elaborate political structure and made possible more leisure, wealth, the development of cities, an increased population with specialized occupations, commerce, and public institutions and buildings. The town was harmonious in scale with the surrounding rural countryside. As a source of fertilizer it balanced what it drew. The increasing wealth that transformed village to town was associated with the development of hard, storable grains and improvements in farming techniques. The upper limits of town size were dependent on the water supply and local productivity. Further distinction between village and town or city was the bold, esthetic manipulation of a social center in the city, especially laying paving and building a temple. The first cities were possibly Mesopotamian, with perhaps populations of 20,000 or more.

Early cities were largely under theocratic administration. A priestly corporation controlled crop surplus. It and they were associated with a major structure, a temple which began as a ziggurat, an artificial mountain. As the city became an "inverted oasis" it manifested artificial equivalents of the natural habitat in addition to the mountain, such as vegetation and water systems. Its walls, shelters, arcades, pavement, reservoirs, aqueducts, granaries, and sewers insulated the inhabitants against the vicissitudes of climate, substituting as a "source" for nature and for the earth. Independence from environmental accident urged an illusion of independence from nature. Metallurgy and trade in inorganic materials further fed this sense of autonomy. Where aggrandizement and colonialism supported still further population growth, the old organic harmony within the environment changed.

I am aware that the above description of cities is vastly oversimplified. My point is that their origin is inextricably associated with a surplus agriculture, that cities tend to grow beyond what the local agriculture will support, and that there is an urban attitude toward nature which is insular, cultivated, ignorant, dilettante, and sophisticated. At the same time, by virtue of the very polarity in the landscape that cities create, they contain and educate and produce men who retreat to nature, who seek its solitude and solace, who study it scientifically, and who are sensitive to its beauty. The very idea of a sense of place is an abstraction, a sort of intellectual creation like sex or climate or fashion, which is impossible except in a world of ideas whose survival depends on the city. The dilemma is that those who yearn for the warm garment of landscape security are already deflowered. They can only go back so far. They can regain the hunter's, pastoralist's, farmer's nonverbal responses, limited to an extent by their self-consciousness; but the yearning is thrust upon them in any case, for they were all children once and they had wild ancestors and they dream and to some degree all have premonitions of special places.

Chapter Three

The Image of the Garden

A garden locked is my sister, bride,
a garden locked, a fountain sealed. . . .
Awake, O North Wind,
and come, O South Wind!
Blow upon my garden
that its spices may distil.
—Song of Solomon

THE BIBLICAL EDEN ("delight") is probably the valley
of the Tigris in the vicinity of Babylon, a green strip extensively irrigated by an elaborate and ancient system of canals
for nearly six thousand years. The Tigris and Euphrates are
major river oases in the arid subequatorial regions of the
Near East, part of the "fertile crescent," the home of civilization. Man was "created" here in the Hebrew-Christian paradise. "Paradise" is Persian for "garden." The uplands of this
area, now central Iran, were probably where cereals and most
hoofed animals were domesticated. These slopes were
gripped simultaneously by deforestation, overgrazing, and
soil erosion. Urban man and domestic animals together
blighted the landscapes of the hilly flanks and intermontane
valleys of Mesopotamia even then.

In the flood plains of these rivers were parks, extensive,
walled places into which animals were released to be hunted,
where the nobility and its retinue went for sport and to escape
the city heat in summer, living in large tents or summer

palaces. In these grazed, open woodlands the court resided in cool spaciousness and directed the business of troop maneuvers, public festivities, legal trials, and religious observances. The practice of keeping exotic animals in the parks probably represents the origin of the zoo.

Temples in ancient Persian cities were sacred artificial mountains covered by terraced hanging gardens. Perhaps the terraces were suggested by the irrigated valley; certainly they were practical solutions to the management of water. Here flowers composed islands of perfume in the horrendous summer stench of an equatorial city (as in Egypt, flowers had religious significance). Here the vacation was invented— retreat from the city during the worst season—and the custom of summertime evacuation of the royal palace spread east to the Orient. The Nile Valley, with its annual floods, was unsuitable for such extra-urban retreat. The Egyptian nobility made do with a small garden architecturally extended from the private villa. It was a small, protected, semi-sacred place for the cultivation of special plants. In these bowers the Egyptians wrote poetry, made love, and staged the important ceremonies of life and death. In scope the Egyptian garden was not greatly unlike that of the Moors, from which the Spanish medieval cloister grew, a distant inspiration to the great Italian Renaissance gardeners.

The Greeks discovered the hunting parks during the Persian wars. Alexander was reportedly so enthralled that he set aside one quarter of Alexandria as park. The Persian parks had shrines and hermitages and long rows of planted trees. Although pre-Alexandrine sacred temples in Greece had not been placed in constructed landscapes, they were parts of an organic whole, oriented to evoke in ritual procession a profound sense of the protective anatomy of the Great Mother Earth. Perhaps the more detached, man-dominated, geometric parks of Media helped undermine the indigenous unity of the older Greek shrines whose sacred groves and mountains were parts of the living body of the Goddess and prepared the way for the later Greek thought of Aristotle and Plato that emphasized dichotomies separating man from nature.

Public parks were native to Greece, and small private gardens were common. The lyceum was a public park reserved for meditation, a quiet stroll, or discussion. The larger gymnasium, with its turf and trees, was a gaming field often in the environs of a sanctuary and sacred grove. The heart of the sacred grove was a spring, sometimes flowing from a cave or grotto. Even during the centuries of deforestation of Greece the trees of these shrines were spared.

Burial in a sacred garden is an ancient privilege. Alexander was buried in a park; Israelite and Jewish kings looked upon burial in a grove as a final sign of status; Jesus was buried in Joseph's garden.

According to Genesis, man was created in what amounts to a Mesopotamian hunting park. There lions, other predatory animals, and hoofed animals were kept, living peacefully, artificially fed. These parks also contained fruit. One can picture the yearning of inhabitants of drier regions such as the Hebrew pastoralists for such lush fabled places. These great parks resembled traditional visionary scenes: rich watered rows of green, colorful fruits, large trees, birds singing like angels, a basinlike distant vista, an unchanging or mild climate through the year, palatial exotic architecture, the odors and display of flowers, a wealth of quietly grazing animals, beautiful amorous women.

The traditions of the hunting park and city park continued in Christian times. Baghdad had nearly a thousand little walled gardens with fountain, court, plants in boxes, mechanical trees and birds, and scented blooms. The Arabic game of polo was played on lawns in the larger parks of Byzantium. The Persian carpet, dating from about the sixth century, is patterned after the ground plan of a little private pleasure garden or paradise. The Persian term for the background design in these carpets means "earth." The carpet's border is a canal within which is a formal arrangement of plants, trees, and flowers. This basic pattern of all carpet design is used, like wallpaper, to bring the garden into the house.

From Egyptian, Persian, Arabic, and Moorish beginnings came the European garden, a paradigm of life in subtropical arid land where water and genesis and the flowery shade and the mystery of life and death were inextricably united. Its fruitfulness contrasts to the city pavement and stony desert. The spring or flowing well is the prototype of the fountain, the overgrazed slope or tree-planted pasture that of the sward. It is the "perfect" environment, the measuring rod of the earth as a habitat. Its fountain and tree of life are the symbols of creation.

In the tradition of the Greek lyceum, the Roman country house carried the tradition of dignified solitude to the country and converted the Greek model to a private work of art. The Roman gentleman retired to a home amid pastoral surroundings, horticulture, and unhurried quiet. At his rustic villa house, garden, and park formed a rough concentric pattern. All rooms opened to a terrace. There were gardenlike rooms in the house and arbor "rooms" outside. There were fountains and mounts. Pliny's rural Hortus was a complex establishment with his rooms opening into a patio linking the garden to the house, a garden room with lifelike paintings of vegetation, and an outdoor room or peristyle. His hippodrome, or park, was laid out regularly with winding alleys, sculptured hedges of box, fountains, and stonework. There were lakes fed by canals and long graveled walks and arbors. A little rotunda in the park, modeled after a Persian artifact, was used for dining. The *nymphaeum* or grotto contained alcoves, waterfalls, and a mosaic floor. Beyond were vegetable and fruit gardens, vineyards, fish ponds, aviary, apiary, orchards, fields, and groves. The walls of the house were concealed by plantings to blend house to countryside. It was located with a view. Though it had elegant formal components the whole was "an imitation of the negligent beauties of rural nature." Such a blending of villa and rural landscapes was not again to become the motif for gardens until the eighteenth century. In this admixture of the planned and unplanned, the extraordinary sensitivity of the Roman poets reached its acme in the two generations preceding Pliny, in the century before Christ.

Byzantine gardens prospered while Roman villas fell slowly to ruin. In western Europe they were survived only by a fragment of the Roman complex: the kitchen garden. Christian monastery gardens were primarily for practical needs, which in a sense is the first theme of all gardens, but the theme of generation has never been merely mundane. The medieval Christian monastery garden included flowers as symbolic decorative objects as well as herbs, vegetables, and fruits. Monastic tradition implies a withdrawal from ordinary social and worldly traffic, toward asceticism and the redirection of attention from the natural to the spiritual. But as Havelock Ellis pointed out a half-century ago, self-sufficiency as well as persecution put Christians in the wilderness. The lands available to monastic orders were usually remote and "beautiful" in the modern sense of scenery. The monks nurtured the Roman tradition of agriculture and erudition with the peculiar anti-nature Christian twist. Yet some sensitive observers among them, such as St. Francis, lived peculiarly dichotomous lives, dedicated to the life of the spirit but deeply and perpetually immersed in the natural environment and agricultural activities. Most Christians treated the environment as an elaborate text composed of fixed lessons in morality. The training of vision to see only a stereotyped iconography of living emblems and parables must have been tested in the gardens. Garden chores were not exhausting and were pleasant, exposing the Christian's soul to tempting textures, tastes, smells, sounds, and sights. Christian thought and symbolism of the garden were not dangerous, since an image or allegory has no smell or texture; but the gardens of this world, however mild and disciplined, confronted the individual with the sensual pleasures leading to Hell.

The garden was a hedonistic affront to ascetic moralism and Christian virtue, full of reprehensible pleasures tempting the pilgrim away from the steep and stony path of righteousness. A manuscript illustration from the eleventh century shows monks on the ladder to heaven, one falling who leaned out too far to smell or pick a flower. It was precisely this against which St. Anselm warned: sin and the enjoyment of the senses; the duplicity of the garden. The tumbling down was to become a rain of bodies beginning almost the very year of Anselm's death in 1109. The herb and kitchen garden persisted in the yards of fortified castles.

If the Greek tradition of the garden as a seminary (meaning "sowing of seed") was perpetuated by monks in the yards of converted villas, its Persian erotic counterpart, the little paradise garden, survived beside private villas and in castle compounds as a *hortus conclusis*. Women cared for the garden, entering it directly from their quarters by a narrow door. It contained flowers and a few trees, bedded plants, Greek trellis or grass. Often there was a fountain in the center with a shallow pool where it was customary for the ladies to bathe their feet.

At the time of Anselm's death the Mediterranean world was again becoming safe for travel after seven hundred years. A revolution then burst upon that world, marked by a shift in consciousness, from emblematic to allegorical thinking and perceiving. The subject matter was not changed so much as transfigured. The idea of a garden emerged from its medieval stereotype. The little private garden of roses, the green places within the castle yard, and the hedges and walls which set gardens off from the meadows outside figured allegorically in the most significant event in the perception of nature in Europe for a millennium. A phenomenal sensitivity to the landscape appeared in southern France and spread to Italy in the twelfth century. It was contemporary to a rising tide of religious pomp and courtly formality. It was inseparable from the transformation of society in the name of knighthood, heralded by a tumult of song and poetry.

In the setting of these gardens and meadows, love became for the first time in nearly a thousand years a serious social and literary theme, intertwined with an awakened interest in bucolic surroundings, plants, and animals. This love drew upon the traditional *Frauendienst* or service of ladies, but was transformed by ancient love poetry, especially Ovid. To what extent it reflected a Byzantine legacy or Crusaders' experience of Eastern ways and gardens is conjectural. Inhabitants of noble houses were the followers of this new theme, including itinerant knights and wandering jongleurs, whose number made knights more abundant than ladies. The new art and religion of love which they created drew upon Ovid's *Ars Amatoria*, performed as an allegory on Christianity, with its humility, devotion, adoration, suffering, pilgrimage, supplication, hells, and paradises. It developed as a "religion of love" among Christians to whom it made possible a bifocal view. Ovid was read as a pious allegory of Christian virtue and as a guide to love-making cloaked in Christian terms; Alexandrian eroticism was married to Christian teaching, as *amatoria*, for instance, by thirteenth-century nuns; the lascivious discovered a guide to piety—seduction with pious phrases and religious fervor.

In short, modern love was born, almost abruptly in the afternoon of the twelfth century. New importance was attached to chastity. Noblemen wandering among feudal estates strove for the beds of their chosen women by an elaborate protocol of social ritual, music, poetry, the tournament and other trials, and a new fashion of double meaning in all communication. After centuries of raw boorishness intersexual society was restored to something more nearly like the courtship of cranes, pheasants, and nightingales.

The interlarding of love and nature is displayed in an allegorical tale of the twelfth century, the *Romance of the Rose*. A young man wanders through a flowery meadow beside a stream and arrives at a walled castle, chastity's bastion. Inside he finds a lawn where couples converse or make music in the shade of fruit trees. There is good food and beautiful flowers. Nearby is a smaller sunken garden surrounded by a thorny hedge, the *hortus conclusis*, bearing a rose which he determines to pluck—the ultimate reward of love's endeavor. The way is thorny and full of obstacles. A new life opens to him, which requires not only a new dedication but a transformation of his own behavior, for only the heart intrinsically noble can succeed. Whether he was born a serf or a prince makes no difference, for the elegance of love's protocol springs not only from gentlemanly demeanor but virtuous devotion.

It then becomes possible for him to return to the fields

beyond the castle walls with new eyes. The *Romance* extends the metaphors of garden, fruition, and generation to the country. The yearning and love in the young man's heart is an extension of universal energy and beauty. Fecundity is the perpetual triumph over death. The endless cycle of reproduction is a natural link with immortality; observe life in the flowery meadow and singing brook: all creatures are bent upon perpetuating their kind. So does the allegory spread beyond the castle wall, extending the particular story toward older pastoral tradition and erotic poetry. In Chartres a group of writers and naturalists strove to reunite courtly and religious ideals, emphasizing the unity of man and nature in reproduction. Beside man's little individual passion how huge loomed nature's immense urge to perpetuate itself. It was as though the whole garden and the meadow and grove in the nearby park were responsive to that intensity of feeling that the courtier cultivated. Paradise, wrote Bernardus Sylvestris, was woods with serpentine river, flowers, and meadows, "wherever earth is most delightful, be it with grassy ridge or flowery mountain top." A hierarchy of landscape is seen in a story by Andreas Capellanus, who borrowed imagery from older mythology. He tells of three groups of ladies on their way to their ultimate rewards. The first was composed of those who, in accordance with the rules of courtly love, gave themselves only to deserving and devoted knights and were wafted to wooded parks with fruit and graceful streams. The second group had broadcast their favors indiscriminately and had violated the feudalization of love; they continued ultimately to a treeless swamp of cold water. The last group had loved nobody and were destined for a desert with thorns for chairs.

In southern Europe the nobility, retreating from excessive complexity and formality of society and city, encouraged by song and poetry, went out from the castle. They yearned for a simple life—not the simple life of the hovel, of rearing swine and chickens, cultivating and harvesting, but for the simple life of the afternoon of shepherds. This rediscovery of the pastoral as a beautiful, nostalgic sentiment of shepherding was one of the great early themes of the Italian Renaissance. Yet its roots are older than the Renaissance or the antiquity it evoked, for it hearkens to a symbiosis with grazing animals which no other rural activity can match.

Pastorality has a unique ecological history, for the horse, cow, sheep, and goat were the agencies of human control of nature and the creation of the humanized landscapes of Western civilization. Where lands declined in fertility, the pastoralist had only to shift from one kind of hoofed animal to another in a series in which the goat is the ultimate form. Besides perpetuating the pastoral scene by preventing the new growth of small trees, grazing and browsing support an economy on lands too steep or poor for cultivation. Although they have nearly extinguished the soil and depauperated the biota of much of the Mediterranean world, the goats and sheep have produced stable if denuded lands, invisibly degraded, for the death of soils and forests is slow and silent, extending over many lifetimes. Generations of men can come and go in such lands, unaware that richer surroundings have been destroyed and are excluded by the animals which they value. Such was the situation in Southeast Asia, North Africa, and Latin Europe from Babylonian times on, sometimes hastened, sometimes retarded by minor climatic change, but generally impelled by an economy based on domesticated grazing animals. Indeed, there is evidence that the region south of the Persian Gulf in Iran is where cattle were domesticated, so that the pastoral complex, including the ways and attitudes of shepherds, has been developing there for perhaps eight millennia. The landscapes characterizing the Cradle of Civilization are a product of centuries of grazing interspersed with lines and spots of farming.

Many of the forests, such as those of ancient Greece, which grazing helped to destroy, were adapted to the dry, hot climate and thin soil. Scores of years might pass in which the action of livestock showed no visible effect upon the trees, for the damage was done by nibbling the seedlings, interfering with the continuity of the whole by cutting off reproduction. A forest of long-lived trees might still last for centuries under such conditions, for it would require only occasional periods of no grazing for seedlings to grow beyond the reach of most livestock, though goats will climb trees where there are suitable limbs. Thus the withering of ancient forests, where not precipitated by cutting for ship timbers, was slow. Yet perhaps its slowness lent to the change an implacable momentum extending behind and before. That is the perspective of the Greek-Judeo-Christian cosmogony: the sterile land a punishment against man by arbitrary gods and a sense of gradual and progressive deterioration of man and nature. To this the Middle Ages added the yearning for the twilight stability of slow wasting, the peace of static biology as a human setting.

Except for hunting, pastoralism is the only life in nature without arduous labor. In contrast to agriculture, with its year-round drudgery, dependence on the weather, and danger from plant diseases and floods, tending livestock is comparatively leisurely and the shepherd's life appears idyllic. Classical mythology unfolded in a pastoral landscape. Grazing animals remove brush and lower limbs and mow the lawn beneath the trees, creating that penumbrous grove in which lovers dance, the weary traveler pauses to drink, the shepherd rests and plays, the philosopher meditates, and the youths compete. This scene was resurrected in a literary genre, influenced by a new reading of the verse of Theocritus, who had come from the Sicilian uplands and expressed his longing to return to rustic simplicity from urban Alexandria. The pastoral ideal was a golden age of youth and of antique man. Vergil used it in his drama of Arcadia; it was Homer's "Mother of Flocks." Pan found a permanent niche in that pastoral scene, as the fusion of man and beast, goat's bottom and man's top, signifying the intimate relationship of shepherd, grazing animals, and environment. Generations of poets, classical and modern, used the pastoral as a vehicle for philosophy, theology, allegory, and panegyric. Behind its stilted verbiage are genuine perceptions and sentiments, such as that original memory of Sicily, or later blunt, bawdy, and ironic verse and balladry of peasant life. But most frequently it was simply a poetic device. In spite of convention, verbosity, and obscurity, the main elements of the pastoral remain visible: freedom to discourse, think, make music, dance, and make love. The currency of this imagery has been inverse to the degree of formality and constraint in routine social intercourse.

In his book *The Waning of the Middle Ages*, J. Huizinga calls this dream of the shepherd's life one of the strongest motives of the Middle Ages. It became the bucolic answer to the strenuous chivalric mold of the courtier's life, a peaceful call to antique splendor. As their immediate predecessors had played at Lancelot and Guinevere, the kings and their courts in the fourteenth century played at shepherd and shepherdess. Not only a refuge from the competition, vanity, and hatred that beset the aristocracy, but the pastoral was, Huizinga says, "the idyllic form assumed by erotic thought."

The image of the Christian shepherd was used by Petrarch to lament the ruin of Rome and to attack church corruption. In the fourteenth and fifteenth centuries, allusions in the pastoral became even more heavily topical, attacking civilized evils, vicious court life, political cynicism, materialism, and rationalism. The pastoral was dramatized in the sixteenth century with Sir Philip Sidney's *Arcadia*. Thereafter, its form and substance were modified by new ideas of man and nature, but the theme of the innocent, ideal life of the shepherd continued to affect the arts and the perception of nature. In spite of its trite unreality and daydream sensuousness, the idea of the pastoral enlarged the new sensitivity to nature that was born in the twelfth century. "However artificial it might be," concludes Huizinga, "pastoral fancy still tended to bring the loving soul into touch with nature and its beauties. The pastoral genre was a school where a keener perception and a stronger affection towards nature were learned. . . . Out of the simple words of exultation at the joy caused by sunshine and shade, birds and flowers, the loving description of scenery and rural life gradually develops."

Speculation about the origin of man suggested that creation in Eden was symbolic of a natural history. Classical ideas of primitive man fell into two categories: early man as a barbarian, little differentiated from the animals, struggling daily against a dangerous world; and man in an Arcadian paradise where the climate and soil yielded food without work, winter, or strife, where leisure fostered art and innocent pleasure. Christian doctrine coincided with the latter, focusing on the moral and intellectual state of Adam before and after the Fall, and humanity before and after the Flood. Some believed because of a particular translation of the Scriptures from the Greek, that nature was cursed along with man at the Fall. The Christian Garden of Eden was reconciled with the Arcadian Golden Age during the first Christian millennium. The word "natural" was a synonym for normality, to the Greeks and Romans, as so to modern man, as man subsequently became unnatural and degraded and cursed. Part of the problem of integrating and rationalizing Classical and Biblical history was the moral status of pagans. Opposing views were held by different theologians, as, for instance, opinions on the Scythians or the Germans and Nordics in the ninth and tenth centuries. By the twelfth century the argument took on new intensity as a result of the infusion of paradise legends, widening historical perspective, and increasing geographic and ethnological speculation. Theories linked golden age and evolutionary views by invoking a progressive, evolutionary return toward a paradisaical state which had been lost. Sannazaro's *Arcadia* and Boccaccio's *Olympia* (c. 1361) unite Theocritus, Petrarch, and Vergil with the new curiosity and pleasure in the park landscape. In *Olympia* even heaven is pastoral. The paintings by Titian, Tintoretto, and Giorgione are pictorial glimpses of this association of erotic theme and the park landscape. Giorgione's *Concert champêtre* is set in a landscape which is a natural garden. Spenser and Milton displayed the English love for the forest edge; the imagery of *L'Allegro* is primarily pastoral. This aspect of the landscape attracted Chaucer and Shakespeare.

The landscapes of northwestern Europe emerged from twenty-five hundred years of pioneering with livestock. These meadows and pastures were abruptly demarked from the forest. The pattern of village growth was nucleate, a cluster of buildings separated from the forest by a zone of meadows and crop lands, seldom at first partitioned by hedges. Sometimes there was a small ring of woodland for fuel left very close to the village, while pasture, crop, and grazing land separated these woods from the vast surrounding forest. Parts of the meadow near the village were common ground. Villages that expanded into towns incorporated the commons within the settlement. Planned villages, such as those self-consciously established in colonial America, included a built-in common. Although the function of this public meadow was originally pastoral, it became the place of many social activities. Games of the lawn, frequently involving the use of a ball, archery, horsemanship, and athletic events belong to the meadow, as well as social dancing and other public celebrations and religious ceremony. Childhood games, wedding receptions, funerals, burials, graduations, and the lawn party are associated with the yard in the forest opening. Public use of the northern common is the counterpart of the southern pastoral. Northern gardens were never the same antithesis to the countryside as those of the South. The lushness of grass and abundance and richness of all verdure was greater in Northern Europe than in the Mediterranean park. Only one great innovation in the history of gardening has come from the North: the English landscape garden. For the most part, its gardens have been imitations and adaptations from the South. But its social lawn, or glade, ringed by the forest wall, is distinct from the Mediterranean grove. It is an inverse oasis, an island of open space in the continuum of forest. In Old Saxon "paradise" was translated as "meadow."

To those privileged or professionally obligated to hunt, this habitat was the counterpart of the classical hunting park. Besides conducting many of the exercises held in the meadow, the feudal lord was responsible for protecting and hunting the king's game. From the thirteenth century in England, the official hunting park was a royal grant or prescription, enclosed to contain the stag, fallow deer, wild cow, or boar.

It may be distinguished from the royal forest or chase, which had laws of public use, officers, and was not enclosed. Hunting signified status formalized to varying degrees, from the feudal baron's rights in the fields and forests of his domain to special hunting parks reserved for royal use. Except for a few kinds of animals, such as boar or stag, hunting was not limited to the forest interior. The hunt spilled across lands that had been earlier cleared and abandoned as well as the grazing areas at the periphery of the village fields. True falconry was carried on entirely in the open. In general, hunting was an activity of the forest edge, always beginning and ending with a procession across the lawns and meadows near the village or castle.

The small kitchen garden and the peasant cottage with flowers are also northern. They and the hay meadows suggest the poetry of Burns and Cowper. But the modern idea of a garden infiltrated from Italy, where at the time of the Renaissance it emerged as a major art form. The formality of pastoral poetry materialized in the great Italian gardens at the end of the fifteenth century. As the *villa rustica* or *villa urbana* became fastidiously decorated, its gardens were improved also. By mid-sixteenth century these gardens came close to an ultimate achievement of their kind. They were intensely ordered constructions, with rigidly geometric forms, the parterres, near the house; new plants had become available; new engineering achievement and political conditions opened the way.

The immediate predecessor to the Italian Renaissance garden was the formal cloister around a central fountain, united to a great house, a modified monastic patio severely dominated by orthodox symbolism and beautifully integrated into an over-all religious architecture. Like the Moorish private gardens from which it in turn arose, the Spanish patio was designed by artists working to subordinate every aspect of natural form to a religious idea. The elegantly ornamented Italian gardens which burst forth as major works of art in the sixteenth century abandoned that Spanish puritanism, taking from it or sharing with it only that underlying geometric rationality. Not that there is much historical descent from one to the other, for there is evidence in the fifteenth-century Italian tradition, particularly as it was illustrated by woodcuts, that classical elements of design were already nourishing the new Italian esthetic.

So it was that the Italians created in the sixteenth century some of the most brilliant gardens of history. They were large, walled, geometric spaces adjoining private villas. Arranged axially, they were boldly drawn with hedges and topiary, straight paved paths, and rectilinear ponds interconnected by flumes and water staircases and punctuated by incredible fountains and cool, sculptured grottos. The abundant water was made possible by the reconstruction of the Roman water supply. Still, there was little grass and few flowers, although there was often a park surrounding the formal area, with a diversity of meadows, vineyards, fish ponds, aviaries, plantations, and artificial mounts.

Although they continued the tradition of refuge from the mundane world, the magnificent Italian gardens, such as those of the Villa d'Este at Tivoli, were reoriented toward esthetic and intellectual ends, away from both erotic and religious motives to which the garden had been subordinate for a thousand years. The new abstractions were coupled with science and display, for they became showplaces of botanical science where new plants were incorporated and systematically developed.

It may seem odd that a society rediscovering and reinterpreting ancient rural idylls, more motivated to escape the city than the Romans and Greeks, should have so formally sculptured garden space. The answer is, I believe, that their rigor defines an attempt to encompass—as well as to control—nature. However severe the design of those gardens may look to us today, they were regarded in their time as *natural*, in the sense of essential reality. Wild nature had not yet been seen as orderly. It contained the germ of beauty, dormant and imperfect without human help. The garden was becoming a more deliberate abstraction of the cosmos than it had yet been, and its unconscious symbolism subordinated. It is perhaps significant that an art implying by its existence and affirming by its fashionableness that nature is coherent should have emerged in a semiarid land, or I should say, in a Mediterranean land with wet winters and bone-dry summers. Behind the figures in Italian Quattrocentro painting are bits of landscape in which that discovery is anticipated, where trees and shrubs grow as isolated specimens, indeed, as horticultural objects. Or perhaps it took the Flemish mind, tutored in Italy, to see pattern in that sparse growth and to nudge Italian consciousness. It was as though every tree had been arranged by the hand of man, while in fact it was as much the intolerance of one root for another in dry earth. The painters must surely have influenced the gardeners who, though adequate water was at hand, created not thickets and banks of flowers but rows and whorls of mathematically spaced shrubs, hedges, vines, and trees.

The Arabs, Greeks, Spanish, and medieval Romans had, alas, too little water for gardening on a grand scale. Yet it is in just these lands that water is most appreciated and revered. Northerners from more humid lands comprehend only with difficulty the joy of the wading pool in castle grounds or the cool grace of the urn in the summer drought. There had been fountains in gardens for millennia, but the lavish and creative use of water made by the Italians emphasized its endlessly fascinating animation.

Even the frivolous, elegant, rococo use of water was part of a visual realization and abstraction of characteristics of wild nature. We are reminded of Persian rugs and Flemish tapestries in which the spatial arrangement of forms is the first order of understanding and the precise though stylized identity of types the second, both brought to consciousness with the formality of a minuet. The pattern of spacing between trees in a wild woodland, the disposition of shrubbery relative to trees, the disposition of leaves upon each plant, the symmetry of growth forms are but a few of the features which have implicit geometry, while perhaps the streamways and paths seem more subject to the aimless disruption of accident and were consequently given the most intense treatment as part of garden design.

There is no reason to believe that the formality of those gardens inhibited the personal behavior of those who built and enjoyed them quite the way it does that of Anglo-American visitors to them today. In contrast to the hushed decorum or museum mumbles which they now elicit, those gardens in their day were gay and joyful, where water music and other tricks, pageants, and concerts were formal expressions of an optimism which the garden itself evoked. The religious idea of the garden as paradise had been reassuring in its own way, but the Italian formal garden was a return to a secular or pagan theme which dealt not with the next world but with this one. And the message was essentially that *this* world was beautiful too, that behind its tangle, sorrow, and decay were intelligence and goodness.

By the time the political and social situation in France permitted the undertaking of landscaping on the Italian model, the form had reached its zenith in Italy. To the basic Roman garden with its horticulture and fountains had been added medieval flowerbeds, knots, and arbors. Revived during the Renaissance and subordinated to the symmetrical and sculptural intensity were terraces, vases, statues. By the end of the sixteenth century villas and their grounds were being designed with the unity of a single composition. Peace in France permitted the construction of new country villas and redecoration of moated castles with extension of the garden beyond the walls. These new country houses which began to appear early in the seventeenth century opened the French estate to unrestricted improvement. The famous architect André Lenôtre designed extensive manorial grounds to an extent impossible in Italy, where garden space was usually limited and the villas and grounds had taken direction over years of creative development. The new French gardens were therefore bigger, more symmetrical, and in some instances on a superhuman scale. French aristocrats took to gardening as a sign of status and the competition extended in some cases to hundreds of acres. What the Italians had begun, the French went beyond, at least in quantity. Painters were retained to record the results and the effete, insular world of upper-class play. Music was composed to be

played outdoors, pageants and plays and masques to be performed in special sunken arenas and on spacious lawns. The
labyrinth was recreated in high hedges as a puzzle and entertainment, far from the ancient temple labyrinth of Minos and
its ritual symbolism, and yet anticipating the delicious sense
of getting lost in the transcendental wilderness of the nineteenth century.

Some of the French royal gardens were so large that
they went to the horizon. The abstract symbol of the world
became in a sense the world itself. The water scheme grew
into a watershed and the Italian ponds became artificial lakes
with real, miniaturized warships. Where hedges had been
trimmed and marked by topiary, whole forests were sculptured. Paths became avenues, garden temples palaces. At
Chantilly and Versailles the extensive formal grounds were
fringed with hundreds of acres of formal parks: lawn with
regiments of trees. Garden art was shifting in transition from
architecture to landscaping, from nature's vital meanings
contained in the city to their spread upon the countryside. It
foreshadowed what was to come in England, but we must
remember that it was not a "return to nature" that lay ahead
so much as a shift in the extent and kind of abstraction and
therefore of art in the perception of nature. In Molière's
Florimen, a masque of 1635, there were shepherds and shep-
herdesses who, presumably, appeared to be consistent with
the sculptured elegance of the royal gardens although they
were "natural" beings. Illustrations of paradise appearing at
that time were formal gardens. Perhaps it is as many historians of garden art have said and English gardeners wrote
later in retrospect, that the English revolution against the
geometrical avenues of yew and box was a reaction against
formality, royal ostentation, extravagance, affectation, and
the rigidities of the autocratic mind and system of which
those gardens were tokens. And yet if psychology has taught
us anything in the years since the eighteenth-century Englishmen explained themselves, it is that the explanations men give
for their actions hide the truth as often as they reveal it. It is
the fashion of our times to explain history in political, eco-

nomic, and ideological terms—indeed, it had already begun to be so among those Augustan, rationalist thinkers of the eighteenth century. No doubt there were many who were prepared to see in the great gardens of the privileged few the antithesis of the democratic ideal which was then emerging. But social convictions are insufficient to explain the changing meaning of nature and man's relationship to it. The latter encompasses the first and it may be more useful to think of the garden as the symbol of environmental forces creating society than of society arbitrarily creating gardens.

The change was engendered partly by the intellectual ferment of the last fifteen years of the seventeenth century. Opulence in the formal garden had run its course. A Newtonian universe could not have been more clearly epitomized than in the mathematical regularization of gardens. The English invention of the landscape garden, or Informal Gentleman's Park, did not deny that universe so much as it modified and extended it according to other streams of thought. It was romantic literature, for example, which held that the alternative to a chaotic world was not necessarily a disciplined one. In Lord Shaftesbury's *The Moralists*, a protagonist is said to love nature

> where neither art nor the Conceit or Caprice of man has spoiled . . . genuine order, by breaking in upon that primitive state. Even the rude Rocks, the mossy Caverns, the irregular, unwrought Grottoes and broken Falls of Waters, with all the horrid Graces of the Wilderness itself, as representing Nature more, will be the more engaging, and appear with a Magnificence beyond the formal Mockery of princely Gardens.

Every word of this pronouncement of Shaftesbury's was to be realized a hundredfold in the tide of feeling and attitude which followed in the two centuries after its publication in 1709. It was not a completely new idea. Sir Henry Wootten had said in 1624: "As Fabriques should be regular, so gardens should be irregular." And others had called attention to the Chinese garden as a statement superior to that of the formal type, whether Italian, French, or Dutch.

The English park was destined to become the model for public parks in America and the motif for the yard around the American private dwelling. Although new, it resembled a miniature of the hunting parks of the sort built by Assyrian kings. Elizabeth Manwaring has shown convincingly in her book *Italian Landscape in Eighteenth Century England* that the new landscape parks were born out of a symbiosis of painting and architecture. Yet it had deep and numerous roots, for it was a return to the mainstream of pastoral imagery. To the hunting park and the classical pastoral it added an indigenous Gothic element which drew upon the esthetic of the northern forest glade, openings like windows in the forest, with fog and wet green, unknown to the South, where every rock and building was etched with age by the carbonic acid from plant roots.

The great parks, which have become perhaps the most characteristic feature of the central and southern English countryside, were built at a time of economic revampment. Commons were being appropriated by estate owners, the long-field system was being abandoned, and holdings and boundaries were being reorganized with the official sanction of the Enclosure Acts. Paradoxically the enclosures opened rather than closed the lands insofar as large areas were incorporated into single holdings and there was a great removal of borders and fences. The fence or hedge, like the garden wall, had protected the fruit and kept the unwanted out and tame animals in. It had shielded people and domestic animals from the wilderness—or at least had given the medieval clan and village an emphatic claim and erected the signs of territory. This economic-political transition was not motivated by changes in taste but was spread over two centuries of the development and emergence of modern industrial and agricultural England.

But it opened the door to renovations based on new esthetic awareness. H. V. S. Ogden, a student of English art history, has observed that the English learned in the seventeenth century to see their land esthetically. Their teachers, Dutch and Flemish painters, went to and fro across England, contributing to private English collections, focusing English attention on country houses, doing estate portraits. Toward the end of the seventeenth century, the precursor of modern tourism emerged, bent on capturing culture and scenery on a Grand Tour. The "enthusiast," the literary dilettante and connoisseur, brought to England landscape paintings which shed Italian light on the English walls and whose mythological and Biblical references were familiar to any educated person. The Dutch paintings showed fat cows in forest glades, but the Mediterranean scenes contained allusions to classical pastoralism and provided the visible clues of a venerable land: the rough skeleton of a worn earth and the ruins of ancient civilization. Classical architecture had long been admired, but nothing except rubble was left of the Roman buildings in England. A revival of interest in the Gothic swept England and Europe, not as religious enthusiasm but as evocative source of artistic imagination. Whatever object or scene looked well in pictures was picturesque; and the Gothic ruins did. Where there was no abbey the English architects of the eighteenth century built Gothic objects into the new landscape garden.

Before the enclosures the old country house stood bleakly amid the medieval fields, isolated by dense woodlands; the formal garden, hedged in, was no longer imperiled by the disorder, menace, and avarice of the outer world. Reorganization of the estate embraced land units of hundreds of acres. The great forest that had immemorially surrounded the settlements had slowly shrunk to relic islands. Contacts were made between adjacent forest openings and groves were planted in isolated fields. In the language of physics, a phase reversal had occurred in which the countryside became one of patches of forest instead of clearings.

Coming from the Grand Tour, at the end of the seventeenth century, English gentlemen praised the green meadow as opposed to the formal garden. Pope and his ilk wrote of Flora, Pomona, and Pan. The ancient gods and their environment had been evoked with classical poetry, inspiring paintings by Frenchmen in Italy in the seventeenth century.

Englishmen collected these paintings of landscapes by Claude Lorrain, Nicolas Poussin, and Salvator Rosa, and their imitators. In England these paintings became models for the new park gardens.

Joseph Addison made the tentative suggestion that a whole estate might be turned into a "kind of garden" which included the cornfields as well as the meadows. The landscape architect Stephen Switzer declared that gardening was greater than surgery because God made a garden before he took out Adam's rib, urged country gentlemen to read the poets, and wished that "all the adjacent country be laid open to view and that the eye should not be bounded with high walls, woods misplaced, and several obstructions that are seen in too many places, by which the eye is as it were imprisoned and the feet fettered in the midst of the extensive charms of nature and the voluminous tracts of a pleasant country." The reconstruction of the estates into gardens was begun in 1719 by William Kent, a frustrated painter. Sir John Vanbrugh urged the consultation of painters in planning new "natural" gardens, and William Shenstone later declared, "I think the landscape painter is the gardener's best designer." An early step was to remove walls and fences from sight. Charles Bridgman, an early gardener, retained formal elements around the house but allowed the park to grade off into the countryside. He modeled his famous work at Stowe in 1726 after a picture. Pope phrased the new objectives:

> He gains all ends, who pleasingly confounds,
> Surprises, varies, and conceals the bounds.

By mid-century even the formal elements about the house had begun to disappear. The view from winding walks and drives was planned as a series of scenes. Streams were directed in serpentine curves or dammed for Claudian effects, or built into falls after Salvator. "Capability" Brown directed the new landscaping of hundreds of acres of the grounds of great English houses on a formula of unbroken turf, sinuous streams, vistas amid clumps of trees, and a surrounding ring of woodland. Echoing an earlier sentiment of Bacon about the beauty of lawn, Edmund Burke wrote: "Most people must have observed the sort of sense they have had of being swiftly drawn in an easy coach on a smooth turf, with gradual ascents and declivities. This will give a better idea of beautiful than almost anything else." Even Samuel Johnson defined the sensation of happiness as "being swiftly drawn in a chaise over undulating turf in the company of a beautiful and witty woman." The beautiful, Burke decreed, was associated with pleasure. It sprang from love and distinguished love from mere sexual attraction. Beauty was characterized by smallness, smoothness, gradual instead of abrupt variation (corresponding, he said, to Hogarth's "line of beauty"). An effort was made to capture the repose and passivity of the pastoral, gentle in sound and texture. It fit the landscape of Claude Lorrain. The beautiful landscape was characterized by symmetry, graceful curves, grazing animals, and a mixture of lawn, water, and trees. In contrast to the sublime, which stimulated feelings of self-preservation, the beautiful was said to affect the "subconscious" with ideas of procreation.

The new professionals built picturesque models of Middle Age architecture, painterly compositions with a sense of the "genius of the place" woven into pastoral scenery. The formal areas near the house were first retained, then swamped as a sea of grass reached the foundations of the buildings. Toward the century's end the landscape garden moved toward a baroque climax. From a rather simple, sometimes austere, midpoint at the hand of "Capability" Brown, its variety grew. From the smoothly flowing beauty of the rolling lawn with its lake, ruin, and grazing animals, the plan broke out in grottoes, caves, little cliffs, hermitages, falls, statuary, exotic objects, and macabre scenes. In the closing years of the century the practitioners and critics formed two camps, those who followed painting as the model, and those who preferred a simple repetition of lawns and woody clumps. The genteel child of the eighteenth century lived in a world dominated by the landscape arts. His nineteenth-century counterpart occupied a habitat shaped by the maturing forms of the great era of informal gardening. Nor was the villager and peasant immune to the ideals of improvement and beauty dotting the countryside on hundreds of English estates.

The landscape park was said to be natural and its proponents spoke of nature as the model. It was an unconscious education for the discovery of nature's visible order in the rural countryside, although that order was not easy to perceive. In the man-broken forests of the temperate and Mediterranean habitats the acceptance of natural order could first be discerned. Garden historian Marie Luise Gothein says, "The romantic landscape was best pictured as a garden . . . for what the hand of man did in a garden was the same as that which 'Nature with her wonderous art' had accomplished in open country. . . . Decades later, everywhere outside England the feeling for nature was inspired in the main by the artistic beauties of the garden."

With the removal of the garden wall the earth could be seen as an extension of the garden. Once the wall was down, observes landscape architect Christopher Tunnard, the meadows and woods' edges looked somewhat untidy and the whole landscape came to be judged as the garden. Rousseau called the new English park a "wilderness garden." The "naturalness" of the English park nurtured an esthetic which would be directed to the actual wilderness. The parks blended imperceptibly with the distant groves and fields, seen between clumps of trees beyond lake or stream. This would have been impossible in Persia or Italy where watered land was sharply demarked from unwatered, where trees were individual and horticultural. The removal of garden walls was an extraordinary turn in the ecology of human consciousness. It happened in the lush English landscape totally unlike the ancient home of gardens.

The hermitages and ruins and other artifacts were "man-signs," although the philosophy prevailed that improvements on nature were neither desirable nor possible. The garden had been a sanctuary where men retired from the evil of the world. Removal of the wall marked the faith that all nature was a kind of garden with that same function. It was man-made things from which retreat was desirable, and therefore, said Rousseau, sanctity lay in unadorned nature. Goethe wrote that "men must retire from the world from time to time, for the world with its lewd and superficial activity interferes with the awakening of the best." And Schiller said, "The man who wants to be himself, who strives for inner harmony, must live as a stranger to his surroundings . . . remove himself from the belittling influences of the ambitions of the multitude." The city was cursed with the vices of men and the chains of society with its false values. By the beginning of the nineteenth century many people believed that nature was not cursed—as fundamentalist Christians and their puritanical antecedents had supposed—but, indeed, rural and wild landscapes were pure and the wholesome inhabitants of the countryside as innocent as children. That children themselves were innocent was a renewed idea too. Though new in its romantic and transcendental expression, natural morality was part of an old tradition of escape and solace, retreat and meditation. If retreat had at one time been into the monastery and its garden, it had also been to the cave in the desert. New travel literature encouraged the conviction that savages were instinctively noble. Wordsworth, an avid reader of travel books, has come to exemplify for the whole of English literature and thought this aspect of the retreat into nature—which meant to him the woods and fields, mountains and lakes of an England greatly modified by the land reorganization and gardening of the eighteenth century.

In some ways the creation of those gardens was the antithesis of other, contemporary developments. Changes in the legal aspects of landholding emphasized land as property. Land reform was directed to the creation of such free property in land and the abolition of patrimonial jurisdiction and police power, as well as the reorganization of farms and farming practices. As land became alienable and subject to debt, to be held in fee simple with few restrictions, the formal nature of human obligation toward it changed. The loss of familial attachment to land increased speculation, misuse, dismemberment of property, and accumulation of debt. However, the larger landowners were able to experiment, to make broad changes based on unified management in keeping with agricultural progress, and to undertake the new style in gardens.

Royal parks in England had been enclosed for hunting since the thirteenth century or before, and the "forest" or "chase" was the site of royal hunting parties before that. The park had not really disappeared since the time of the Persians; in the interval it had merely surrounded the formal garden in a horticultural form or marked the grazing zone at the forest edges. The "informal" English landscape gardens or parks were not "natural," but were intensively and elegantly planned; tons of earth were moved and fortunes spent in their construction.

The adaptation of the lawn with its scattered trees and distant groves is the principal innovation of the English landscape garden. It was "a great plain adjoining to a noble Seat." According to an eighteenth-century gardener's dictionary, "it should be as large as the Ground will permit; but never less, if possible, than thirty or forty Acres." It was a microcosm of the classical pastoral scene into which one escaped for solitude and tranquillity, which on occasion was preserved even at the price of having the mowing done at night. Late in the nineteenth century John Sedding reported that these charmed silences were "broken by the healthy interests of common daily life—the romps of children, the clink of tea-cups, the clatter of croquet-mallets, the melee of the tennis-court, the fiddler's scrape, and the tune of moving feet." It was the type of sound, and not the silence, the listening and not insensitivity that made solitude.

The unfortunate connection of these natural parks with the idea of democracy and the formal gardens, particularly Louis XIV's sumptuous Versailles, with decadent autocracy was probably one cause of the destruction of hundreds of fine formal gardens in England and elsewhere.[1] The aping of

---

[1] Most historians rather disdain gardens, in the spirit of St. Anselm, as founts of distraction and sensuality which periodically swallow up notable personages, thereby delaying the march of great events.

fashion no doubt played its part, too. It is interesting to speculate how different Washington, D.C., might look had the cultural lag in America been shorter, or Thomas Jefferson's esthetic of classical rationalism less persistent. Had it been designed thirty years later, Washington, D.C., might have been an English park instead of what it is.

It was not until the early nineteenth century that the American landscape became transformed in the vision of its inhabitants by the new shapes of morality and art. The painter Asher B. Durand wrote of England, "In the country as far as I have been all is like a vast garden of the richest cultivation." He was echoed by James Russell Lowell: "The green pastures and the golden slopes of England are sweeter both to the outward and to the inward eye that the hand of man has immemorially cared for and caressed them." Wordsworth's following was so great that he required an American editor, Henry Reed, who wrote him that his poems fostered "a taste for landscape that finds its indulgence in the worthy admiration of regions that are accessible to us." At the age of seventeen William Cullen Bryant had read *Lyrical Ballads*. He wrote in turn:

> Stranger, if thou hast learnt a truth which needs
> No school of long experience, that the world
> Is full of guilt and misery, and hast seen
> Enough of all its sorrows, crimes, and cares,
> To tire thee of it, enter this wild wood
> And view the haunts of Nature. . . .

If the English park was a diminutive Italian landscape, it was nonetheless destined to become the model for the public park and private yard in America. Patterns of settlement and landholding, rural and urban, fertilized by Jacksonian democracy, created the "house with the front yard" as the most characteristic single feature in the white settlement of most of the continent. The landscape became a public amenity in the nineteenth century. Where there was any doubt of the moral value of certain natural features, nature could still be improved, as when Frederick S. Cozzens recommended that the

Palisades be painted white for the esthetic and moral improvement of people in Yonkers. Picnicking and walking in rural areas was popular by 1830. In 1825 Dr. Jacob Bigelow, of Boston, condemned the city cemetery as unhygienic and fervently urged that a new one be built outside city limits. With influential support from Daniel Webster, Judge Joseph Story, and the Massachusetts Horticultural Society, a site was found at Mount Auburn, four miles from Boston. It was consecrated in 1831, "the first example in modern times of so large a tract of ground being selected for the processes of landscape gardening to prepare for the reception of the dead." In his dedication address Story described the site as inspiring the feeling of a "solemn calm, as if we were in the bosom of a wilderness . . . a spectacle well fit to excite in us a noble emulation." Philadelphia's Laurel Hill had thirty thousand visitors a year, many of them picnickers. Scenic cemeteries were established in other cities in the thirties; all of course remained nearly empty of tombstones for many years.

Bryant began privately agitating for a public park in New York as early as 1836. English-style town commons existed in many New England cities, planned originally for pasture, parades, and meetings. Bryant was probably influenced by the new rural cemeteries as well as the parks he saw in England. Landscape architect Andrew J. Downing knew the English parks and Count Rumford's "English Park" in Munich. In 1849 he quoted for Americans Humboldt's *Cosmos* to the effect that the garden should be amends for our having to live at a distance from free nature. For two decades Downing revamped American estates along English lines. He associated patriotism with improvement of one's habitation. He pointed out that by primogeniture in England land-use practices were passed on from one generation to the next, an advantage large landholders had there in directing improvements among their tenants, while in America it was up to each landowner and each generation to improve the beauty of his place. The English pleasure grounds, he asserted, are superior to others in Europe because they contain the "spirit of *nature*, only softened and refined by art. . . . [They are a] miniature of primeval paradise." These gardens were beautiful because of the "broad curved line" of the landscape. Downing's reputation spread from the owners of elegant imitations of English estates to modest householders, whom he urged to plant flowers to beautify the yard.

Frederick Law Olmsted, destined to become the principal architect of Central Park in New York, entered the picture in 1851 as friend and student of Downing. Olmsted's view of a park was also that of a retreat, where cares should be forgotten and the open landscape present "the greatest possible contrasts with a restraining and confining condition."

New Yorkers argued, pro and con, over the proposed park for ten years, during which time the main themes of opposition to the preservation of nature to be used repeatedly during the ensuing century were marshaled. When construction of the park got under way in 1858 the chief engineer made his first report, which probably approximated the view of the city council. He wrote, "Public opinion has, within the last few years, been awakening to a sense of the importance of open spaces, for air and exercise, as a necessary sanitary provision for the inhabitants of all large towns, and the extention of rational enjoyment is now regarded as a great preventative of crime and vice." It is apparent that many of the arguments for preserving nature still given coin today also had prominent utterance. His report proceeded to note that Europe could not be our model. We must have something better because it was to be for "all phases of society." The opulent, he continued, should be induced to surround the park with villas, which were to be enjoyed as well as the trees by the humble folk, since they "delight in viewing magnificent and imposing structures." A kind of American doubletalk reconciling villas with democracy and privilege with society in general had begun.

In improving the park, the natural glade or pastoral landscape was said to be the model. The hills and streams were "nature's pencilling. . . . To alter them would be desecration." Lip service paid, the chief engineer outlined plans for drives, walks, spaces for drilling, cricket, and arboretums. These things, he said, must be done: thorough drainage of all wet places; removal of stone walls and buildings; removal of brushwood and briars; removal of useless roots and vegetation; preparation of a nursery; leveling parade and cricket grounds; building an enclosure; and excavating ponds.

A leading citizen suggested that the grass be rented to a shepherd whose flock would make footpaths. Olmsted himself saw the park as beautiful meadows, with "clusters of level-armed sheltering trees," with "dainty cows and flocks of black-faced sheep, while men, women and children are seen sitting here and there, forming groups in the shade." Sheep were actually run in the park for many years.

As in England the estate owners of America first built park landscapes, but the idea of public parks of that kind was close behind. Once again the timing was significant, for the rural prosperity that attended the clearing of the New England forest on an industrial scale and the agricultural and pastoral bonanza which followed were narrowly sandwiched, as the broader strokes of history go, between the frontier wilderness which preceded them and the economic decline which may be said to have begun with emigration to Ohio and the canal linkage to the Great Lakes. But there was a glowing period of perhaps forty years when it could be observed that "with the exception of Maine and the mountainous sections of Vermont and New Hampshire, the whole country was a continuous prosperous agricultural settlement." A self-consciousness about the emergence of a New York–New England gentry lent its force to the new fashion for scientific agriculture and landscaping. James Fenimore Cooper, for example, was strongly imbued with a sense of landlordship. Fifteen of his novels pivot on the acquisition, possession, or loss of land. Up and down the Hudson River gentlemen's parks on the English model flecked the shores. The theme of the pastoral, ranging from portraits of fat livestock through classical motifs to the clearing at the edge of the primeval forest, many of all types based on real places, was central to the Hudson River school of painting. Ultimately, these were the American equivalents of the English designs and ideas derived from northern Europe and Italy. These pictures usually contain tiny figures looking into the vast scene, poised in equilibrium between virgin wilderness and the art of landscape.

Perhaps in America as nowhere in Europe it was possible to follow what had begun there to its conclusion: to go out a few hours from a great city and to look upon true wilderness in the biological sense as a garden. What makes such an event so peculiar in its form and art is that there was so little true pattern for it. The wilderness had never really entered the history of gardening. For the garden is an odyssey of unbroken sod and shade trees, purling streams, nodding flowers, singing birds, and quietly grazing animals—and above all a happy man and woman. Although an old and stereotype image, it is forever being seen with fresh eyes, by someone who tells again of the sweet music of the meadow and grove in contemporary terms. The garden is a formal human recognition in art of the beauty of the forest edge, the amenity of clearings in the forest, the gift of hoofed animals. Hence it is at once an embodiment of history and an objectification of paradise. It is no surprise that its imagery is part of the permanent gallery of the human psyche.

To understand the relationship of the psyche and the garden, we must examine some aspects of animism. What was called animism in the nineteenth century ranges from the endowment of certain land forms and moving things with an inner spirit and totemic rituals to the paganism of early Greeks, whose gods grew progressively more humanized. The ancient idea that birds and insects arose spontaneously from muck and the myth that man was born from an oak intuitively apprehend the blurred understanding of generation and the zone of uncertainty between life and nonlife, between men and animals. By the twentieth century animism was relegated to the limbo reserved for sentimental poetry and quaint illusions. Nature's reflection of human mood in literature was labeled "pathetic fallacy" by the literary-minded, choosing their support from psychology and an-

thropology that it was a regressive childish or primitive urge
to personify the world. It was as though the positivist critics
thought that all of nature was pushing to copy man's image
and none of it deserved the privilege. The general idea found
further refutation from the scientific denial of consciousness
to bird, tree, or mountain.

As in so much of human thought, there is a to and fro in
this opinion on the sentience of the nonhuman world. Opinion
shifts one way and then another. Biochemists and other scien-
tists now propose that life was spontaneous, however humble
in origin. Their idea differs mainly in its conditions from the
popular seventeenth-century assumption that decaying meat
turned into flies. Perhaps opinion is coming full circle, too, for
the ancient belief that the natural world is composed of a
myriad of living patterns or beings in social union. Charles
Hartshorne, for example, a Whiteheadian philosopher drawing on Fechner, argues in *The Logic of Perfection* that this is
the key to understanding the universe. A biologist, Aldo
Leopold, discussed in "Thinking Like a Mountain" the
changes that a mountain might witness on its own slopes, a
new version, as it were, of the Land of Counterpane. It was
only a helpful simile, Leopold seemed to say, but his essay
was a transmittal of ecological information about order and
disorder on a mountainside. That order was a pattern of
arrangement and behavior of the men, plants, and animals
there. Their mutual interactions were guided by the information, genetic and cultural, which they possessed. So it is that
the essay and the cluster of creatures and mountain are both
shaped by information. In that sense information may be one
of the most widespread phenomena known. It is possible to
speak of a mountain knowing, or, with Jacquetta Hawkes in
A Land, of the quiet sentience of rocks. Pond, oak forest, and
city, like the body of a man, create dynamic patterns from a
stream of materials and energy (both, perhaps, forms of the
same something). Although only an individual creature can
be regarded strictly as an organism—on the basis of what is
now known about the integration of a pond or forest—there is
value in envisioning such larger aggregations as creature-

like. Such envisioning has motivated the studies leading to what we do know of the pond as an entity. It may be an example of a larger class of perceptions by which we are able to know anything at all.

There is in totemism, the religion of the hunter, implicit affirmation of the landscape as an organic entity. It affirms that man is related to and dependent upon innumerable beings, certain animals dominant among them, extending in a web of reaction to every human action throughout the world. Some creatures are lower than others in such a system. Though no longer totemists, we now speak of other creatures as being lower by the degree of self-consciousness they exhibit, that is to say, their difference from humanity. In this connection the evolution of the cerebrum seems to offer man a choice. In one direction is independence: intensified awareness of the self-body emphasizes uniqueness, difference, and separation from other kinds of life. In the other direction lies continuity. In our fascination with the biology of growth and maturation and function we may recognize the living record of the past, in which our own individual development parallels evolution. That past contains the events by which we are confirmed blood kin to other life, the rock and air of the planet.

No one can be sure how a conception such as animism came to be inherent in men. But it is clear that the patterns which it enables us to discern in the world are just those which reflect our personal and social experience. For example, there is the polarity of male and female, and the final shaping of our attitude toward the earth by our understanding of gender. Perhaps it happens something like this:

The growth of brain and nerves that ends in seeing is begun in the foetus and may seem to be finished autonomously. But in spite of genetic momentum it is not completed without visual experience. Experience literally changes the brain and can determine the nature of future visual meaning. Sensitivity to light reflected from distant objects is the last of our senses to be organized. We must learn to particularize objects within the visual field and coordinate their appearance with sound and touch and taste. All of this focuses upon the nearby form of mother and the food she gives, then spreads slowly to the world. The world is at first mother and food. The eye and mind separate mother and food from the background, then they go on to isolate self and the father. The confusion which modern man can make among these four components of the world is measured by the magnitude of modern psychiatry. Do we ever unlearn that early blissful unity of mother and self, the nourishing environment, or the later division of the world into mother, father, and self? The world may be animate and bisexual because we are sexual and educated from infancy in sexual roles. The social sexual role and the sexual polarity of the world would be inevitably and inextricably meshed.

The most momentous corollary of that discovery is that the female and not the male gives birth. Mother is both the embryonic landscape and the infant environment. How does this affect the lives of boys and men as opposed to girls and women? Perhaps it results in the frustration of the male in accommodating his ego to the world. We have yet to realize the full implication of the mother as a primary landscape. There can be no mistaking it as simply a cultural phenomenon. From a literary view Simone de Beauvoir has uncovered its far-reaching branches, in a somewhat negative tour de force, in *The Second Sex*. The mytho-anthropological evidence is presented by Erich Neumann in *The Great Mother*. Karl Stern's psychiatric study *The Flight from Woman* explores it as an unconscious basis of perception and personality. Although these books largely explore Western thought, they leave little doubt that the identification of earth and mother is a general human phenomenon.

The sexual anthropomorphism of the world is not a primitive vestigial idea or a gross miscarriage of perception. The fabric of its imagery is gossamer though enduring. It operates in hidden ways, perhaps less hidden in dreams, myth, and visions than in the contemporary arts and public media. It is an abstract, vigorous, elusive part of most of our responses to nature more complicated than a reflex. It is embodied in forms which seem to be special keys to the depths of the psyche and to be properties of mankind collectively, like Jung's archetypes. It is possibly a last defense against naive reductionism and the pseudo-materialism of the technological society which confers death and uniformity upon the landscape.

In dreams and art, under drugs and hypnosis, fragments of this archetype emerge in symbolic form. But it is not limited to esoteric representation. Certain land forms have because of it been incorporated into religious ritual, as though parts of the natural world trigger a certain response and endow those mountains or lakes with special meaning. The ritual confirms among its participants that common thought stream. For example, in his study of the pre-classical Greek temples, *The Earth, the Temple and the Gods*, Vincent Scully examines the precise physiognomy of the horizon as an essential element of the architecture. His book is a breach in the prevalent conviction that the Greeks were not much interested in the landscape or in nature on the grounds that they left no great body of landscape painting, garden architecture, or nature poetry. Having not yet reduced nature to scenery, they could still sense the divinity immanent in it. Certain details of the mountain profile seen beyond temple altars correspond to what G. Rachel Levy calls "the gate of horn" in her fine book by that name.

The gate of horn may be taken as the symbol of the passage or the way. Its flesh-and-blood equivalent is the vulva. To say so raises objections from those who would not have such important components of religion and art reduced to body parts—even if they are magnified on the scale of a mountain—especially if they are the more disreputable body parts. The difficulty here raises some questions of the nature of syllogism and of metaphor to which I will return. The evidence that it is such a symbol, however, is both psychological and anthropological. Sigmund Freud distinguished between female forms (pits, caves, hollows, houses, water, blossoms, fruit) and male (sticks, pointed rocks, certain trees, the sun). He wrote:

The female genitalia are symbolically represented by all such objects as share with them the property of enclosing a space or are capable of acting as receptacles; such as pits, hollows, and caves. . . . The part of the body called in a dream "a mountain" is similarly termed in anatomy the *mons veneris*. . . . The pubic hair in both sexes is indicated by woods and thickets. The complicated topography of the female sexual organs accounts for their often being represented by a landscape with rocks, woods, and water. . . . If you have chanced to wonder at the frequency with which landscapes are used in dreams to symbolize the female sexual organs, you may learn from mythologies how large a part has been played in the ideas and cults of ancient times by "Mother Earth" and how the whole conception of agriculture was determined by this symbolism.

From a psychiatric standpoint, architecture and land forms are a continuum, an interlocked series entangled with the body image. Presumably that entanglement dates far back into the hunting life and cave dwelling which fostered the emergence of mankind. That those cultures existed for hundreds of thousands of years is the testimony of their success, against which all the progress of humanity for the past ten thousand years may yet prove but a downward spiral. We shall probably never know how they related the anthropomorphism of the earth to the self and the society. What skimpy evidence we have from the cave art and the relict hunting tribes of today is that the images of both the self and the Mother Goddess were not so boldly fashioned. We are dealing with an evolution of style in consciousness. To say that the dichotomy which men felt between themselves and their environment was less does not mean that the intensity of life was less; on the contrary, the color, smell, joy, anguish, and awe were probably more deeply felt. But with the domestication of plants and animals—with agriculture—there was set in motion the processes of thought and perspective that would eventually isolate the ego from the rest of the world.

It is a widely recognized observation of human psychol-

ogy that the power of creativity and control is central to the
ego. Agriculture dealt the male ego a blow so terrible that his
vengeance may yet destroy most of nature, for its havoc is
everywhere around us. The necessities of cultivation were
inescapably feminine. The whole cycle of vegetative growth
from the earth, the permanent hearth, the passive waiting and
receptivity corresponded as though foreordained with the
ambiance and psychology developed by the woman in the
hunting society.

Regardless of the botanical knowledge the ancient
Egyptians or others may have had, there is about the birth of
plants the appearance of an immaculate conception. The earth
needed no men to inseminate it, only the magic touch of
women as midwives. For centuries women planted and
worked the fields as guardians of the generative mystery.
Men could participate in elaborate ritual dances of copulation, but those were always once removed from the operation
itself and were performed in supplication of a goddess. Although the rain and sun were analogous to semen, they were
beyond direct control. It was not until the elaborate rituals of
sacrifice and the mythology of the divine king were attached
to sky gods—invisible, distant, abstract, concerned with
urban society—that the balance began to shift. The eclipse of
the female forum by a patriarchal succession, from Yahweh
to Mohammed, corresponded to the application of increasingly efficient tools to agriculture, the development of irrigation works, storage facilities, and the social paraphernalia of
trade and commerce. The dark strain of hatred in Christianity
against women approached paranoid outbursts of ascetic male
egos aimed precisely at the mystery of reproduction.

That fury was not entirely elicited by the great goddess's authority over fertility, but over death as well. She was
both the giver of life and the receiver of the dead, reigning
over the processes of decay as well as those of generation. She
was witch as well as goddess, controlling the whole cycle, the
"great round," a vessel retrieving all that springs from it. She
was the governess of birth and death and all the metamor-
phoses between, possessor of powers that could be used for

good or evil. These aspects of the female, manifest in mythology from the unconscious and intuition, provide the source of one of the richest stores of symbolism in human history. In the ages of nomadic hunting and gathering men had slowly come to distinguish themselves in space and time, among spirits and creatures unlike themselves who were physically and symbolically regnant. The hunters' vision was never wholly lost. It is incorrect to think of them as superseded by the goddess with her dominion over seeds, germination, gestation, dormancy, birth, menstruation, fertility, growth, and death. Alongside the rise of matriarchal power there remained the hunting mythology and hunting itself. Side by side with the evolving worship of celestial rhythms dictating the seasons and the weather there existed an underground whose roots were infinitely deeper. While the language itself was shaped by the celebration of farming—the verbs for sowing, copulating, nourishing, and tending growing from the same roots and streams of thought which would lead to the conception of man as a microcosm—men continued to hunt at leisure, and some groups kept hunting as a livelihood.

In surveying such a vast change in the nature of human existence, one is tempted to conclude that the great goddess created her own antithesis where none was before. Western nomadic pastoral peoples developed a philosophy of life which perhaps came from and certainly parallels that of hunters. But the similarity is superficial, for there is a desperation among those nomads and an antagonism toward farming and women and female gods for which there is no evidence among true hunters. Pastoralists depend on domestic animals, although they may occasionally hunt wild animals, and can scarcely be imagined worshipping by the kind of sympathetic magic which produced European cave art.

Broadly speaking, the society of true herdsmen is male-oriented. Women may be bought and sold and appear (to an outsider) to be treated as chattels, though we cannot assume that they are always unhappy. In surprising contrast to the dreamy security of classical shepherding, the nomadic herdsman's environment is fraught with hazard. Its potentiality for instant malevolence embraces bandits, predators, storms, disorientation, aridity, and any debilitating accident when mobility is essential. The sky is like a massive eye, perpetual and yet ever altering, in whose minutest change clues of crucial importance—weather, water, direction—are hidden. The wind, too, is something apart from the earth, more portentous in its subtle flux of pressure, smell, or sound than farmers and city men can imagine. These men look up. The magic machinery of the soil is of little consequence; indeed, there is no deep bed of soil full of unseen worms and bones. Their sheep or camels or horses are bred at will. Paternity is the intelligent application of cause, not an enigma. Desert and seagoing people create an empirical astronomy, which evolves a kind of mathematics. So does trade and commerce, for which the mobility of herdsmen makes them especially suited. The virile arts—shooting, riding, and love-making—are greatly admired. It would be astonishing if such a people did not embrace male values, the rational act, the abstraction, the extraterrestrial god.

With urban society and civilization in the Near East came the victory of the male gods, Jehovah, Zeus, and the Christian Father over the ancient goddesses Ishtar, Astarte, and Cybele. The downgrading of the great goddess and the domain of the female emphasized her negative sides: decay, death, unconsciousness, and witchcraft. The West had yet to rise out of its disgust with human origins and final corruptions. The preoccupation with feces, sores, agony, and torture which suggest an arrested infantile stage of consciousness were elevated to religious concerns by the same twist of mind which has caused puritans always to be preoccupied with the objects of their scorn. The womb pond and the birth canal, so close to and so like the alimentary passage, the individual's ultimate disintegration among a nightmare of consuming worms, and the pleasure which can attend the bodily functions are sources of prudish revulsion. In the fourth century St. Augustine attached himself to the cult of Manichaeism, which simply considered all earthly things as evil. The New Testament's granting of this world to the Devil was about as far as it was possible to go, although it was seven hundred years before there was to be any substantial change in Christian thought.

That horror of nature continues to erupt from time to time, marking a hostility scarcely below the surface. The pictorial art of the Renaissance, wedded as it often was to the Church, includes numerous examples of the landscape of the negative goddess. For Italian painters, who had never seen a heavy forest, the wilderness was near that of Judeo-Christian tradition, deserts such as that of Transjordan. There was associated with the desert the ascetic of the hermitage, the cleanness of sterility. It was a wilderness of paucity, the very landscape seeming to suggest fasting. North Europeans knew better, for they knew the toughness and fecundity of the great forests and what it meant to be submerged in vegetation. It is there, among the Protestants, that the full modern form of the hatred of women and the fear of organic nature bloomed its last pre-industrial flower. There were said to be wild men in those forests who consorted with witches. They had fallen from grace and reverted to a hairy primitivism. As Richard Bernheimer has said in *Wild Men of the Middle Ages*, the wilderness was the background against which the drama of Christianity was played. To go into that forest was to risk the loss of one's soul. How different it was from the hermit of the desert who went out of the oasis city, from temptation and corruption, into the desert to meditate. Like the unicorn, the forest wild men were susceptible to capture and sometimes reclamation. The adventures of Tannhäuser-like anti-heroes in the south were framed largely by geomorphic anatomy, the *mons veneris*, while in the north the legend always involved vegetation, a dark chasm, and a forest tangle like a pubic jungle. In Grunewald's sixteenth-century Isenheim altarpiece in the Colmar Museum, St. Anthony has exposed himself to the gloomy inbetween realm of a foetal swamp. Beyond it, through an opening, an earthly paradise is visible. In the opposite panel the saint endures the earthly demons. A scaffold in the background is a tumbling ruin, pulled to pieces by monsters. These Gothic specters were the spirits of organic life.

Other Renaissance painters treated the great goddess differently. The Netherlanders Pieter Brueghel, Joachim Patinir, and Hieronymus Bosch have left a body of work which art critic and historian Kenneth Clark has called landscapes of fantasy. But their fantasy is not arbitrary. It records the struggle toward the birth of landscape art working its way up through the deep unconscious, never entirely free of that archetypical vision of the goddess's body. El Greco's "View of Toledo" in the Metropolitan Museum of Art is balanced at the knife edge, a real city in the light of a real day and yet an embodiment of Freud's observation.

The beginnings of landscape painting and modern garden art in the fifteenth century were part of a revolution in thinking which is still going on. As men had ceased to identify themselves with the biota at the time of the birth of agriculture, they passed another mark in the evolution of consciousness which Owen Barfield has called a transition from the "intellectual soul" to the "consciousness soul" in his anthroposophical treatise *Romanticism Comes of Age*. It was a remarkable "passing over of life and meaning from the macrocosm to the microcosm" in which ideas became—as nature had become long before—general property rather than part of the fiber and bone of the individual, and words became the tools for mining them. It was a further shaping of the ego which would leave men in the dilemma of knowing that the price of stepping back from the world to see it objectively was separation. Barfield is right in recognizing that the new intellectuality was not simply scientific in the narrow sense of the word so much as a step in the evolution of perception and thought. Nonetheless, science and mathematics are usually associated with the suppression of values identified with the goddess and with the conquering of nature. Among the few innate traits in which the male human is superior to the female (see Ashley Montague's *The Natural Superiority of Women*), mathematics is the most one-sided. "It is possible to trace the modern history of science through an apostolic succession: of mathematicians and astronomers," observes Dr. Charles Raven, who proceeds in *Natural Religion and Christian Theology* to show that this is a widespread error among historians of science. Science, with its characteristic mode of curiosity, doubt, cautious reliance on the senses, and withholding of final judgment, is not a struggle to dominate nature for man's benefit. Much of what is done in its name is mathematical and male-oriented, but science is also the spirit in which twelfth-century leaves and twigs were rediscovered as objects of great beauty and wonder, as we see them carved from life into the walls of the Gothic cathedrals, as on the cornices of Southwell-King. It is the spirit with which Conrad Gesner, the fifteenth-century botanist, discovered the beauty of the Swiss Alps and their vegetation.

With so many diverse threads, our theme seems to have shifted from a consideration of anthropomorphism to various aspects of culture and history. But so has human thought become diverse and the evidence widespread on the concept of woman-as-nature. Perhaps it is easier to see such ideas in past cultures than in our own, because ideas of this kind are expressed symbolically and it is precisely the function of a symbol to intervene between the individual and certain kinds of collective wisdom.

Sometimes it is not so obscure—the cluster of ideas centering on "virgin land" in the nineteenth century, for instance. "And here we are once more upon the prairies," wrote James Henry Carleton in 1845, "and surrounded by nature in all her purity and her bloom. No plough has ever furrowed these fields, nor has the axe sullied the loveliness of these groves." Victorian gentlemen preferred that their wives come to them as virgins in somewhat the same way that members of the front echelon of pioneers settled upon lands where no smoke from another hearth was visible. The talk of travelers on the Midwestern prairies in those years was larded with the imagery of virginity and gardens. Frontier settlements were the sites of erotic evangelicalism reminiscent of the bacchanal. Communistic cults on the frontier were characterized by novel forms of sexuality. Any number of current historians have shown the prudish Victorians to be secretly sex-obsessed. Indeed, there is undoubtedly a psychological connection between this antithetical behavior and the equivocal use of land in amplitude—from devastation to preservation. Given the nature of man as highly sexed, perhaps the conservative ethos of an inhibited society is always symptomatic of two-faced nature attitudes. In Texas the whooping crane, one of the world's rarest birds, is vigorously protected in its winter habitat. Other Texans kill golden eagles from airplanes and experiment with plows that cut eight feet deep. A few years ago J. B. Priestley reported his impression of Texas in a book with his wife called *Journey down a Rainbow*. He found that fashions in female anatomy revised as rapidly as the landscape was changing along the highways. In Dallas, he observed, the ideal woman is never old or even mature. She is large-busted, long-legged, and boy-hipped. Not breasts, he said, for lactation, but as erotic signals. No hips for issuing children. Nor is fecundity the look of the land, where wealth comes from wells and an agricultural-industrial complex. The creator there is man, not nature. There is no such thing as a farm, since the land is only a kind of matrix awaiting chemical-mechanical treatment. Priestley's worst premonitions were realized a decade later when, in the mid-sixties, the women's fashion centers in Paris seemed to have capitalized on the transvestite image and their designers to have pre-empted the creative role, the energy of which was spent, ironically, in defeminizing women. Meanwhile the machine in the form of the automobile had become one of those complex objectifications of the arrested psyche which Robert Searle has so richly cartooned: the mixture of womb, breasts, phallus, and the mechanical power to detach oneself at great speed from one scene to the next.

The feminist revolution is a ruse. An issue of the UNESCO *Courier* pictures a female riveter on the cover and proclaims women's assumption of roles in industry, military service, business, and so on, which are traditionally activities of men. Capable as they may be in these jobs, they do not actually replace the men but join them. They are swallowed by a system which is antithetical to their innermost natures. A movement which should enhance rootedness, creativity, disarmament, the arts, and an organic philosophy of life could do no worse than fall into such a trap. As Priestley says, "Momism" and the talk of a woman's world are the sop that confuses the issue—the alleged tyranny of housewives who drive their men to a frenzy of earning in order to buy gadgets, who misuse leisure for the enslavement of the family and for inconsequential pastimes, who push their children to succeed as organization men, whose aggressiveness, masculine posture, and sexual frigidity create an atmosphere of neurosis and intellectual dishonesty. The tigerishness of American housewives does not prove the dominance of the female spirit, only its monstrous subversion. Our society is focused on rational, practical, exploitive, political, commercial, abstract behavior and values, not on intuitive, esthetic, organic, social, and individual ideals. It is not much interested in mysticism, magic, internal space, religion, tradition, children, nature, or the arts. The low social and political status of women coincides with the general absence of devotion to place and of a mythology of rootedness in nature. In agricultural rather than commercial or pastoral societies special attributes of the female—menstruation, reproduction, lactation—have been part of ritual celebration. Such a society is slow to change itself or to alter its environment, is resistant to moving and migration, nonaggressive, and reluctant to accept "progress" when it means the substitution of ideological for organic principles.

The garden is a kind of stronghold against this imbalance and is likely to preserve by its very existence an attitude toward the environment which is unsympathetic to currently prevailing values. The male society tends to be exclusive. When the role and figure of the female is supreme, a partnership exists in which male integrity is preserved; in spite of cultural variations, the man is still the master of marriage, the taller and stronger, the trainer of beasts, the hunter. Abstraction is itself masculine and the garden is an abstraction of the essential femininity of the terrain. In the genesis of gods, the earth has been predominantly female, the sky, male. The Great Mother is the spirit of generation and nutrition. The garden is the threshold of her mystery, of birth and death, the place of giving and taking life.

If men innately regard the land as organic and animate, then the importance of that belief probably goes far beyond the simple response to caves and tunnels as orifices, to ridges as thighs, mountains as breasts, trees as hair, and lakes as eyes. It means that the relationships between men and women partly determine how people use their environment. It suggests that, like the normal human copulation, there is a healthy counterpart in the nexus of man and nature, and that a mature human respect for the mystery of motherhood may be reflected as an attitude toward wife and nature. Skyscrapers epitomize the cleavage between men and the environment, resemble the ancient phallic worship stones of Syria. The two are part of the same development which began with commerce and male gods. The role of trade was not merely incidental, for it was like nomadism associated with an anthropocentric philosophy and with a creeping deterioration of the natural environment. Its present protagonists display what Priestley calls "nomadmass," with its indifference to the endless and hideous landscapes of filling stations and cheap joints endlessly alike across the country. They could only be patronized by people who were rejecting or were apathetic to any functional sense of organic resonance with their surroundings.

That land is female is more than allegorical. Insecurity, frustration, outbursts of violence, and immaturity reveal men's underlying apprehension of the distortion of values which he experiences not only as progress but also as impermanence, sexual patchwork, unimaginative living, and social poverty. It is reflected in land use also. The violence of strip-mining for coal and compulsive social charity are part of a pattern with the degradation of the feminine and the establishment of parks. Urban men are sometimes said to be unaware of the significance of the devastation of nature. They may not fully understand the chain of reactions, but beneath the wash of daily events they are profoundly affected.

In the construction of high dams, which involves blasting and ramming an enormous upright block of material into a stream valley, no engineers exceed those of the U.S. Army Corps of Engineers. It has become apparent in recent years, through the ultimate inefficiency and semifailure of these constructions, and their almost traumatic determination to continue to build them at the utmost speed and in the greatest possible numbers, that forces are at work which completely obscure our modest needs for such dams. Those engineers seem to be at the opposite extreme from the esthetes who attempt to etheralize their sexuality. Yet the engineers' authority and dominance over the land carries the force of sexual aggression—and perhaps the guilt as well.

A major lumber company proclaims itself a leader in forest conservation, though its greed in the past was unrestrained. It makes public amends in national magazine advertising in the form of landscape paintings of "forest cropland." These expiatory pictures always contain some form of wildlife, often a mother with young. To us mammals, motherhood means lactation, which is the essence of nutrition and nurture. It involves the oral act which ties mankind to woman and to the landscape which produces his food. This advertising filters maternal idealism into commercial channels. The inference is of course that the company now subscribes to the laws of nature, and yields to the nurturing perfection of Mother Earth. This may be true in a way, but the company also sells lumber and expiates our public shame.

The richest, most evocative of the milk-and-landscape imagery belongs to the Italian Renaissance. A nursing woman in a landscape strikes chords deep within us, as in Giorgione's mysterious "La Tempesta." The lactating and pregnant women of pre-industrial Flemish and Italian art signified the generative mystery of the feminine and exploited it in the interest of religion, ideology, or simply eroticism. One effect of Protestantism was to weaken the cosmic role of the mother, and by the seventeenth century a different symbol had replaced her in northern painting. This was the passive, domesticated, serviceable cow: the sign of controlled nutrition and affluence. This symbol was less common among the Latins. Perhaps they were not so prudish.

England and then America took up the cow theme. Since the cow requires a meadow and protection—signs of a high degree of the domestication of nature—we find in American landscape paintings of the nineteenth century the odd juxtaposition of sleek cows in the wilderness. Only as a sign of America's promise as a land of material wealth is this bovine sanctuary amid the craggy slopes and forests comprehensible.

If the geography of the obscure land of the unconscious is one of nature perceived in human forms and social and anatomical realities symbolized as natural features, perhaps it follows that mental health as well as personal fitness and social vitality depends on the survival of the natural environment. This healing property of the outer world includes the transforming power of the wife. A young theologian, Ralph Smith, suggests that the female transforming character and the great round of life and death parallel two concepts of modern ecology: gradual succession in the natural community toward a more perfect identity, and the final stage of equilibrium that persists indefinitely and contains the multifarious cycles of life and death. The transforming agency is love. Man need not study nature in order to love it, nor is it an intellectual idea that he loves. Perhaps all it asks is existence, and his occasional walk in the field will permit it to love him. We may then rejoice in a fresh understanding of the words of Leonardo da Vinci:

> So then we may say that the earth has a spirit of growth; that its flesh is the soil, its bones are the successive strata of the rocks which form the mountains, its muscles are the tufa stone, its blood the springs of its waters. The lake of blood that lies about the heart is the ocean; its breathing is by the increase and decrease of the blood and its pulses, and even so in the earth is the flow and ebb of the sea. And the heat of the spirit of the world is the fire which is spread throughout the earth; and the dwelling-place of its creative spirit is in the fires, which in diverse parts of the earth are breathed out in baths and sulphur mines, and in volcanoes, such as Mount Aetna in Sicily, and many other places.

Simone de Beauvoir has written in *The Second Sex:*

> Man has his roots deep in Nature; he has been engendered like the animals and plants; he well knows that he

exists only in so far as he lives. But since the coming of the patriarchate, life has worn in his eyes a double aspect; it is consciousness, will, transcendence, it is the spirit; and it is matter, passivity, immanence, it is the flesh. Aeschylus, Aristotle, Hippocrates proclaimed that on earth as on Olympus it is the male principle that is truly creative: from it came form, number, movement; grain grows and multiplies through Demeter's care, but the origin of the grain and its verity lie in Zeus; woman's fecundity is regarded as only a passive quality. She is the earth, and man the seed; she is Water and he is Fire. Creation has often been imagined as the marriage of fire and water; it is warmth and moisture that give rise to living things; the Sun is the husband of the Sea; the Sun, fire are male divinities; and the Sea is one of the most nearly universal of maternal symbols. Passively the waters accept the fertilizing action of the flaming radiations. So also the sod, broken by the plowman's labor, passively receives the seeds within its furrows. But it plays a necessary part: It supports the living germ, protects it and furnishes the substance for its growth. And that is why man continued to worship the goddesses of fecundity, even after the Great Mother was dethroned; . . . Man venerates the Earth: "The matron Clay," as Blake calls her. A prophet of India advises his disciples not to spade the earth, for "it is a sin to wound or to cut, to tear the mother of us all in the labors of cultivation. . . . Shall I go take a knife and plunge it into my mother's breast? . . . Shall I hack at her flesh to reach her bones? . . . How dare I cut off my mother's hair?" . . . Aeschylus says of Oedipus that he "dared to seed the sacred furrow wherein he was formed." Sophocles speaks of "paternal furrows" and of the "plowman, master of a distant field that he visits only once, at the time of sowing.". . . In Islamic texts woman is called "field . . . vineyard." St. Francis of Assisi speaks in one of his hymns of "our sister, the earth, our mother, keeping and caring for us, producing all kinds of fruits . . ." The religion of woman was bound to the reign of agriculture, the reign of irreducible duration, of contingency, of chance, of waiting, of mystery; the reign of

Homo faber is the reign of time manageable as space, of necessary consequences, of the project, of action, of reason. Even when he has to do with the land, he will henceforth have to do with it as workman; he discovers that the soil can be fertilized, that it is good to let it lie fallow, that such and such seeds must be treated in such and such fashion. It is he who makes the crops grow; he digs canals, he irrigates or drains the land, he lays out roads, he builds temples; he creates a new world. . . . Nietzsche writes: "Inorganic matter is the maternal bosom. To be freed of life is to become true again, it is to achieve perfection. Whoever should understand that would consider it a joy to return to the unfeeling dust." Chaucer put this prayer into the mouth of an old man unable to die:

> "With my staff, night and day
> I strike on the ground, my mother's doorway,
> And I say: Ah, mother dear, let me in."

And Erich Neumann, in *The Great Mother*, says:

The tree belongs to that stratum of life and growth which is most directly attached to the earth. Older than this stratum is only that of the sacred stones and mountains, which along with water are direct incarnations of the Great Earth Mother, part of herself.

For this reason the female powers dwell not only in ponds, springs, streams, and swamps but also in the earth, in mountains, hills, cliffs, and—along with the dead and unborn—in the underworld. And above all, the mixture of the elements water and earth is primordially feminine; it is the swamp, the fertile muck, in whose uroboric nature the water may equally well be experienced as male and engendering or as female and birthgiving. The territory of the swamp has been so thoroughly explored by Bachofen that there is no need of discussing it here in detail. Among the Germanic peoples, the water lady is the primordial mother and the linguistic connection between Mutter, mother, Moder, bog; Moor, fen; Marsch, marsh; and Meer, ocean, is still evident.

Numinous sites of a preorganic life, which were experienced in *participation mystique* with the Great Mother, are mountain, cave, stone pillar, and rock—including the childbearing rock—as throne, seat, dwelling place, and incarnation of the Great Mother . . . It is no accident that "stones" are among the oldest symbols of the Great Mother Goddess.

Neumann raises the question of whether the idea of the landscape as female is a historical or psychological concept —or both.

There is no doubt that the development leading from the group psyche to ego consciousness and individuality, and from the matriarchal to the patriarchal dominance in psychic life, has its correspondence in the social process. The development of the ego brings with it not only the acquisition of an individual "soul," of an individual name and a personal ancestry, but also of a private property.
Whether the social process is the foundation and the psychic process an epiphenomenon, or whether conversely the psychic development is the base and the social evolution one of its manifestations, is a question that today must be re-evaluated. The materialist view of history is pre-psychological. . . . The relating of all ideologies to their foundations in human nature is one of the decisive intellectual gains of our time. . . . There are well-nigh unlimited data arguing that the decisive configurations of the primitive psyche—religion, art, social order—are symbolic expressions of unconscious processes.
The purposive ordering of inherently independent impulses and instincts, for which the human body is the prototype, is experienced as "nature"; that is, projected outward as the world of plants and animals. The history of the natural sciences shows that a man's view of nature develops parallel to his experience of his own nature.

As for its contemporary reality, Rebecca West found it in the unlikely circumstances of the trial of Alger Hiss:

To Whittaker Chambers the American countryside was not merely earth that had a look of purity. It was a person that made claims, that offered help. When he and Alger Hiss visited the derelict farmhouse in Maryland, the two men were not alone. For as the features of a face, as the limbs of a body, were the wisteria that smothered the porch and pushed through the shingles of the roof, the two cedars tall beside the barn, the apple and sour cherry trees in the orchard, the wind that blew along the valley through the unscythed grass.

So, we may turn again to the garden, and the Song of Solomon:

> Fondling, she saith, since I have hemd thee here
> Within the circuit of this ivorie pale,
> Ile be a parke, and thou shalt be my deare:
> Feed where thou wilt, on mountain or in dale;
> Graze on my lips, and if those hils be drie,
> Stray lower, where the pleasant fountains lie.

The little garden enclosed is the vulva of the earth, an anatomic metaphor evident in the love and garden literature of the ages. In architecture the spring becomes a fountain. When the design of the fountain is phallic there is a mixture of sexes; but, then, as the individual human is physiologically both male and female, so are the symbols of sexual morphology dual. In southern Europe the earth is barely fecund enough to support the human population. Aridity and sterility are the synonymous forms of the evil besetting nature and man. Misery is never equated with fecundity. Elaborate social-psychological mechanisms hide this cause of the human dilemma. The nearest approach to conscious confrontation is the comparative evaluation of male and female offspring. In the Mediterranean world the garden is the oasis of pleasure, the source of all fruitfulness, the exclusive privacy of which the bridegroom is assured. The details of the external genitalia of the woman are built into the garden, taking the variation of expression which always asserts itself between the elemental image and the art form. There are the grotto and the fountain; the mount is the traditional expression of the *mons veneris*, the pubic hill. The labia and pubic hair are transformed by art and, like a dream, transfigure literal identification of forms, and we are left with the peculiar synesthetic and unconscious awareness of their presence.

The voluptuous experience of the enclosing womb is enjoyed by the foetus, perhaps imprinted on its nervous system as a sort of ideal environment. It is no longer new to examine architecture in the light of this prototype. Such analysis does not "reduce" humanity to a "physical level." Art and the humanities are not sullied by blood and tissues, but given life.

City buildings are for people. In spite of roaches and rats, urban houses and pavements have no little transition to nature, no intermediate ground shared with the external world, except for gardens. Like the cathedral, the garden or park represents the point at which the interpretation of experience in nature is transitional between mythical and rational, between an internal, personal sense of identity and the universe. The garden is composed of real nonhuman organisms with their own independent existences, but which are perceived metaphorically and reassuringly. Unlike the buildings which turn the individual in on himself, the garden is the landing from which outer space is confronted.

In the nineteenth century the English landscape garden became baroque, full of architectual inventions illustrating mythical and historical events, concoctions for evoking emotions on the theme of time, death, or love. Flowers and color and perfume invaded. The clean line dissolved in a hundred rococo directions. In the twentieth century the small formal garden once again is common, with abstract visual designs and attention to texture and space. The garden has not returned simply to the symmetry of earlier times, but to a balance deliberately broken by various means. The garden has a new mission, says Christopher Tunnard. "In an age which has divorced itself from the life of the soil, we need nature's materials (not her image), her sticks and stones and leaves, the stimulus of her proximity." The Japanese garden is a "new" direction, with its emphasis on substances, forms, textures, and the elemental processes which they represent. In its smallness, its formality, its privacy, its interest in abstract design, the new garden is far from the great parks. But it does not really break with history, with an evolution, or with the tradition of a function not immediately evident. The newness of its mission is only relative. Modern gardens are no exception to the broad purpose of gardens.

The garden is the perfect human habitat. So far as there is one paradise for all men, all gardens in all times and places are alike; their peculiarities measure the unique experience of each society as it confronts nature. The garden is midway between nature and art and may be debauched either way. As a pattern of symbols communicating something in a very special way, art is put, in the garden, in the position of using not only the forces of Nature, but the land itself. Allowed to go wild it becomes a natural landscape. Tightly organized in formal abstractions it reveals less of nature and more of the mental representation of spatial relationships and sculptural abstractions.

The search by creatures for comfort is never perfectly realized. There are too many variables in the environment and too many barriers between the individual and the distant places. Tunnels, nests, and houses are effects that create environment in new combinations of sensory experience. They provide comfort, but it is limited because a hideout is a refuge from the world rather than the perfect mixture of solace and contact. The garden is abstracted from the world as a whole. It is designed to provide the best of all possible relationships to nature, unimpaired by the practical routines of house and field. It combines fruitfulness, refuge, and the deepest insights into the living world.

Man is not only a natural species but a historical idea. There is much evidence today that that idea points to his individual drama. We need to assimilate this evidence—from anthropology, psychology, the arts—not to reduce him, but, as Karl Stern says, to add dimension and insight, to enliven the concepts touching on theology. While avoiding the "nothing but" reductionism that would merely boil down the ingredients, we should use any information for recovering a view of an orderly world, intrinsically connected at various levels and interdependent throughout. Syllogism, analogy, metaphor have been led into disrepute as mere devices. Their legitimate function is the communication of levels of correspondence in a world of mysterious, multiple meanings.

At a time when the garden is regarded as a mere housewifely pastime or recreation for jaded suburbanites it may seem pretentious to allude to it seriously as an essential part of the human environment. We live in an avalanche of sensation and excitement with a thousand artificial ways to get pleasure and comfort. Few of them are directly dependent on other organisms and none except gardens are designed as a microcosm of nature. Since the garden is an abstraction of the natural organic world, it is not surprising that it is depreciated or perverted in our machine-oriented society. Perhaps the same set of values cheapens the place of women, whose organic creativity is both materialized and etherialized as the garden. The garden has not ceased to be important as an art form, but its present destitution marks our "conquest" of the natural world.

Chapter Four

The Itinerant Eye

"SCENERY" comes from the Greek word for "stage." The idea that the world contains scenery marks one of the great evolutions of human perception. It converted the human habitat into a kind of coinage by creating a generalized scheme of reference. It was the birth of the visual esthetic experience of nature. The observer of scenery has a disinterested attitude which would be inconceivable if he believed the surroundings to be haunted by spirits and art to be a form of magic. Scenery comes with science and with museum art, a product of analytical and detached vision. Petrarch has been identified as among those who first made a clear distinction between the pictorial quality and utility of a place. But surely it was not only an intellectual discovery. The art historian Otto Pacht has said, "The discovery of the aesthetic values of landscape was the final outcome of a complex ripening process in which every form of imagination was involved and which concerned the entire attitude of man towards his physical environment."

The history of scenery is the history of painting and tourism. Pictures had been prohibited from Christian churches by a Constantinian canon as heretical until the early ninth century. The Greeks had long before employed frescoes of the landscape as decoration; manuscript illustration and scriptural decoration with some backgrounds were not uncommon at the time of the earliest Crusades, but they had nothing to do with what came to be called "the view."

While those marginal illustrations serve as a kind of reference point, the herbals of the middle ages exemplify the development of visual consciousness which led to landscape painting and which, in fact, became part of it. The ancient herbals had been uncritically copied for many centuries, had accumulated errors and become dangerously stylized. Just before the earliest Gothic cathedrals were begun the herbal had come to life like a seed germinating. In the early stages of this renascence only the useful parts of plants were represented, although newly drawn from real models. The herbal evolved from such representation of leaves and stems by stages to a book of scenes including the plants of interest.

In a parallel development, the medieval calendar had begun by the eleventh century to include illustrations with an ever widening sense of the human scene. From the labor of the month, with some of its roots in the illustrated herbal, the modern calendar has descended by way of the poetic calendar of Italian literature. Even as the Quattrocentro painters struggled with the fundamental problems of the painter's art and created a visual iconography of symbolic forms, the herbalists and calendar illustrators were incorporating genre and natural history of their own times and places.

For the painter of saints and Christian episodes the important things were invisible, and could be represented only in some symbolic way, while the unimportant or merely real objects could be represented by signatures or emblems, deliberate stereotypes. It is difficult to imagine how those early paintings looked to the mind of a fourteenth-century observer. Perhaps the window itself—particularly church windows with stained-glass designs and scenes—generated a place for them. What paintings there were in churches between the tenth and fourteenth centuries were portraits, including that of the Madonna. The Virgin Mary had been acclaimed as "the Temple and Sanctuary of the Trinity." Her impregnation with the Holy Spirit was represented in Gothic cathedral architecture by light from windows. It seems that the puritanical Manichaean imagery of light and darkness as good and evil ultimately lent itself to St. John's metaphysic of light, and the whole provided a mythological rationale for letting the light of day in through a window. Once the window was in, the machinery of the psyche proceeded to accommodate itself to the similarity of what could be seen through it and pictures.

It remained only for the birth of allegorical thought to break down the habit of seeing trees as providential clichés. The emblems of medieval iconography not only ceased to obscure the tree from the observer, but the tradition of the emblem as representing something more than itself engaged the modern mind with nature in an incredibly catalytic way, for the whole landscape became suffused with hidden meaning. Explicit symbols disappeared into a general scene of "corporeal metaphors of things spiritual," as St. Thomas put it.

Influenced by marginal illustrations from manuscripts, the herbal, and the calendar, and nurtured by allegorical thought, painting emerged as a kind of window. Not that windows transmit pieces of nature as cleanly as a knife slices a pie. Nature changes as soon as part of it is isolated, whatever the means. Vaughn Cornish, in *Scenery and the Sense of Sight*, observed that a tree seen through a window seemed to increase in size as the size of the window decreased. A whole field of experimental psychology has grown up around window isolation and perception, and students of visual perception, notably J. J. Gibson, are exploring the non-Euclidean world which we occupy. They find, as Cornish did while sketching landscapes thirty years ago, that the visual scene is pear-shaped, with the observer standing opposite the stem. The insistence by artists and critics that painting is never simply a two-dimensional duplicate of nature is true for more reasons than they know.

Walking through any large art museum today, one is plunged suddenly from a visual dialectic by Florentines—by Giovanni di Paolo, Benozzo Gozzoli, and others—to the world of the Sienese and the Flemish, to respectively the sentiment for and the visual pleasure in nature. There are dozens of fourteenth- and fifteenth-century painters whose work has some kind of intermediate or transitional aspect. One of the most startling and most revealing is Leonardo da Vinci. His close attention to the details of individual human physiognomy, the immediate background of genuine vegetation, and the generalized crystal mountains in the far distance are the perceptions of a man poised at the threshold of the discovery of the beauty of the world. Solutions to the problem of coherence and meaning in that world based on abstract retinal effects lay far ahead. What deep organizing processes could the human spirit furnish for the perception and representation of unity in the world? Da Vinci struck out, as everyone does in some degree, on a speculative apprehension of the world as a body, an organism, in which certain forms correspond—sometimes by their appearance but just as often by a process by which visual forms in nature or in art trigger unconscious responses which somehow inform us about the topography of our own minds. Kenneth Clark has said that landscape painting marks the stages of our conception of nature, a perennial attempt to create harmony with the environment. The tacit question is always "What is man's relationship to nature?" That nature itself holds an answer is one of only two or three general approaches. Although handicapped by a very young language of forms and technique, the early landscape painters—including those who painted landscapes only as backgrounds—were struggling to discover significance and unity in their surroundings. Da Vinci, like others of his time, was prepared to affirm a sense of terrestrial natural order although he had nothing but faith to go on when it came to the far distance, and forms to use for it only from fantasy—the fantasy of his own unconscious.

The shift from landscapes as backgrounds to Biblical subjects on altar decorations toward windows into the world was exemplified by the painting by Jan Van Eyck and Giovanni Bellini. Van Eyck is said to have first painted "the impact of light on the retina." He went further in extending the subject matter of painting to history, as his contemporaries, both Flemish and Italian, were extending it to portraiture. The Netherlands painters proceeded to examine the villagers, village life, and local woodlands and fields in detail. A northern visual scrutiny of the texture of life was initiated which would influence the visual experience of the Western World. Michelangelo accused the Flemish of fooling with "stuffs . . . the grass of the field, the shadows of trees, the bridges and ruins . . ." Later on, the prosperous Dutch wanted their own portraits. Henry Peacham's text on the art of drawing in 1606 noted that "landskip" was a Dutch word involving "hills, woods, castels, seas, ruins, valleys, hanging rocks, cities, towns." They painted "prospects," a sweeping view from a high place which seemed to exude a comfortable sense of plenitude. Itinerant Dutchmen filtered through England, selling sketches and doing villa portraits for English country gentlemen. They were to become an important source of the English enthusiasm for the picturesque, but more than that they encouraged the evolution of esthetics from a narrow association with pictures to the landscape as a whole. Values were transferred first from "ideal" pictures to "topographical" pictures to the landscape itself.

Giovanni Bellini stands at the source of modern landscape painting also, if for no other reason than that his paintings suggest an observer who has simply stepped back so as to enlarge the view. Like Van Eyck he anticipates the great central problems of modern painting as the control of light and space. But more than anything else, it is a love of *this* world, its men and its life, that comes across in Bellini. It was not a new idea. The poets had for two centuries secularized the love theme from Christianity and aimed it at other humans and at nature. But, if the Flemish devised the terms of visual exploration, it was Bellini and his students who could paint light itself as an expression of love. If Giorgione and Titian after him emphasized sensuality, it was Bellini's doing as well, for the ultimate form of the love of this world is the love between men and women.

In the course of the seventeenth century, landscape painting came into its own, simultaneously with the art of travel. People in the "classical" landscape paintings are small and subordinate, though important. Painting caught up with poetry in the sense that Roman and Greek themes from classical history seemed to call for a kind of Golden Age setting for which the northern Italian countryside could still provide a stage. New stereotypes developed: formulas for leaves and trees, for the disposition of cows, temples, and trees; the format of the classical landscape was essentially a landscape from a slightly elevated viewpoint, with mountains in the distance beyond a still body of water, a temple or ruin in the middle ground with shepherds or a pagan ceremony in a parklike clearing, and the near ground with a few identifiable plants and large trees or buildings framing the scene. Such composition in three planes and muted color has in the course of three centuries so deeply etched itself on the collective memory that it unmistakably influences general ideas of beauty and scenery.

How this came to be so belongs to the history of egalitarian esthetics. Gentlemen of the seventeenth century mostly learned the meaning of taste and something of connoisseurship. Having learned the clues to scenery from looking at pictures, they were prepared to look for the picturesque wherever they found it.

The idea of the "picturesque" began early in the eighteenth century as "the scenery's capabilities of being formed into pictures." Nature as scenery did not simply expand the field of esthetics, but was an entirely new bearing on the meaning of the environment, of space, color, objects, and the visual process. Man withdrew from the picture and turned to look at it. The pictorial quality affected and brought together other arts at this time: music, literature, gardening. The great German musicians composed pastoral and sublime pieces and the poets such as Gray and Thompson turned their talents to scenery. The English gardeners declared that their greatest guide was the painter. What some art historians call Dutch naturalism—as represented in paintings by Cuyp, Van Laer, Ruisdael, and Hobbema, a waxing sense of the immediate surroundings—continued to develop in England with

Gainsborough, Richard Wilson, John Chrome, the landscape
painters of the Norwich school. In this the English followed
the Dutch, whom Horace Walpole called the "drudging mim-
ics of nature's most uncomely coarseness."

This was the period of the Claude glass—the convex,
low-toned pocket mirrors carried in leather cases, for looking
at the scenery, framed and darkened after the fashion of
paintings by Claude Lorraine—and of mechanical devices for
tracing a scene projected on ground glass. The so-called
"objective" cityscapes by Canaletto, circular panoramas, the
trompe l'oeil, English sporting pictures, and the "topographical" records of the country estates have all been called literal,
imitative, or a copy of the visual world. But they are not
literal; all perception and representation is conditioned and
symbolic. These "descriptive" painters followed some mechanical rules of proportion so that some aspects of their
paintings resembled photographs. But in spite of all their
striving neither artists nor critics have yet achieved the mindlessness of a machine or the simplicity of a computer. The
paintings done before photography seem to be photographs
primarily because the observer shares certain biases with the
artist about appearances and what is real. Whatever the verdict may be about them as works of art, they are not copies.

The pursuit of this type of realism-in-perspective was
but one of the picturesque bypaths. The separation of the
visual from literary and other associations was to become the
basis for modern abstract painting. It began with the framing
of a scene and the developing of techniques for using the
environment as a picture, representing a selected section of
"reality" on a two-dimensional canvas. Any landscape could
be seen from the painter's view: one learned to see the picturesque with Rubens or Rosa.

William Gilpin, an English vicar, put "picturesque"
into wider use by relating it to his search for pictorial places.
He walked over southern England, calling himself a "picturesque traveler" in search of "visual effects" and making
bland aquatints. The principal discourse on the nature of the
picturesque came in three volumes in 1794: Uvedale Price's

Essays on the Picturesque. A connoisseur, landowner, and critic, Price redefined the source of the picturesque as those irregular details, rough surfaces, and coarse textures in nature and art that pleased the eye with their shadowy chiaroscuro. The picturesque was characterized by roughness, irregularity, abruptness, variation, and the broken interplay of light and shade. It was not to be found, he said, in parks with their lawns and clumps, their monotonous and merely beautiful smoothness. Price told gardeners how to achieve picturesque effects by controlled erosion and the disruption of land contours, stream courses, and lake strands to "avoid insipid curves" and sameness. He referred to landscape painters to illustrate his argument and catalogued picturesque items: bark, rocks, knobby trees, ruins, the pelage of donkeys. Old oaks and rustic bridges were his equivalents of the Dutch rutted lowland roads and knotty trees.

The picturesque joined the sublime and the beautiful as a good and admirable quality in scenery. It accounted for visual pleasure in informal, close surroundings, an adaptation to rural, rustic places, and a rising interest in the peasant cottage and the common man. It was possible to look for picturesque objects in the local countryside or to build them into gardens.

About the same time Richard Payne Knight, another theoretician of art, drove painting and historical allusion further apart. He admitted that a work of art might still be judged by the ideas and emotions it aroused, but he held that color was in a different category, sufficient by itself, affording an abstract pleasure undiluted by ordinary meanings. J. M. W. Turner and the French impressionists realized that philosophy in their painting and, thereafter, landscape painting—most art, in fact—was to be analyzed in a language of abstractions such as power, force, line, color, mass, symmetry, balance, tension, and texture. Since the middle of the nineteenth century, the "subject"—what a picture is about—diminished in importance. Formal criticism has pronounced representational art dead. But do we know that nonobjective forms are not representational? Perhaps such pictures are representative of that part of nature for which there is no verbal equivalent, and the facile language of abstract analysis misses the essential point.

The Tourist

The relationship of scenery and pictures is inseparable from travel. Painting has been an attempt to discern relationships and to communicate them with visual symbols. Modern scenery-tourism has been the attempt to apply the esthetic learned from art to the landscape as a whole. History and science played a part in determining what was interesting, but pictures made objects and places into scenery. Mountains, for instance, remained visually unassimilated until travelers, particularly between Italy and the rest of Europe, discovered them.

But the roots of tourism precede the pictorial arts. The prototype of modern tourism is religious and medieval. In early Christian times the rural retreats of the Greeks and Romans were almost forgotten. There were exceptions, such as Sidonius Apollinaris of Lyons, a poet who took a classical tour to Rome in the fourth century, quoting Vergil in his journal as he went. On the whole, however, travel was difficult, dangerous, and uncomfortable. Journeys of piety began about 500 A.D. There were two kinds of religious traveler, the exile and the pilgrim. By peregrination the exile renounced home and safety for a purposeful vagrancy. His journey was a purification, a wandering impelled *pro remedio animae*, "for the love of God," and "to gain a country in heaven."

The pilgrimage followed an itinerary to sacred relics. The pilgrim traced the path of Christ, other Biblical events, or went to participate in a religious celebration. He bathed in certain pools *pro benedictione*. A sixth-century pilgrimage by Antonius of Placentia included besides the trail of Jesus the chamber of Elijah, the pail and basket of the Blessed Virgin, the chair in which she sat, the scene of the marriage feast, the synagogue in Nazareth, tombs, the sites of miracles, and various monasteries and churches. Before the Arab conquests cut off Palestine in the seventh century there had developed an elaborate system of inns. The curative aspect of the pilgrimage was literal as well as allegorical. The inns had separate quarters for diseased travelers. Sickness had long been associated with curses, sin, and the Devil, and miracles were invoked for cure. The records of these travels, like those of the Crusades later, include almost no account of the countryside, except for the places having therepeutic or Biblical interest.

Tales of fantastic animals and human freaks were common in medieval travel writing. Alexandrine legends of fabulous lands contained just enough truth to be considered travel literature. The opening and closing of routes due to war and bandits magnified the peek-a-boo reality of distant empires. A century of access to China from 1235 to 1345 allowed enough travel to stimulate widespread interest in Eastern civilization. The route was thereafter closed by the hand of Islam, whereupon the East acquired that garb of mystery in which it still appears in the Western imagination.

The mode of the pilgrimage, the concept of the hidden paradise, the hope of renewal, the reenactment of great travels, the quest for strange knowledge were inherited by secular tourism. In the Jubilee year of 1300 some 200,000 pilgrims went to Rome. For this celebration guidebooks were available. Already exploration and learning were tempering and secularizing the pilgrimage.

In Europe and the Mediterranean travel associated itself with the great Italian universities of the thirteenth century and the ferment of activity around them. Chaucer went south twice in the fourteenth century—an example of professorial exchange, as Italian tutors went to England. The scholarly voyage began an Italian tutorial for young Englishmen in Italy. The young courtier was sent out with a tutor for the "benefit of his wit, for the commodity of his studies, and the dexterity of his life." The motif came directly from religious wayfaring, combining scholarship and gentlemanly pursuits with Christian devotion. With this Elizabethan ideal was born the travel book—the first, appropriately, Guylforde's *Pylgrymage* in 1506. From it grew the genre of literary travel. One might serve one's country by publishing travel observations. Books such as John Evelyn's in the early seventeenth century abandoned the ideal of pious erudition.

The earnest tutorial system deteriorated after the Restoration, but tourists took up the trail to centers of ancient and Renaissance learning, to private collections, and to the architectural foci of Italy. Architecture was no less venerated in ruins than intact. Scholarly discipline dissipated into connoisseurship and collecting. The transition is apparent in Richard Lassel's *Voyage of Italy*, a 1686 anecdotal gazetteer by an erstwhile Roman Catholic tutor to instruct and entertain tourists. The Grand Tour had arrived. Travel books for the rising middle classes developed rhetoric of the sublime, alluded to classical literature, and pointed out oddities.

Longinus, the Greek who first extolled the sublime, was not concerned with scenery but with oratory. His essay was the classical guide to the grandeur of the inspired passion and noble phrasing. Joseph Addison observed in 1701, nearly two thousand years after Longinus, that the sublime was only the echo of true danger and awe. In Addison's time there was much sorting out of influences on the mind and accounting for them as subconscious associations, subconscious in that their cause was not apparent at the moment of emotion, but accessible to the rational intellect—what psychoanalysts would now call the preconscious. By Addison's time a pilgrimage was not yet simply a vacation but had abandoned responsibility to church or family. It was a journey to acquire proficiency in art and history. Addison himself followed the routes of some of the classical poets. His sensitivity to the Alps made him an early enthusiast for mountain scenery. Partly as a consequence of Addison's writing the tour shifted its emphasis toward scenery. The famous trip through the Italian Alps by the novelist Horace Walpole and the poet Thomas Gray marked the linking of scenery and history.

New classes of travelers appeared in the eighteenth century: women, children, merchants on pleasure trips, reluctant gentry who would rather have stayed home with hawks and hounds. The didactic travel book reported not only history and geography but directed the traveler where to look and what to feel, as well as where to eat and lodge and how to travel. There were notes of injunction against being cheated and means of avoiding illness and bandits. It was a fulfillment of practical directions made as early as 1695, when Maximilian Mission's guidebook *A New Voyage to Italy* suggested that the traveler carry a cane with measured intervals and a fifty-fathom cord knotted at each foot for determining the heights of towers. Other guidebooks recommended keeping data on the "causes of the Decrease of Population and Remedies to Prevent Them" and on methods of farming ("How much is paid per day for ploughing with two oxen? With two horses?"). Sketches of landscapes, machinery, and costumes were recommended. This documentary attitude had an antecedent in the traditions of merchantry, which were established by the Arabs before the sixteenth century; the Italians, whose merchant-travel literature forms a distinct body of work; and the Jews, who penetrated deep into Africa before it was even mapped. It was logical that the trader's eye should be adapted to the travel motif of the pilgrim, as the two were intertwined throughout Biblical history. Theodosius, a sixth-century archdeacon, described the Lord's Field in his *Topography of the Holy Land:*

> The Field of the Lord in Galgala is watered from the Fountain of Elisha; it produces six bushels more or less. In the month of August half of the field is ploughed, and there is a crop at Easter from which the oblation is taken for Holy Thursday and Easter Day. And when that is out, the other half is ploughed and there is a second crop. There too is the vine which the Lord planted.

A land rich with grains and orchards attracted the Renaissance traveler. A well-stocked land for human profit was consistent with an optimistic Christian outlook. Lassels considered Lombardy and the Campania beautiful because of their productivity, and, if contemporary landscape paintings may be taken as indicative, the Dutch and Flemish had the same standard of judgment for their own lands.

But admiration for the rural countryside was never merely utilitarian. The beauty of the farmed land is seldom felt by the farmer, or, if felt, seldom articulated. Farmland is admired not by those who work it, but by those who live in the city and travel through the countryside. Its esthetics emerged with nationalism and a new cosmopolitan respect for native institutions. Any intelligent observer knew that agriculture was the economic foundation of society. The French Physiocrats held that agriculture was the only creative work and farms the only real wealth.

By contrast the wilderness was not only unproductive but frightening. Adam of Usk had himself blindfolded and carried across St. Gotthard Pass in 1401. For real or imagined dangers some travelers wore mail for that trip. The Pyrenees were "not so high and hideous as the Alps," but "uncouth, huge, monstrous excrescences of Nature, bearing nothing but craggy stones," said Dr. Johnson, recoiling from the Scottish mountains. "An eye accustomed to flowery pastures and waving harvest is astonished and repelled by this wide extent of hopeless sterility." It was Johnson who, during the revolution of garden design to incorporate pictorial scenery, said simply, "That garden is best which produces the most fruit."

As early as 1635 mountains were said to be useful as barriers, watersheds, home of exotic animals, and sites for producing healthy inhabitants, but it was not until the eighteenth century that they were much enjoyed as scenery.

As a cultural satellite of Europe, America has no distinct tradition of tourism until the nineteenth century. Its educated classes went abroad for art and history. Even then the American experience was an obstacle to the enjoyment of certain kinds of scenery. Andrew Robertson, an English drawing teacher, wrote about 1835:

> The author once took an American gentleman possessing no common power of understanding, and quick-

ness of observation, to an eminence commanding one of the most beautiful, varied and extensive views, near London. The whole scene was a garden in cultivation, every field enclosed by hedgerows. As these receded in distance, less and less could be seen of the fields, but trees could be seen to the extreme distance. "And do you call this beautiful?" said my friend. "In America we would consider it one of the most desolate scenes that the mind can conceive. It resembles a country that has never been clear of wood."

The difficulty was not only that the American forest *was* formidable, but that an adequate body of literature and painting did not exist for the cultivation of sensibility to particular places. Scenery is no scenery without the right cultural baggage. There were few Americans who could carry the esthetic momentum from European art into the American landscape as the instrument of tourism as well as, say, Chateaubriand. He had seen the virtue and nobility of the wilderness through the eyes of Rousseau and was ready to put Rousseau's art of revery to work in the wilderness west of Albany, New York. Rousseau had said, "It is on the summits of mountains, in the depths of forests, or desert islands that nature reveals her most potent charms." Chateaubriand went into the primeval forest to see unspoiled savages in their paradise. The guide led him to an Indian village. Out of a hut came a Monsieur Violet, a French dancing teacher, who with a sweep of his hand introduced Chateaubriand to *"ces messieurs sauvages et ces dames sauvagesses."*

The American tourist, far less adroit than Chateaubriand, who made himself ridiculous in America, was destined to play the fool. Jacksonian democracy ushered into the world a body of tourism unmatched in its gullibility, naïveté, and silliness. The artlessness of the American tourist has been his hallmark ever since. But there have been and are islands of solid ground. Whenever the tourist has been motivated by something more than form and whenever he has carried to his destination some body of technical knowledge, however slight, then he has shared in a universal mainstream which has an ancient and honorable lineage.

For example, a revolution in geology was occurring at about the time it became fashionable for large numbers of Americans to tour in the eastern United States. James Hutton's *Theory of the Earth* opposed Biblical cosmogonies and cataclysmic origins of landscape features, proposing instead that such formative processes as fossilization and stratification were continuous, that one needed only to go out and look. At the same time, mineralogy was coming into its own on a chemical basis and the relationship of minerals to soil fertility was a subject of great interest. The idea that the momentous processes that shaped the earth's surface could be seen, on however small a scale, was a rather new idea. When it was combined with that sentiment expressed by S. T. Coleridge, that he hoped his child would wander in nature to

> . . . see and hear
> The lovely shapes and sounds intelligible
> Of that eternal language, which thy God
> Utters, who from eternity doth teach
> Himself in all, and all things in himself . . .

the outcome was a combination of intellectual and emotional motivation that moved large numbers of amateurs to travel. As tourists with a purpose they clattered into the field halfway between Hutton and Coleridge, disciples of the shifting middle ground, convinced that what could be learned in nature was most worth knowing. Said a writer in the *New York Review* in 1839, "The tendency of intellectual and moral and social progress now is to copy and draw from nature. Men in all ranks and classes from the philosophical geologist to the rural picnic party now seek in nature for their present happiness."

The enthusiasm for natural history is illustrated by the housing of Peale's Museum in Independence Hall. The academies and lyceums proliferated, the latter numbering more than three thousand by 1835. Stimulated by Robert Owen's American text on geology early in the century, interest in the subject increased greatly. Compulsory education and a vast increase in book and magazine publication contributed to a spirit of agricultural improvement, teaching about soil minerals and similar information. Lyell's work in 1835 and *Elementary Geology* by Hitchcock in 1840 were widely read. After hearing a lecture by Yale's Professor Silliman, a farm-journal editor wrote: "How narrow minded must that man be, who looks upon the face of nature, and settles down to the belief that the hills, the dales, the ocean, and the innumerable tributary streams present the same appearance that they did at the moment they were called forth into existence by the Creator." This concept of change was essentially a new point of view. Controversy between the vulcanists and the neptunists over the origin of the earth's rocks added to the excitement.

Geology was fascinating not only because of its bearing on theology and agriculture, but because certain geomorphic forms were felt to be sublime. Since the concept of the sublime had religious sources, the discovery of harmonious laws in the earth's formation was appropriate. Architectural ruins were focal points of beauty and contemplation. America had few, but there were the ruins of the mountains to which geology held the key. In Silliman's *American Journal* of 1828 was a letter by a reader which said:

An occasional outburst of the sun threw a glorious flood of golden light over the enormous peaks that were grouped thickly around us, and disclosed the immense bosoms of the valleys and the green forests that opened among the wild ocean of mountains; the deep and wide chasms produced by vast slides presented horrid features of devastation, attesting the ravages of Alpine floods, bearing down before them a forest, soil, and rocks, with every movable thing, and thus gashing the solid framework of the everlasting hills with deep wounds. . . . The piles we trod on were the ruins of the stupendous granite mountains, elevated in ancient time, lashed by the storms, cracked by the frost, and mutilated for untold ages by the sure, although slow, agencies of Nature. . . . The ruins are only evidence of the mighty work of demolition, which is always going on with a real although imperceptible progress.

Such rhetoric was most frequently aimed at the touring public. In an 1833 book for girls, heroine Caroline Westerley makes an extended visit to Niagara Falls. Caroline and Papa return to their hotel "laden with minerals and plants." Meeting British friends, Papa explained, "I wish my daughters should be sufficiently versed in science to view with attention the changes which are now going on in nature, or the evidences which everywhere appear of the past change." A lady asked Caroline the names of her flowers. Caroline said, "I took up a bunch of hare-bells (*Campanula rotundifolia*) and explained to my attentive auditors the meaning of the botanical name, telling them that *Campanula* was the name of the genus, and signified a little bell, in reference to the shape of the carolla." Caroline reported that the rock at Niagara is "geodiferous lime rock" like some at home in her cabinet. She quoted Papa that it is seventy feet thick and lies over "calciferous slate" and is "remarkable for its tendency to decomposition, and to form new productions, by a different combination of its elements. It sometimes produces salts, or *sulphate of magnesia* composed of sulphuric acid and magnesia." She repeated an overheard remark that the channel below the falls must at one time have marked the site of the falls, all the way down to the lake, and that its walls "for ages to come . . . will remain as monuments of the great and surprising changes this country has undergone."

Caroline's interest in natural processes and several branches of natural history is characteristic of the era of naturalists dominated by such figures as Louis Agassiz, who arrived in 1846 to lecture on the plan of creation and the harmony of science and scripture, and stayed to discover the glacial past of New England. Until after the Civil War, almost every educated man was something of a naturalist, capable of discussing the stinging questions that geology raised about Scriptures: the Old Testament date of 4004 B.C. as the creation of the world, the location of the Garden of Eden, the plausibility of the Great Flood, the origin of fossils, the role of holocausts and cataclysms, and the degree of permanence of hills and oceans.

Natural history was in the nineteenth century—and remains today—a great *modus vivendi* in tourism. Given an ordinary mentality, the traveler would at least have some new knowledge and experience which he could enlarge in future trips or broaden by study at home. That men of imagination and talent should travel for even more promising benefits was the central thesis of the father of modern tourism, Alexander von Humboldt, whose *Cosmos* was translated from German in New York in 1850. Humboldt believed that the Western mind was fired with new imagery and "enlargement of powers" by travel during the Crusades and to the western hemisphere, especially the tropics. He urged both naturalists and artists to see as much of the world as possible, to get "the true image of the varied forms of nature" before they settled down to a life work in a parochial orbit. He was especially sensitive to the role of the landscape painter in influencing attitudes toward the landscape. He wrote:

> "An enchanting effect might be produced by a characteristic delineation of nature, sketched on the rugged declivities of the Himalaya. . . . This is calculated to raise the feeling of admiration for nature; and I am of the opinion that the knowledge of the works of creation, and an appreciation of their exalted grandeur, would be powerfully increased if . . . a number of panoramic buildings, containing alternating pictures of landscapes of different geographical latitudes and from different zones of elevation, should be erected in our large cities.

It was almost as though Humboldt had waved the starting flag. Reacting to his words or to similar encouragement, painters and naturalists dispersed west into the American wilderness, down to the southern hemisphere, and north to the Arctic. In the cities temples were built to show geologic panoramas, and natural-history museums and collections flourished. When the painter Frederick Church went to Quito he sought out the same family who had housed Humboldt.

To the tourist the painter, as well as the photographer after 1850, was a source of interpretation. The rhetoric of

most guidebooks was more of a veil than an illumination. The
old gazetteers were insufficient. A story from childhood, a
painting seen in a gallery, a story told by an old man—it is
through such odd fragments that the tourist pieces together
what he sees. Except for abstract visual qualities, the traveler
appreciates very little *ad hoc*. So the need for an interpreter
ensured the survival of the naturalist after gentlemen turned
to other avocations and young men interested in nature began
to specialize in science and technology. This was the conscien-
tious role of John Burroughs—interpreter of nature to Theodore Roosevelt and to Eastern ladies who, in the eighties and
nineties and in the twentieth century, no longer found time
themselves to collect minerals or bird eggs. The naturalist
survives today as a guide in the National Park Service, as a
narrator for a travel film, a photographer for Walt Disney,
the zoo keeper with a television show, the education director
for the natural-history museum, a feature writer for the mag-
azines, and as the manager of a private wildlife refuge. A few
naturalists lurk about the wild places collecting for the zoos
and museums, but generally they have ceased to be solitary or
private and have taken on the mantle of official interpreter to
the city man and suburbanite. The naturalist cultivates a new
visual facility in the individual who lives in a frozen world.
To most people all of the environment that is in any way
"important" is learned so well by constant practice that its
essential features are instantly recognized by clues. This
makes for efficiency, the efficiency of the honey bee, whose
compound eye is wonderfully sensitive to certain flickering
patterns, such as the shapes of certain flowers as seen when
the bee is in flight. The flashing pattern is like certain visual
fragments in our lives. Dignified by the psychological desig-
nation of gestalt, they gain us efficiency and blindness.

Bird recognition is a perversion of natural history when
bird watchers aspire to no more than the bee with its tiny
cerebrum can do. The guide books with their short lines on
the prominent marks and patches of color that identify each
species should be only a beginning. Birds have always been
wonderful metamorphic symbols, but the new, technological,

unionized pursuit is "by the numbers." They identify them and then check them against a "life list," and keep score.

Genuine perception of birds proceeds beyond this, first into the life history of the identified creature or geological form and then into its relationships within a larger field. Few naturalists prosper at this more difficult level of interpretation. The naturalist's best moment is when he catches the observer away from routine pathways whose familiar signs or identity marks have petrified perception.

Another legitimate and perennial theme of travel, as we have already seen, is the pursuit of health. In this, Americans were never far behind their Anglo-European counterparts. Strictly speaking, the resorts which grew up around mineral waters and hot baths do not belong to tourism, but with the rise of the vacation as a general restorative or an escape from disease, and the philosophy of the beneficence of nature in general, the distinction broke down. The egalitarian vacation was invented in America, although retreat from the city's summer stench by the wealthy is as old as urban civilization. Mature slums had developed in New York and Philadelphia as early as 1820. Immigration put a strain on housing, flimsy construction hastened dilapidation, and the breakdown of sanitation precipitated outbreaks of smallpox, cholera, and other communicable diseases. But the negative push of vacating the city does not carry the urban dweller very far; it does not imply any benefit other than escape, nor prescribe the kind of place the vacationer will visit. He is directed in part by the availability of accommodations and transportation. In contrast there emerged in America after about 1830 an active tourism based not on health or natural history but on the pleasures of travel and the pursuit of scenery. Before 1850 the vacationer would not have needed to go far from the cities if he only wanted a rest in rural surroundings.

The kind of scenery that many Americans wanted to see was the kind that would have interested the visitor to England who regarded uncleared land as desolate. Like the Elizabethans, many Americans were esthetically satisfied with signs of rural prosperity. Jefferson and Crèvecœur believed with the Augustans that agriculture produced the only real wealth, that every man had a natural right to land, that cultivation earned the right of ownership, and that labor in the field dignified the farmer and purified him by exposing him to nature. The freehold concept, the theory of the noble yeoman, was near the heart of American idealism from the beginning. Usually the yeoman himself had no such sentiments. It was an agrarian philosophy, the esthetic utilitarianism of gentlemen who had time to travel and reflect on the politics of man and nature. Jefferson admired sublime objects, such as Virginia's Natural Bridge, but he was aware that the bridge was, after all, too steep to be cultivated. He had read Shaftesbury and Burke, but he knew Locke and the Physiocrats too. He said, "Whenever there are in any country uncultivated lands and unemployed poor, it is clear that the laws of property have been so far extended as to violate natural rights. . . . The small landholders are the most precious part of the state."

Tourism on a large scale was not feasible in Jefferson's day, nor was the agrarian esthetic capable of drawing travelers. It required something more. There was a time of transition, when the first flickering of sublime emotion at American wilderness and mountains was to be seen but when the most admiring words were still spoken for the fruitful settlement. Timothy Dwight and his nephew Theodore, Jr., were enthusiastic travelers before travel became popular and widespread and before compulsory education was the general rule. Theodore particularly went into unsettled areas of Vermont and New Hampshire, and yet his pleasure was so pensive that one feels that he went mainly for the relief of getting out. "The rocks overhang, the hills look darker, more uncultivated and inaccessible, the music of singing birds gives place to the discordant notes of birds of prey, and the streams hurry by in a wild and impetuous manner." Of the Saco River, he said, "it may be conjectured what romantic region, what shady valleys, what retired caverns, what headlong precipices it has visited in its passages." But headlong precipices were not his preference. He looked for the "single seal of cultivation in

solitary clearing," turning away with relief from a region
"designed for eternal solitude," where nature "sternly forbids
the approach of man," and where the visitor feels "like a
citizen of the world." He disliked the "painful exertion we
make in contemplating things too great for our powers," and
concluded that the principal value of sublimity was in improving the beauty of fertile valleys by contrast. The wild areas
"have never heard of the blessings of wise laws and refined
institutions," and nature here was "an enemy of civilization
and humanity." The sterile soils of the mountains were de-
grading to the mind, while everyone, he said, admired that
part of the Saco Vale where the beauties of cultivation, lambs
and orchards, "soothe the harshness of nature, and pacify the
rage of what is by creation ungovernable." On the farms he
found families whose domestic tranquillity was a strong
moral contrast with the increasing turmoil and "lawless violence" of the stream itself. He was reminded of the uncivil-
ized regions of South America, where "science and virtue"
were yet to come, where natural beauty would then be discovered. There, he concluded, "the sun, which was formerly
worshipped on some of her shores, is but an emblem of the
civil, intellectual and moral light which will soon overspread
her hills and valleys." He added that the many small fields
of New England reminded him of human industriousness, "in
covering such a wide extent with one coat of verdure" and
with "ten thousand patches of corn" and the "fruit of their
engrafted orchards." New Englanders were a people, he said,
"of well-known customs, good old maxims, a firm moral
sentiment, and a dutiful reverential attachment to the country
of their origin."

If the admiration of American countryside was to be
based on the signs of peaceful industry and utilitarianism,
why should it end with farming? Even Ralph Waldo Emerson had observed: "We may easily hear too much of rural
influences . . . let us be men instead of woodchucks and the
oak and the elm shall gladly serve us." Shot-towers, rail-
roads, bridges, waterworks, and mills were always interesting to the traveler. Bayard Taylor, a travel writer, said in

1852, "With the rapid progress and wider development of the great locomotive triumphs of the age, steam travel and steam navigation, the vulgar lament over their introduction is beginning to disappear." Four years later another writer could conclude, "It is remarkable that the anti-romance of the railroad is mere prejudice. The straight lines piercing the rounded landscape are essentially poetic, and the fervid desire of sight and possession which fires the mind upon approaching beloved or famous places and persons, takes adequate form in the steam-speed of a train." The following year, in 1857, the Baltimore & Ohio Railroad ran a special three-day tour for artists. An anonymous contributor to *The Scenery of the United States* boasted that "there is nothing impossible to modern enterprise, which, within the last two or three years, has penetrated to within a few miles of the wildest recesses and most secluded nook. . . . How great, how glorious is man, the conqueror of nature—and the immortal co-worker with God."

Running waters were beautiful and the music of empire was in them too. One writer was horrified to see an engraving of the Hudson River without ships. "It would outrage one's sense of justice if that broad stream were to roll down to the ocean in mere idle majesty and beauty." Nathaniel Hawthorne overheard "two traders from Michigan" at Niagara Falls agree that "the sight was worth looking; there was certainly an immense water power here," but that "they would go twice as far to see the noble stoneworks of Lockport, where the Grand Canal is locked down a descent of sixty feet." Another tourist concluded that the great falls must ultimately "be compelled to become utilitarian, and perform an active part in the great drama of life." Of Concord was said, "A day spent here in visiting the Insane Asylum, the Prison and the State House, and in looking up the landmarks of old Pennacook, will furnish some of the most pleasant reminiscences of the traveller." In this view the countryside is but an extension of the wealth of town. The editor of *Sartain's Magazine* wrote in 1851 of the serpentine bosom of the Delaware River, winding among ornamented grounds of rich country seats between the towns with their mills, manufactories, colleges, churches, spires, and railroad depots, which "have given the river a setting worthy of its own really grand dimensions"; he had lost his heart to the depots and not the river. The Jersey shore, he said, was once desolate with stunted pines, rank weeds, and unreclaimed meadows where "rude gusts of wind drove into the air vast clouds of moving sands." Now

> the wealth and luxury of a great city have spread energy and enterprise over all that surrounds it. The meadows, well-drained, are carpeted with rich green grass, and stately cattle rove knee-deep in the vegetable floss. The almost Arabian desert has become, by cultivation, an Arabian Felix, and instead of a slender crop of Jersey Horse Mint (*Monarda punctata*), and red ants, in a coat of mail, that resist the weight of the human tread, we find there the thousand thriving luxuries of the truck-garden . . . trees of more valuable quality and larger growth crown every little apology for a hill.

The editor described an ideal tour:

> The stranger, when relaxing from the cares of business and the hurry of travel . . . may promise himself a day or a half-day of unalloyed pleasure, if he will step on board any of the numerous up-river steamers, and take a quiet trip to Burlington, Bristol, Bordentown, Florence, or Trenton. Everywhere, except at Florence, which is yet too young, he will see evidence of the indomitable energy and the characteristic constitutional go-aheaditiveness, of the American race; —particularly the latter; for at each place he hears the grating of the saw, the heavy sound of the forge-hammer, the rattle of machinery, but more especially, the whistle of the locomotive and the thunder of the steam pipe; everywhere he finds himself involved within the meshes of the vast net of railroads, or intercepted by the long canal. Then, when he wishes to reflect on these things in the quiet of a purely rural scenery, though surrounded with all the comforts and luxuries of civilized life, let him land on his downward route at Tacony, and, gazing on the quiet

sailing vessels and the more noisy steamers, continually passing and repassing, let him listen in dreamy revery to the splash of the small waves on the pebbly beach.

There was little conflict in those early years of American tourism between the admirers of wild nature, or of natural scenery, and those who preferred the grating of the saw and the thunder of the steam pipe. There was, however, a confrontation over the development of Central Park in New York City.

New York Judge J. Harris, who approved the mayor's official application for acquisition of the land which is now Central Park, explained that if such a park should turn out to be a mistake in half a century the land would nonetheless be many times its 1858 value and could be sold by the city. A petition opposing the park was presented to the City Council, arguing that the park would delay the city's development as a boundary to expansion: the city would "be brought to a premature stand-still, and its glories, so vividly pictured, never realized." It was pointed out that the Jersey shore was more attractive for the seekers of health, comfort, or pleasure, and that, at the same time, "our wide streets and avenues, and the neat pleasant squares so easily found, render it more agreeable, as well as less fatiguing and expensive to resort to . . . for 'breathing places.'" The number of lots and streets to be closed to commerce was given. The park was said to be too ideal ever to be realized, too expensive, and undemocratic as a place for "royal display."

We have seen that the opinion that a field of grain is the most beautiful of nature's scenes is certainly not new. The Dutch found it so in the seventeenth century and the French in the nineteenth. But, esthetically, it was to become a difficult position to delimit as the century progressed. Francis D. Klingender, in his *Art and the Industrial Revolution*, traces the attempt to apply the esthetics of the sublime and the picturesque to industry, the heroic effort to align the utilitarian and the beautiful. As pictorial art became more clearly defined in terms of forms rather than ideas and divorced itself from content in the sense of a particular dramatic assembly, it was freed to find aspects of beauty in almost any kind of visual experience. Count Hermann Keyserling, after a trip around the world in the 1920s, wrote in *The Travel Diary of a Philosopher* that Kansas was the most fully exploited landscape he had ever seen and therefore approached a kind of perfection.

What Keyserling saw in Kansas was the early industrialization of the rural countryside, and what he felt was the recognition that the traditional poetry of rural England, of James Thomson, Robert Dodsley, William Cowper, was meant for a certain kind of rural countryside and did not exhaust the range of esthetic pleasure possible in the patterns of land use which man could create. The forests and the watersheds would be next. On a trip through the woods it is no longer necessary to be bound by monotonous green chambers and corridors, silence and solitude. One might go through a managed forest with the forester to see the production of pulp, some machines planting trees and others cutting them. The lumber companies and those geographers who are gladdened by the achievements of engineering enjoin the acceptance of cut-over land, industrial parks, vast monocultures, phalanxes of earth-moving machinery as worthy esthetic subjects. General Pick, former Commander of the U.S. Army Corps of Engineers and the co-author of the "Pick-Sloan Plan" by which those engineers united with the U.S. Bureau of Reclamation to "develop" the Missouri River watershed, defended the proposed impoundments and dams as objects of great beauty and their environs as prime recreational areas. He proposed an ideal American vacation: an automobile trip up one side of the river and its reservoirs and down the other. So does the tradition of the pilgrimage to a place of miracles and wonders, in the past oriented toward the supernatural, turn itself upon man's works. No one can argue that such constructions as Boulder Dam do not attract great numbers of tourists, and if the landscapes created by the Pick-Sloan Plan have not yet drawn their share it may only underscore how far ahead of his time General Pick was.

Scenery still means something very different from Gen-

eral Pick's landscapes to many people. It is derived directly
from the traditions of eighteenth-century England. As native
painters and poets, prose and travel writers discovered the
scenery of New York and New England early in the nineteenth century, their patrons and imitators and the fashion-
makers came too. The public followed in its own way,
seeking to discover the enchantment of the Hudson cliffs, to
confront the falls in a moment of stupendous glory, to experience the luminous insights of the artist, to find for themselves
the virtue that was said to sanction special places and scenes.
There was a wave of feeling for native soil that wanted
landmarks. When the Erie Canal opened in 1826 a human
flood descended on Niagara Falls, which was to remain for a
century a major spectacle. Many of the tourists, new to matters of sensibility and taste, foreign to the leisurely quality
that had been essential to the Grand Tour and to the mien of
the dilettante, required an exaggerated stimulus, a supernor-
mal signal, to kindle their responses. The literature of travel
and the guidebooks achieved a purple rhetoric from which it
has not yet recovered. Said one:

> What can we imagine more beautiful, more truly
> sublime, than a majestic river suddenly contracted into
> less than half the former width, after tumbling over a
> bed of loose rocks, precipitated, roaring as it were, with
> very terror, into a dark cauldron below, maddened and
> lashed into foam white as the driven snow, and throwing
> up a thick column of spray towering to the very arch of
> heaven?

There were those who were willing to accept such descriptions and to give themselves to the experience. A Mrs.
Ossoli, for example, who wrote a book about the falls a few
years later, "felt a strange indifference about seeing the aspi-
ration of my life's hopes." She wandered about her hotel
while "a solemn awe imperceptibly stole over me." At the
falls "my emotions overpowered me, a choking sensation rose
to my throat, a thrill rushed through my veins . . . I
thought only of comparing the effect on my mind with what I

read and heard." For her Niagara was as overwhelming as the guidebooks said. For Nathaniel Hawthorne, who undoubtedly had read much and who shut his eyes to avoid seeing the falls as his coach approached the hotel in 1834, it was a different story. Uncontaminated by an accidental glimpse, determined to make the most of the confrontation, he went to his room and began to concentrate, to build mood. But he knew too much, and the falls failed his expectations. It was several days before he recovered from the anticlimax enough to enjoy the spectacle.

Innocence, expectancy, determination, and frequent disappointment are the most touching things about the tourist, then or today.

A trend toward going farther afield compounded the tourist's problems. The Reverend F. W. Shelton joined a party to climb Vermont's Mt. Mansfield "to behold the CREATOR's glory." The mountain was a "temple of nature . . . in sublime and savage trim," a product of "awful convulsions." Leaving their buggy at "the last bounds of civilization . . . a farmhouse on the edge of a vast primeval forest," they continued on horseback. They were drenched in a rain for which they were not prepared. When fallen trees blocked the trail they abandoned the horses and struggled over windfalls, remembering that "obstacles are the very pavement to great deeds." Crossing a primeval hemlock forest, the Reverend Mr. Shelton counted his steps and notched his cane once for every thousand. Another shower found the party crouching in the vegetation, thinking of a "scene from Sterne." Meanwhile the author had lost his bottle of pickles and his telescope. Without sufficient blankets to sleep comfortably, they spent a chilly night in a small shack on the mountain telling ghost stories.

On the descent Shelton experienced "tremulousness of muscle in the extremities" and lay down to rest, whereupon he made the only close observation of the vegetation on the whole trip. T. Addison Richards recorded the joys of a populous wilderness in his *American Landscape Annual* in 1845: "Frequently, in traversing a gorge of the Catskills, every turn has either brought me upon an enraptured student, or has shown me the traces of one in an unfinished canvas, carefully secreted in the cavities of the rocks; or in scattered eggshell and other remains of their frugal noon-tide bivouacs." Many published accounts of travels at mid-century are primarily personality and character sketches. In addition to people there were rocks that looked like people or like animals. The face in rock, the "old man of the mountains," was well known, and the exploitation of caves developed upon this same general theme.

The novice traveler, unpracticed in the study of nature and the reading of literature, was at the mercy of impossible ideals, in a juggernaut of tourism. He was almost inevitably disappointed. Emerson, whose forays into nature consisted primarily of rowing a small skiff around a pond and to whom the forest had a "sanctity which shames our religions and reality which discredits our heroes," was disappointed as naturalist and tourist. It was no surprise that he found that nature "converts itself into a vast promise. . . . There is in woods and waters a certain enticement and flattery, together with a failure to yield a present satisfaction. This disappointment is felt in every landscape." Edgar Allan Poe had the same sort of reaction but his own way of solving it: "We can at any time double the beauty of an actual landscape by half closing our eyes as we look at it." "People love the country theoretically, as they do poetry," said the travel writer George Curtis. "Very few are heroic enough to confess that it is wearisome even when they are fatigued by it. The reason of which reluctance I suppose to be a lurking consciousness that we ought to love it, and we ought to be satisfied and glad among the hills and under the trees."

Efforts by tourists to adumbrate the secret or not so secret disappointment produce some of the more artless vagaries associated with travel. One of them is connected with the nature of crowd psychology and that transformation which seems to come over any event witnessed by many people instead of one. "Is it not something to mourn over," asked a nineteenth-century tourist, "that the spectacle of this *bivouac* of hills should have been so seldom seen by tourists in New Hampshire?" The quietly gnawing doubt that disappears in a crowd is likely to come back in solitude. A report by a hiker to the top of Mt. Washington in 1856 contained little excitement except for meeting other hikers. "Forewarning me of an indescribable sense of loneliness when I should get beyond the limit of trees, they departed, leaving in my mind a somewhat more somber tinge of things to come." As soon as the company left, "there was an aspect of desolation in the scenery around . . ."

Perhaps the haste characteristic of tourism is also related to disappointment. An ideal itinerary was outlined in *The Scenery of the United States* in 1855:

> If we wished to impress a stranger with what is most characteristic of this country, in many ways, we would take him from the steamer upon his arrival in New York, whirl him along the Erie Railroad to Niagara, and return him by the Central Albany Road, and down the Hudson. He thus would see the wildness of regions already long settled, according to our computation; he would feel the shock of the new young life that goes running over the mountains, and roaring through the woods, and out upon the Niagara, and hear the mighty cataract thundering its sympathetic welcome to his splendid career.

The tourist today who drives through six national parks and six thousand miles in a two-week vacation belongs to the main tradition of a century of public travel. One of the odd things about the hurry is that, even at a great pace, the tourist frequently had trouble filling the day, or "keeping busy." The proliferation of divertissements, what Bernard De Voto once called "amiable diversions" in connection with the national parks, has become a commonplace. As early as 1838 a billiard room was established on Goat Island at Niagara Falls, and it was observed that visitors also spent their time "dressing, reading novels, playing at chess or backgammon, or an occasional ride." The journey itself was punctuated by innumerable coach stops to buy meals, fruit, and wine, and

then resumed in a rush. When passengers began wildly leaping from the train as it arrived at Niagara Falls in 1856 an
observer "looked upon them at once as a select party of poets,
overwhelmed by the enthusiastic desire to see the falls." But
he found instead "that they were intent upon the first choice
of rooms." In view of that milieu, it is not surprising that the
educated tourist or observer was likely to be cynical. George
Curtis described the development of Catskill Falls, which was
associated with an Indian legend, was located near the famous Catskill House, and had been painted by Thomas Cole
and others of the Hudson River school:

> The process of "doing" the sight, for those who are
> limited in time, is very methodical. You leave the hotel
> and drive in a coach to the bar-room. You refresh! You
> step out upon the balcony and look into the abyss. The
> proprietor of the Falls informs you that the lower plunge
> is about eighty feet high. It appears to you to be about
> ten. You laugh increduously—he smiles in return the
> smile of a *mens conscia rectum*. . . . The proprietor of
> the bar-room is also the genius of the Falls, and derives
> a trade both with his spirits and with his water. In fact,
> if your romantic nerves can stand the steady truth, the
> Catskill Falls is *turned on* to accommodate poets and
> parties of pleasure.

The visitor then paid twenty-five cents. A boy opened a sluice
and the water plunged down. The tourist was "boxed up
again" and delivered to the Mountain House in time for
dinner—which was always formal.

Curtis was obviously not the only cynic present at the
falls. The odium, the enormous disrespect, in which the tourist is held by merchants and innkeepers reflects the general
awareness of the falsity of the position into which the tourist
has been thrust, his gullibility and his agonized squirming.
The tourist's dilemma is measured by the impossibility of his
situation and the folly of his behavior. He is not only disappointed and hurried. He is homesick and he has a mild infection. Nature has proved publicly expensive and privately
monotonous. The enormous gap between the touring shop-

keeper's view of life and the unfamiliar surroundings has been avoided by undue attention to trifles and routine arrangements. Awareness was—and is—clogged with the anticipation of and anxiety over accommodations, the nuisance of pests and small dangers, the pursuit of conveniences, and social adjustment to other tourists. Silliness and bickering were perhaps inevitable in the pursuit of formula travel by large numbers of people on vacation.

The pain of doing what you actually dislike is not the only price of tourism. The traveler expects to pay in more ways than one, until paying itself becomes an activity, a kind of masochism. William Dean Howells complained of Niagara Falls that "their prodigious character was eked out by every factitious device to which the penalty of twenty-five cents could be attached." The cynicism of the tourist industry stems from recognition that the tourist is usually impossible to please and that he may in fact be gratified most by suffering and spending his money.

However it may mock the original purpose, tourism retains the Christian idea of suffering and sacrifice. The giddy nineteenth-century self-styled pilgrim to the falls seems to us now foolish and naïve. When it was assumed that clues to higher truth and beauty were accessible to travel, some of the manifestations of tourism approached a grotesque epitome which has not yet receded. The tourist emerged as a harassed fugitive from city routine, following a Grand Tour formula derived long ago from the religious pilgrimage and recently from the cultural polishing of educated social classes. The first-generation vacationers of America in the nineteenth century distracted themselves with minutiae and the means of insulating themselves against the landscapes they had gone to see, or indulged in pseudo-literary passion, exemplifying the sentimentality which marked that century as much as any other single characteristic. Either way the tourist has been a kind of boob in the moonshine of travel, the sucker of the open road, taken seriously only by those bent on fleecing him.

Or so it seems. But one cannot lay all these charges blithely on the grave of the nineteenth century, or its roman-

tic antecedents, and turn away. There are reasons for thinking
that century to be not so great a retrogression of intelligence
and sensibility as a majority of the critics of the first half
of the twentieth would have us suppose. Had taste really
deteriorated so badly—or was it just that we have unusually
good records of many travelers? A historian says of the
sixth-century travel of Antonius of Placentia, "In it we find
the superstition and muddleheadedness of its class developed
more fully than in any previous example." Antonius says that
he sat in the seat in which Christ sat "and there I unworthy
wrote the names of my parents." Perhaps the amateur traveler has always scribbled his name, wasted his money, lost his
belongings, bought trifling souvenirs, got lost and homesick,
and preoccupied himself with the thought of food, lodging,
and comfort.

Those American tourists in New England and New
York in the 1830s undertook an incredible adventure, which
had little chance of wholesale success. Faith in the goodness
and sanctity, morality and beauty of wild nature may be
traced in Europe from Lord Shaftesbury and John Ray
through a host of educated writers, painters, poets, and naturalists, all living and traveling through landscapes humanized
over a period of two thousand years by burning, cultivation,
grazing, clearing, domestication, and the migrations and waxing of whole societies. The wilderness sentiment was born
where there was no wilderness. Even the high Alps, as Leslie
Stephens pointed out, were familiar and comfortable, while
the remote Himalayas held no lure for him. The Americans,
moving in this tradition, were presented with the dubious
opportunity of trying out the nature esthetic at the edge of a
real wilderness—an esthetic which had been known to Western civilization for only three hundred years at the most. The
Wordsworthian-Bryantian cathedral of the forest was readily
available. It was like dumping an inexperienced hunter into
an arena with a wild bear and giving him an unfamiliar
weapon designed by someone else and tried out on cows. As
the multitude was vomited into the edge of the primeval
wilderness by democratic travel a few salvaged perceptual

trophies of great value, which would lead later to the extraordinary founding of the national parks. Others met it as a
stimulus to their rhetorical notions. The majority did what
men anywhere would do—they avoided it with great celerity,
if not much dignity.

By the mid-twentieth century tourism had not lost its
connection to pictures—witness the appeals to conventional
scenery in travel publications and advertisements. But art and
technology have both led the itinerant eye onto new paths.
Some of the best reasons for modern travel bear the dignity of
traditional virtue and test the world against a venerable sense
of fitness. An example is J. B. Priestley, traveling in Texas:

> It is good for people to travel, to leave their homes
> and again discover how other people live, to spend their
> days in wildly unfamiliar surroundings, their nights
> under strange bedclothes, to make every meal an experi-
> ment, to sit behind exotic drinks and listen to foreign
> tunes and unimaginable lyrics, to try to understand alien
> habits, customs, values, and to be half repelled, half
> enchanted; and then, with bursting bags and memories,
> to find themselves back home once more. But this is the
> opposite of *Nomadmass* life, which offers movement
> without any essential change. It is a street three thou-
> sand miles long. At each end are the same cigarettes,
> breakfast foods, television programs, movies, syndicated
> columns, songs and topics of conversation. You burn a
> hundred and fifty gallons of gasoline to arrive nowhere.
> You are never really at home nor away from home. You
> neither cultivate your own garden nor admire other peo-
> ple's; the gardens have gone. So has the past, for every-
> thing here is brand new, just unpacked from the factory,
> with gadgets replacing old skills, endless entertainment
> and no art, filled with the devices of second-rate men
> and utterly removed, perhaps forever, from the noble
> passions, the tragic insights, the heroic laughter, of
> great minds.

The truth of Priestley's words is evident to anyone who
has lived long enough. And yet even he has gone by automobile or train. In a lament for the disappearance of the "Horse

and Buggy Countryside," the botanist Edgar Anderson recalls the words of Willa Cather on country roads and his own
joy in the variety of vegetation, the encounters with local
farmers, and, above all, the sounds—the sounds of wind in the
trees, of the onset of snow, of birds and insects. And so we
might find each generation concluding that the quality of
travel had deteriorated, which, in truth, it has for them.

The scene to which Priestley objects may be described as
Beckett's Road, for upon it man is certainly alienated from
the landscapes of Anderson and those of the automobile thirty
years ago. In Beckett's *All That Fall*, says Robert M. Newcomb, a geographer, there is a journey, the theme of which is
the search for self-identity. In *Waiting for Godot* the set is a
country road and the drama unfolds as arrivals, departures,
waitings, meetings, and missed meetings. He speaks of the
road in these and other plays as a "dramatic device," a
"symbol for confronting man with his external environs and
fellow inhabitants"—but so it is for Priestley and Anderson,
and so it has been for all travelers. John B. Jackson considers
today's "abstract world of the hot-rodder" as being a search
for nature and contact with reality "less familiar and less
pedestrian" and freer than that of the past. The hot-rodders
have had enough, he says, "of contemplation, and of the old
sublimities which a century of poets and painters and musicians had interpreted over and over again." Moreover, they
want risk, mobility, and change as an end in itself, "a nature
shorn of all memory and sentiment." It is travel as participation in movement, the sensation of acceleration, what Jackson
calls the "abstract preternatural landscape of wind and sun
and motion," and he concludes that because of it we will
"eventually enrich our understanding of ourselves with a new
poetry and a new nature mysticism."

Jackson, who is himself a traveler of wide experience,
defends the immediacy of the hot-rodder's search because he
believes that participating is important and that the "classic
perspective," however genuine, precluded participating by
placing a kind of awe between men and their environment.
But he also declares, "I still do not see how we can interpret

any human activity without some reference to its chosen setting; I do not see how we can discuss purely in sociological
terms any sport which is obviously designed as a form of
psychological exploitation of the environment," and he concluded that it was a problem which he himself had not resolved (in 1957).

He brings us then to the threshold of the problem, the
crux. The theme of search and discovery is always there.
Original explorers—Marco Polo in China, Christopher Columbus in the Atlantic, or even Clarence King in the Sierras
of the American West—were themselves enacting ventures
long known to their own cultural mythology. And the traveler
who comes after is re-enacting and recapitulating in a
mytho-historical sense; yet for himself he is the original.
From tribal mythology to the half-real traveling monks of the
Dark Ages, to the cosmic voyages that served as literary
devices at the time of the Enlightenment, in all worthwhile
travel the search for God and reality and truth *must* occupy a
center which is both philosophical and psychological. If
Adam was the first man he was also the first traveler—as he
took a trip out of paradise, a journey which still continues
and is still linked to knowledge and to the sense of alienation.

Individual societies will use the mythical tableau of the
journey in their own ways. According to W. H. Auden in *The
Enchafèd Flood*, the metaphorical meaning of the journey has
changed. Once the ship represented society, the garden, the
normal human environment; and the trip on the sea and
desert, a necessary evil. By the nineteenth century these
meanings had been reversed: the voyage was the normal state
of man; in its course occurred the decisive events of history.
The desert had similar iconography. In both desert and sea
were freedom, loneliness, and solitude. But the sea is potential, primitive, the beginning; the desert is the end, a place of
purgation, chastity, and humility, and is crossed only with
faith. The desert was barren not because of nature but because of historical catastrophe, and awaited a stranger to
rescue and rebuild it. The islands of innocence, sea and desert, were real earthly paradises or the works of black magic.

The acceptance of the voyage as the true condition of man was a charter to tourism. It made every man a tourist on earth and every journey the potential epitome of travel. The early idea that calamity produced the desert did not change—perhaps the green veldt which the Sahara had once been lingered in the dim, penumbral fringe of human memory. The hero who would rebuild the fallen nation was a stranger, a traveler, the tourist as hero.

At another level, the question of the redeeming qualities of tourism is part of a larger problem of the use of leisure. That subject receives much stereotyped attention, but is given little serious thought. Josef Pieper has restated its fundamental nature as "the basis of culture" not as *recuperation* for more productive work, but as the antithesis to work. It is the only reason, he says, that labor is tolerable or meaningful; yet it is not idleness, nor to Pieper is it synonymous with spare time, but a matrix for the evolution of the *cultus*, the basic religious body. Leisure is an attitude producing a form of silence prerequisite to apprehension of reality—a contemplative celebration. The *cultus* is related to God through sacrifice, and from its rituals come the behavior and values of a society. He recalls the Middle Ages distinction between understanding as *ratio*, which is worked for, and as *intellectus*, which is given. The latter is "the capacity of *simplex intuitus* of that simple vision to which truth offers itself like a landscape to the eye." It may be concluded that the use of leisure exposes a personal or social relationship to the universe. The greatest contributions to civilization are made principally in leisure, not by *ratio* or mental work but by contemplative, intuitive, religious, or romantic responses to a release from travail. The Sabbath ritual, suggests Erich Fromm, is derived from a pre-Biblical theological truce between man and nature that reestablishes a golden age of paradise or of harmony among all the things on earth. "Rest" on the seventh day meant not interfering with the natural world and its processes.

Auden has shown that our idea of travel is intimately connected to Christian mythology, and Pieper that philosophically it is a part of the great contemporary problem of leisure. But neither has confronted the question J. B. Jackson has raised: What is the role of *place* in the philosophy of leisure and travel?

In 1612 Henry Peacham added a chapter to his hand-book on drawing to discuss the relation of travel to painting. Landscape painting and travel and gardening developed together as the art of vision, for discovering the genius of place. Those arts were responsible for the creation and preservation of places, of scenes, plants and animals, whole countrysides. From them came the idea of scenery.

Today the traveler has at his disposal the technical means of extracting pure sensation from travel. At the same time the world is changing rapidly and profoundly. From leisure and travel could come the incentive to modify, direct, or stop some of that change.

Like the sportsman, the tourist moves in a sphere which has no immediate connection to the conduct of his daily business. He observes the pattern of stream life in which lives the fish, and the whole watershed may assume some significance. The beauty of his activity is its complete immediate uselessness and its ultimate value for the survival of a culture and civilization. It has the merit of low amusement and high re-enactment values. Even though he is currently hypnotized by his own enigmatic and abstract and sensual responses to the environment, the tourist continues to follow a classical pattern. He moves through novel landscapes which have a minimum of stereotyped sign value. Out of his daily niche, his potential for perception increases. He replays the history of the pioneer, and wherever he goes he is the discoverer. Even in a city he is in a wilderness with the possibility of becoming lost or attending a miracle. His possibilities know no bounds, for he is on a pilgrimage or he is wayfaring, the best thing for his soul. He is at the same time retreating from routine and diversion. In this plastic formative mood he is essentially a new and different person. Travel is broadening because of the nature not of travel, but of the traveler. He is apt to be a boob, but he may be the hope of mankind.

Chapter Five

The Virgin Dream

THE SPIRITUAL EFFECT of the wilderness runs deeper than any other encounter in nature. Great distances and vast empty spaces, impenetrable forests and mighty waves suggest the power and omniscience of the supernatural, a presence ultimate and final, somehow more real than small-scale places, closed yards with apple trees and sparrows. To those who sit by the lone sea breakers come the heartbreaking terror and the mantle of prophecy, the ecstasy of divine fear, and the sudden, awful awareness of self in space and time.

Our response to the sight of the Grand Canyon is deeply moving, a romantic experience. Yet, in the Western world that experience has had little to do with formal philosophy in general. Religious thought has not seriously entertained the notion that man in the wilderness is any closer to God. Pantheism is generally regarded as obscuring the ancient Hebrew foundation of Christianity, that God is not of this world. This creation of two worlds where there had been one was begun by the leap of Mediterranean pagan gods onto Olympus and from there into the sky from the disenchanted terrestrial earth, and it was completed in the eighteenth century when Immanuel Kant launched the ship of existentialism, of indeterminism, setting men and their egos apart from nature. In those lands where the gods have not yet leaped, missionaries continue to cleanse primitive minds of demons and to separate spirituality from nature and earth from heaven, and everywhere technology demonstrates that nature is merely the stuff from which men create worlds.

But the human heart is fickle. No creed absolutely disavows guidance, divine or otherwise, in nature, however much it etherealizes human experience. Many of my naturalist friends are quick to assume that Christianity is a mortal enemy of the love and protection of nature, but much depends on which saint, which emphasis or doctrine is attended to. As Charles Raven, in his *Natural Religion and Christian Theology*, has pointed out, Christianity is full of ambivalence. It has absorbed the mytho-poetic wisdom of whole cultures and pagan ceremonies. The great moments of inspiration and decision in Christian history occur in certain landscapes. Although Christianity is the great enemy of the natural world, it also contains the most extreme love of nature. It is surprisingly flexible, as Robert Redfield discovered in Yucatan, where Christianity is smoothly interwoven with indigenous pagan gods and the worship of limestone sinkholes. It has the hybrid vigor of multiple origins. The Augustine-Pauline ascetic fires pasteurized Christian theology, denigrating the body, depreciating the animal nature of man—in short, denying life. It was the greatest effort in history to reduce the aim of human existence to abstractions and shadows. Yet, no religious ideal could exclude the vitality of organic existence for long. Pagan gods reentered Christianity ever more rapidly after the ninth century. Ancient calendars, holidays, names, the classical heroes disguised in Biblical garb, art—all came slowly back. However thinly disguised and crudely readapted, they imparted new earthiness and vigor to a system of belief that had become too ascetic for large numbers of people, too unreal in the sense that most people will always mean reality. By virtue of their patience and the validity of their conception, pagan spirits regained their place in the form of astrology, control of the calendar, and thereby the daily and seasonal workings of the universe.

One extraordinary effect of this secular resurgence

within Christianity has been the transfer of our feeling of awe from sky spirits to stars and planets and then to earth. Esthetics was derived from religious experience, adapting from it a mode of feeling that is now commonly assumed to be part of a normal response to great events, works of art, and grand scenery. The division of the universe into heaven and earth had separated God from this world as surely as the other planets were distinct from earth. At the beginning of the Middle Ages, "sublime" referred to God, his angels, to the heavenly bodies and their mythologies. With the renewed study of the heavens by Copernicus, Kepler, Galileo, and Newton, who did not separate science and religion, a step toward the reunion of heaven and earth was taken. Galileo firmly believed in the efficacy of prayer in his work, and that work was a form of revelation. That terrible embarrassment which the Church refused to face—that the universe was composed of suns and planets of which the earth was merely one—nonetheless implied that the earth was a typical planet and a clue to the splendid mystery of other planets and the sublime events of the sky. The earth was, then, itself a sublime heavenly body.

This perspective encouraged a vision of the earth as a whole and descriptions of the earth's surface as if seen from a great height. The landscapes by Patinir are views seen by a bird, god, or angel. Birds had long been considered among the most mercurial and esthetic of forms. An imaginary flight was an excellent vehicle for new geographic descriptions and new literature. Renaissance humanism and medicine affected the new geological-astronomical study, by descriptive analogy comparing physical entities to the human body (mountains were symbols of pride or "pregnant" with minerals). Psychology emerged as the study of sensation, of feelings, and as an attitude of speculation, adding a new kind of self-conscious or self-analytic esthetic to the tradition of visionary flights and voyages whose imagery was a flight through the sky or an ocean voyage.

The early panoramic landscape paintings have been called "Christian optimism," appreciations of the richness and diversity of the world created by God for man. That world was worth knowing for itself, as well as a source of knowledge about the universe. Naturalists such as Konrad von Gesner, travelers after Polo and Mandeville and the ecclesiastics to whom pictures no longer seemed heathenish, as the medieval church had regarded them, and historians and geographers all engaged in a delineation of the world's great places and events.

Then and now the desert provided the purest sublime experience, so acute that even tourism with its evasive maneuvers could not ameliorate its raw intensity. Aldous Huxley has examined at length the metaphor of the desert as that purest gleam at the heart of religious insight. Boundlessness and emptiness are the two most expressive symbols of an attributeless Godhead, in whom we sink with Meister Eckhart "from nothingness to nothingness." These spatial metaphors are abundant in religious literature, silence and emptiness as symbolic of divine immanence. Judaism and Christianity originated in or near deserts. Their imagery lives on, strangely transformed in temperate climates, taught in Sunday School to children who have never seen a desert. One of the anomalies of modern concepts of nature is that an image is often inappropriate or obsolete or at best exotic. Yet, out of the wreck of that obsolescence rises the inspiration to fit new environments such as manmade wastes.

A grand view of earth is also had from a mountaintop. The shifting of attention in the late Middle Ages from the sky to the earth was signified by Petrarch's famous fourteenth-century ascent of Mt. Ventoux, the idea for which he may have taken from Dante. Modern tourism was far away and Petrarch's lively curiosity wilted abruptly as he sat on the mountain, the price of looking down instead of up. The historian Jacob Burkhardt says that "an indefinable longing for a distant panorama grew stronger and stronger in him, until at length the accidental sight of a passage in Livy, where King Philip, the enemy of Rome, ascends the Haemus, decided him. . . . The ascent of a mountain for its own sake was unheard of, and there could be no thought of the companionship of friends or acquaintances." Petrarch took Augustine's *Confessions* along. While on the summit he read, "And men go forth, and admire lofty mountains and broad seas, and roaring torrents, and the ocean, and the course of the stars, and forget their own selves while doing so." That is, they forget their immortal souls and their duty. Burkhardt assumed that the quotation harmonized with the occasion, but it stung Petrarch for his worldliness and he scurried guiltily down.

Men had climbed mountains before, not just "because they were there," but also to find seclusion and send their thoughts flying upward, as at the Thessalian Meteora, the honeycombed cliffs in Spain, and the cliffs of Africa's Thebaid. After Petrarch there was secular climbing to escape the city's turmoil and to survey the countryside, to permit the exploring eye to rove like a wandering hawk, perhaps to relish the sensation of personal smallness and insignificance in the face of cosmic power and omniscience.

A disciple of Erasmus, the naturalist Konrad von Gesner, wrote in 1541:

> I have determined, as long as God gives me life, to ascend one or more mountains every year when the plants are at their best—partly to study them, partly for excercise of body and joy of mind. . . . I say then that he is no lover of nature who does not esteem high mountains very worthy of profound contemplation. It is no wonder that men have made them the homes of Gods, of Pan and the nymphs. . . . I have a passionate desire to visit them.

But it was to be another century and a half before Gesner's views were widely shared. Then it was not from the motive of the naturalist, which in turn was part of the joy and discovery of nature of *fin amor*, but by way of travel esthetics. More typical of Gesner's time is the sentiment of Richard Lassells, who wrote almost nothing of mountain scenery in his widely read guidebook *The Voyage of Italy* except for a paltry paragraph on a climb to the crater of Vesuvius: "With much ado we got to the top of the hill; and peeping fearfully

(remembering Pliny's accident) into the great hollow from
the brink of it, found it to be like a vast kettle, far greater
than those Hell Kettles near Deslington, in the Bishoprick of
Durham, made by Earthquakes. . . . Having gazed a while
at this chimney of Hell (for Tertullian calls Aetna and Vesuvius *Fumariola inferni*) we came down faster than we went
up."

About the same time, in 1671, a cosmologist, Thomas
Burnet, visited the Alps. He thereafter revived a twelfth-
century theory that the earth was originally egglike and that
its shell was broken by the weight of the deluge. It was in
part an answer to questions renewed by the rise of astronomy,
such as whether the earth had been cursed as a result of sin
and whether nature grew old and decayed. A furious controversy surrounded Burnet's *Sacred Theory of the Earth*, with
its account of the origin of mountains as tilted fragments of
the earth's crust, fractured by the Flood. At this time the
heights of mountains were enormously exaggerated. Speculation over the origin of fossils added to the contention. The
subject was further complicated by the popular analogy of the
earth to a human body, likening earth's interior to intestines
and arteries, mountains to bones. But all helped make Europeans conscious of mountains.

Burnet's ideas stemmed from a profound experience in
the Alps. "Places that are strange and solemn strike an awe
into us and incline us to a kind of superstitious Timidity and
Veneration," he wrote. He was "rapt" and "ravished" by the
vast panoramas. Marjorie Nicolson observed that his work,
though intended to be scientific and theological, was even
more important to esthetics. He established a way of seeing
mountains. Since the mountains were pieces of the earth's
crust, the earth was nothing more than a "broken and confused heap of bodies, the rubbish of a great ruin. . . . What
can have more the Figure and Mien of a Ruin than Craigs,
and Rocks, and Cliffs? . . . all these Caves and blind Recesses . . . say but they are a Ruin and you have in one
word explained them all . . . our cities are built upon ruins
and our fields and countries stand upon broken arches and

vaults." In the confusion of the rocks and disorder of caves, Burnet found a magnificence that haunted his imagination, though it was contrary to the esthetic axiom that proportion and symmetry were the ultimate measures of beauty.

Although others, such as Edward Norgate, anticipated the love of Alpine scenery early in the century, it was John Dennis, a literary critic crossing the Alps in 1688, who aptly phrased and organized Burnet's emotions as an esthetic:

> The ascent was the more easie, because it wound about the mountain. But as soon as we had conquer'd one half of it, the unusual heighth in which we found ourselves, the impending Rock that hung over us, the dreadful Depth of the Precipice, and the Torrent that roar'd at the bottom, gave us such a view as was altogether new and amazing. . . . In the mean time we walk'd upon the very brink, in a litteral sense of Destruction; one Stumble, and both Life and Carcas had been at once destroy'd. The sense of all this produc'd different motions in me, *vis.* a delightful Horrour, a terrible Joy, and at the same time that I was infinitely pleas'd I trembled. . . . I am delighted, 'tis true at the prospect of Hills and Valleys, of flowry Meads, and murmuring Streams, yet it is a delight that is consistent with Reason, a delight that creates or improves Meditation. But transporting Pleasures follow'd the sight of the *Alpes* . . . mingled with horrours and sometimes almost with despair.

Burnet was a link between the astronomers and the estheticians, in apprehending the earth as a cosmic ruin. But it was Dennis who formulated this awareness in literary terms, who called the delightful horror of mountains "sublime" and who listed the sources of this elevated emotion: gods and angels, heavenly bodies, mountains, the four elements, wind, rivers, and the sea.

Dennis's superlatives and exuberant excitement make him sound like a voyager in fantasy, a visionary. The "sublime" experience of the visionary refers to the more traditional meaning of the word, to the transported feeling which usually takes the form of weightless aerial travel during a trance. "Transporting" unifies travel and rapture, the perfect expression of the disembodied passage. Though shaped as an esthetic, Dennis's sublime looked back to monastic martyrdom, exiled saints, and prophets in the wilderness. Isolation, abstinence, fasting, ritualistic chanting, sacred foods, flagellation, asphyxia, malnutrition are the stuff of which visions are made, or at least induced. Although landscape painting, like travel literature, depended upon the birth of an esthetic from a religious matrix, it has never separated itself completely from visionary (i.e., visual symbols of the unconscious) experience. Da Vinci's and Brueghel's and Patinir's mountains and whole landscapes by Giovanni di Paolo and Veneziano are visionary in that sense.

The sublime has been called the esthetics of the infinite. As a result of the invention of the telescope and the secularization of Western culture, the sublime was adapted from God and the heavens to a cosmic vision of this world or to scenery of a certain kind. The two were combined in Milton's *Paradise Lost* in the view of the vastness and diversity of the world shown to Christ by Satan from a mountaintop. After his visit to the Alps in 1699 Joseph Addison devoted several issues of the *Spectator* to the vast, "confused," "rude" piles of rock he had seen. They were horrible, yet pleasurable. After him the poets used astronomic or cosmic terms for terrestrial description. The cosmic voyage became the terrestrial excursion. Addison's introspection caused him to separate the sublime into intellectual and rhetorical. The intellectual was an actual confrontation of vast objects; the rhetorical, a vicarious, pleasurable horror from literary imagination or looking at pictures of wild places. His contemporary Lord Shaftesbury insisted that the sublime did not properly have to do with literary style but with a profoundly moving experience and a sense of God. Both, particularly Addison, prepared the way for Englishmen to appreciate scenery on the Grand Tour, the tour that had begun in the sixteenth century as an educational gesture to the superiority of Italian culture by scholars and scions of noble families. By Addison's time the Grand Tour had become commonplace among the new gentry, the princes of industry, and among both sexes as a voyage amid classical remains, for seasonal escape from the English winter, and for social prestige. Dilettantes, connoisseurs, enthusiasts, and artists on their way to see the works of antiquity were exposed to the sublimity of Alpine passes.

Pictures played an important part in this education of "sensibilities." Throughout the seventeenth century Dutch limners were busy in England and English travelers brought pictures home from the Grand Tour. Many Flemish paintings had Italianate scenery, preconditioning British eyes to wonderful and impossible notions of classical and Alpine landscapes by Gothic artists. In the beginning of the century the wilderness and mountains were only backgrounds to figures. The Flemish retained the landscapes as they copied these Italian themes, but replaced the saints with rustic figures such as bandits. Pieter van Laar was an early exponent of this substitution, and Adrian Van Diest, whose *Mountain Landscape* is a pictorial analogue of John Dennis's prose. Throughout the century the proportion of landscape over portrait paintings on English walls increased. After mid-century the English tourists particularly favored and collected the work of a Swiss-born Italian painter, Salvator Rosa.

Few of Rosa's landscapes are panoramic. They show sky beyond dark, windy subpromontories among the large rocky debris at the base of the upper slopes, cliffs bounding streams near their juncture with the valley floor, sparse trees thrusting through rocky outcrops with the flush valley soils adjacent. The figures, gods, angels, bandits, are very small. As bandits were no longer actually dangerous, Rosa found the freedom of their lives exciting. Just as the French nobility of the fourteenth century escaped courtly life by playing shepherd, Rosa escaped the seventeenth-century rational life by joining bandits. Both of these escapes are indicators of changing values and images of nature, one at the peak of neo-pastoralism and the other at the emergence of the wilderness esthetic.

Rosa's figures move along limestone cliffs, bent trees,

rushing streams, and crumbling walls of the Apennines. The implication of escape and individual freedom is another of those anticipations by painters of cultural trends, in this instance, anticipating the attitudes of Rousseau and Byron.

Thomas Burnet had described mountains as ruins, the chaotic detritus of the Fall. Ruins were pregnant with meaning in a world dedicated to the discovery of the glory of ancient Greece and Rome. Georges Louis de Buffon, the French naturalist, upon reading Burnet's *Sacred Theory* and knowing something of fossils, suggested that the day of creation would have to be pushed back at least twenty-five thousand years. Burnet said,

> There is nothing that I look upon with more pleasure than the wide sea and the Mountains of the Earth. There is something august and stately in the Air of these things that inspires the mind with great thoughts and passions; we do naturally upon such occasions think of God and his greatness, and whatever hath but the shadow and appearance of INFINITE. . . . And yet these mountains we are speaking of, to confess the truth, are nothing but great ruins; but such as show a certain magnificence in Nature; as from old temples and broken amphitheatres of the *Romans* we collect the greatness of that people.

By 1700, antiquarians had been delving for two centuries among the ruins of that departed grandeur.

Early Italian paintings of the Madonna and child and the Magi are set amid the ruins of the heathen past, ruins that had completely taken over the scene and were transformed in meaning by the time of Hubert Robert in the eighteenth century. The blasted tree and the broken wall had connoted death and decay since the beginning of the Renaissance. But these symbols suggested the good life which had vanished, a wistful and melancholy thought. The broken rocks represented time slowly working the cycle of empire. The sweep and grandeur of the past uncovered by archaeology was reaching the imagination of that growing audience with a "classical" education. The pilgrimage to Rome took on a new aspect, a veneration for that pagan past and its relics in every ancient city. Of the seventeenth-century paintings of ruins owned by Englishmen, H. V. D. Ogden writes, "Probably no other kind of landscape except the prospect was more admired during the second half of the century." Englishmen thereupon examined their own parishes with pensive pride for sublime scenes and objects. There followed a rebirth of interest in medieval history and Gothic architecture.

Excavations at Pompeii and Herculaneum began in the second quarter of the eighteenth century and by mid-century were widely known and followed in the press. John Dyer's poem "Ruins of Rome" described "Laturnae's wide champaign, forlorn and waste . . . solemn, wilderness . . . deep empty tombs, gloomy caverns, the mouldering wall . . . whose dust the solemn antiquarian turns." To Dyer the sewers were fantastic caverns and Sibylline grottoes. He and Samuel Bowden wrote a poem on Stonehenge and other poets soon began to write about ruined abbeys and castles in Britain. The landscape architect William Kent stuck dead trees in his landscape parks. Pope admired old walls. Ruins and Gothic edifices were constructed in the new informal landscape gardens.

The scientific study of the rhythmic pulsing of nature reinforced concepts of a cyclical human history. Southern artists such as Claude Gellée of Lorrain and Nicolas Poussin painted landscapes with classical temples and mythological figures. In the north Rubens and Ruisdael emphasized the purely visual details of ruins. In Germany the revival of interest in medieval life and architecture was at work with the Christian symbolism of decay and revival. The dead tree continued to appear as a form of ruin, complicated by its other functions as home for wild animals such as bees, as phallic symbol, and as the log home of wild man.

Catastrophe as well as time was the creator of ruins. Rosa painted stormy scenes. Naturalists reinterpreted storm and quake as natural processes instead of punishment meted out by an angry God. Literary and artistic mood pieces used them to communicate horror or terror. The Lisbon earthquake of 1775 provided a new theme for John Dyer, becoming an esthetic event through the medium of the sublime. So had the esthetic of the sublime evolved since Thomas Burnet, considering them merely chaotic, ridiculed the idea that they had visual appeal. But the local ruins of a "broken world" continued to be revealed in miniature. Burnet said, "They make a great noise, but they might all be apply'd to the ruins of an old Bridge fallen into the water," which as it turns out and as Marjorie Nicolson has said, was what happened.

The suspenseful Gothic novel was full of hidden passages and secret places, suggesting the buried cities in Greece, Italy, and Egypt. Ancient hermitages were turning up in cliffs or under city streets. The imitation of such settings in architecture, gardening, poetry, and painting coincided with a renewed interest in hidden openings, especially underground channels and caves. Nicholson calls the grotto "a minor manifestation of the widespread interest in the secret places of the earth, the first appeal of which was more to novelty and irregularity." We feel awe and solemnity in their interiors. Though a kind of sensuality, the sublime has never meant only seeking thrills; it required a religious preparation or, as it developed in the eighteenth century, a classical education.

From prehistoric times, caves have fascinated men. The sublime esthetic lent itself this complex heritage, impelled by a new interest in ruins with dark passages from room to room. A trip through a cave is a *transporting* experience. It is a reenactment of certain experiences which we know only from dreams, art, or the kinesthetic sense of our own bodily internal space. The light we carry into a dark cave has a hypnotic effect. The journey seems to proceed into "the very bowels of the earth." Mythical and religious travels to the other world characteristically enter underground empires, labyrinths, hollow mountains, and voids so great that they display a peculiar similarity to the desert or the heavens at night. In spite of whatever the geologists may have found since the beginning of the seventeenth century about caves, the setting of Dante's *Inferno* remains valid because it affirms a nonintellectual experience.

The roasting of souls has a geographical basis as well as a biological one: the fiery torture of disease when disease was considered punishment. Volcanoes spouting fire were an affirmation of the nature of hell; it is no wonder that dragons belch fire too. Christianity would be different had mankind evolved at one of those periods of the earth's history when volcanism and mountain-building were at a minimum. Possibly there is also a relationship between sacred caves and the distribution of limestone rocks and the geography of mystery religions.

The fiery part of the subterranean body of the earth is related to fire on its surface. Fire provides a manifold stimulus; its infrared radiation penetrates deeply, euphorically. Burning wood radiates odor, sound, and heat. Visually the fire, like the bird and the tree, is one of the supremely mutable, symbolic, iconic forms.

Social arson is the *Wirtschaft*, an ancient practice of controlled burning in agriculture. It persists today in parts of Africa, Europe, and America. It is a hysterical anachronism, wasteful and profligate in a crowded world. It frees for new cycling the mineral nutrients in dead organic materials. Simultaneously those elements become subject to erosion, and the burning of organic debris destroys humus which is necessary to the soil. The vegetation on lands which are periodically burned is gradually reduced to those plants which are heat- and drought-resistant. Woodlands of the temperate climate become parklike, as the forest slowly declines. The ecologist Frank Frazier Darling has suggested that the emotional furor associated with subtle seasonal changes in human behavior may be the most important factor in perpetuation of such fires.

Hesiod postulated a golden age of innocence in Arcadia, followed by fall due to original sin. The alternative speculation, notably by Lucretius, was the elevation of man from barbarism by the discovery of fire. Greek and Egyptian mythology confirm the antiquity of this idea. Citing Lucretius and Vitruvius, Boccaccio led the revival of the evolutionary or progressive theory as opposed to divine creation and supervision. The visual expression of this idea from Boccaccio's

Genealogia Deorum is to be found in the paintings by Piero di Cosimo, a fifteenth-century Florentine.

The art historian Erwin Panofsky interprets Di Cosimo's forest fires, wild melees between men, beasts, and half-men, and incidents from the lives of the gods, with theories of the origin of man. Drawing upon the *Physiologus*, the beastiaries, and encyclopedias, Di Cosimo created an ethnology before modern archaeology, anthropology, or paleontology. Looming behind it is the forest fire, background to the violence of prehistory.

Di Cosimo inverted the meanings of rocky or forested wilderness and pastoral valleys. To the Christian ascetic, desolation and sterility were associated with virtuous rejection of the pursuit of riches and hedonism. "To Piero," says Panofsky, "the same contrast means antithesis between the merciless hardships of unmitigated wildness and the innocent happiness of a pastoral civilization. . . . While reconstructing the outward appearances of a prehistoric world, Piero seems to have re-experienced the emotions of primeval man, both the creative excitement of the awakening human and the passions and fears of the caveman and the savage." The two pastorals, the innocent and the corrupt, are, he says, Vergilian and Ovidian. It was not the latter's approach in Di Cosimo, nor was it a wistful nostalgia of the former, but a conviction that the pastoral environment propels the advance of civilization.

Di Cosimo himself was a recluse. He disliked the city, noise, the church, hot food, and was terrified by lightning. He refused to have the garden plants trimmed, the fruit picked, or his workshop cleaned. He enjoyed the rain and apparently lived on hard-boiled eggs which were prepared in large numbers to save, or to avoid, lighting a fire.

Flames occurred in the fantastic landscapes by Heironymus Bosch about 1490, and broke out subsequently in the work of Patinir, Lotto, Giorgione, and Brueghel. There are other fantastic aspects of the work of these men. Taken together with Dürer and Leonardo we have the authors of "the first pure landscapes" of modern times. These contain

1

1. Giovanni Bellini: "St. Francis in Ecstasy." Giovanni Bellini's wonderful picture of St. Francis is cited by Kenneth Clark as a "supreme instance of facts transfigured through love." It is principally a landscape—one of the earliest. Indeed, St. Francis himself is here a vestige of the waning *raison d'etre* for art, the Biblico-mythic subject to which artists had been shackled by the patronage of the Church. Not that Christian ideas are absent; the painting's metaphysics of light, the hermitic, mystic ecstasy, the diffusion of the forces of compassion, and the psychological evolution by which an emblematic environment became allegorical all belong to Christianity, and yet are fundamental to the birth of the modern love of nature that is usually regarded as secular and anti-Christian.

When the "St. Francis" was painted, the great plagues and the tides of resurgent witchcraft had diminished, the primeval forest had receded from village environs, and a growing sense of the purposeful goodness of creation had yet to be shaken by the Reformation, science, and the debilitation of modern humanism. Optimism of this magnitude was not again to be expressed in pictures for four hundred years.

2. Francisco de Goya: "Fantastic Vision." The deeper terrors of the human heart, like the beatific ecstasy of the other extreme, assume synthetic forms on emergence to consciousness, forms which are composed of fragments of perceptual experience. The dank chasms, evil fens, and ominous massifs — in short, the geophobic wastes — are at once creations of our minds and realities of nature. The most terrible visions create a mythology of fear, whose forms, embodied in art and story, evoke when confronted in nature some measure of disquiet in even the placid observer. Such are the landscapes of Goya, Grünewald, and Dali.

3. Claude Lorrain. The discovery of pastoral beauty fully liberated the abstraction "scenery" from nature. It may well have been the most important esthetic event of modern times, for since the earliest domestication of plants and animals, the rural country had been the source of physical resources and great men for urban civilization. Nostalgia attributed to it innocence and old men found in it solace. As both environment and image it has drawn the energies of educated minds and of art, of popular enjoyment and tourism. From the noble sentiments of twelfth-century poets, through the great Italianate painters of the seventeenth century such as Lorrain and the eighteenth-century landscape architects, to the emergence of suburbia as a pastoral grove, it continues to be a dominant esthetic form by which the visual world is perceived.

4. Asher B. Durand: "White Mountain Scenery, Franconia Notch." Historians have traced "influences" from Italian landscape painters to English landscape gardeners, from the Dutch limners to the English Norwich school and their picturesque topics. Tracing influences is an endless academic game, as superficial as the concept of "taste" in art. Beneath the surface connections are hidden the dynamics of cultural continuity and nature attitudes. Put side by side some landscapes by Claude Lorrain, John Wilson, and Asher B. Durand and you may be tempted to seek influences, to ask what pictures Durand saw or what masters Wilson studied. Influences are important to art critics, but the similarities have more profound significance as a main road of the evolution of perception and the imagery of nature. Durand was a member of the nineteenth-century Hudson River school that discovered the beauty of the American landscape. Their paintings were, in turn, the tools by which Americans thereafter assimilated that discovery.

4

5. Illustration from *Roman de la Rose*. The garden was the first modern image of nature. It had been since the beginnings of civilization the purest microcosmic expression of the man-nature relationship. By the thirteenth century, when it provided the *gestalten* in which nature and love could be rediscovered, it stood halfway between the projection of unconscious symbolic forms and the mystery of nature itself. The garden was destined to become an allegorical hybrid of the two, an allegory referring to love — to the anatomy of love, both literally and figuratively. Through garden architecture the modern world continues to express its verdict on love and nature.

5

6

6. El Greco: "View of Toledo." If El Greco's "View of Toledo" does not immediately strike the observer as the torso of a woman it is perhaps because we do not trust the metamorphic nature of landscapes and bodies, being a literary rather than mythologically oriented people. Or perhaps it is because we have convinced ourselves that all is divided into the material or the spiritual, the lower or higher, visible or invisible. What seem to be alternatives in our time have the one crucial characteristic of degenerate perception: the form of dichotomy. Even in the religious context of El Greco's day, and surely to his own mind, the alternatives were more like polarities and the homological symbolism of the human body had not yet become the quaint and historical phrase "microcosm and macrocosm." That El Greco's vision was pervaded by a mystic sense of layers of organic continuity is apparent not only in the Toledo "portrait," but in such paintings as his "The Death of Count Orgaz," which depicts the birth of a child.

7. Delagrive: A Plan of Versailles. A long history of geometrizing nature — which began perhaps with the horizontal and vertical axes of the vertebrate eye — reached its ultimate expression in the royal French gardens of the seventeenth century. It was a history which sifted the whole of Western thought for order in the universe, essential to all things and demonstrable in regularity and symmetry. The projection of straight lines upon the mesocosm of the landscape was a mixed legacy from Platonic idealism, astronomic and cartographic science, and that side of the Italian Renaissance which made an esthetic of its own conceit.

7

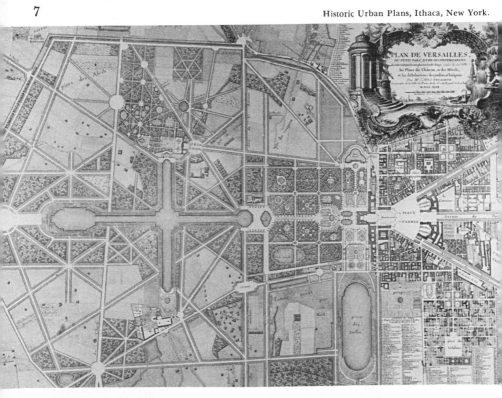

8. Giovanni di Paolo: "Madonna and Child in a Landscape." This painting of about 1456 represents a time of transition in the history of the perception of nature. It was the Virgin Madonna around whom the visual landscape seemed to form itself. In earlier pictures there are only the sketchy, emblematic forms to signify this world. Their skies had been flat gold — a finite cosmos; their hills, trees, and plants but stylized decorations, the emblems of a fixed, damned, and, in effect, unseen world. The new vision did not emerge at once. Its expression in painting lagged far behind its expression in poetry, but perhaps the pictures more nearly depict an evolution of consciousness. First there were the flowers immediately around her, then a bit of lawn, and the blue infinite sky. Finally, in the century after Giovanni di Paolo, the middle distance and the mountains yielded their frozen stereotopy. The great early masters of landscape painting — Bellini, Giorgione, Rubens — emerged, not simply as figures in an "art history" but as reflections of the visual evolution of modern man.

9. Salvator Rosa: "Tobia e l'Angelo." Salvator Rosa was not the first to make pictures of wild places; Adrian van Diest, Pieter van Laar, and others were before him. But Rosa created for a cosmopolitan audience the pictorial romance of wilderness and wildness. Where now we see in his canvases square yards of shadow and a repetitive formula for the silhouettes of leaves, his admirers were bent upon finding in that darkness the forms of a new nature esthetic. It was Rosa's lot, by his machines, to enable enthusiasts, gentlemen, collectors, and travelers to convey to themselves the conviction that there was a sublime order in the most savage scenery.

10. Vasily Kandinsky: "Rain." With the emergence of art collection as secular activity in the sixteenth century, there arose schemes for criticism and analysis that tended to isolate art from life. The evolution of the capacity to abstract — that is, to sort out purely visual and formal aspects of vision — proceeded by degrees to create a dialectic of art separate from symbol, rite, and representation. This anatomy of lines, forms, colors, textures, spaces, motion, and symmetry is sometimes held by academicians to be the exclusive esthetic reality. Perhaps those who insist that art must not follow nature misunderstand the meaning of nature, since art is within nature.

Since abstraction concerns fundamental and formal truth, its creation requires wisdom. It will always be measured against a reality that is not the private property of the artist, hence a criterion of a work of art such as "Does the artist achieve what he set out to do?" is the ultimate frivolity of the dialectic. Kandinsky demonstrates, as few painters who begin in landscape do, that nature imitates art imitates nature.

10

11

11. Albert Bierstadt: "Sunrise in the Hetch Hetchy Valley, California." The dream of a virgin nature, wild and yet beautiful,
sublime and yet pastoral, was a dream of splendor that
extended the essential utopian expression of the will to love.
The combination of geomorphic and biotic elements fell into
place in the nineteenth-century enthusiasm for wild nature, a
fusion of all the disparate images of admirable landscapes that
had gone before: the poetry of meadows, the romance of the
forest, the awesomeness of time in the decay of mountain
walls, and, above all, the unblemished purity of a new world.

incredible jagged rocks or knotted trees, aerial perspective, and other visionary forms. The painting of sublime landscapes came forth all at once, as though some fullness of life, manifestly urgent, overflowed. The sublime was an emerging perception of nature, not a vogue, style, or art cycle.

The primeval forest was to the north what rocks were to the Mediteranean: the wilderness barrier—mysterious, antithetical to man, and awful. The forest's harshness is reflected in early Celto-Germanic epics, distinguishing them from the Egyptian *Book of the Dead* and the Greco-Roman hero tales. In Greek tragedy men were fortuitously caught between two groups of contending deities, while the Gothic man conceived of his soul as a battleground between the powers of light and darkness in which God's victory was a human victory. The vast cosmic schemes by the Mediterrancans, generalities from which details were deduced, contrast to the Northerners' examination of minute details in the natural world which make broader inferences and induction possible. Galileo against Leeuwenhoek, the Rubens landscape against that of Rosa. Yet, no such generalization can be wholly true. The Old Testament tradition is Gothic in some respects. Hebrew life, says Charles Raven, was a collage of isolated organisms, a document of a delight in the detail of a beautiful country. The Aristotelian heritage (Gothic in the sense above) tended to prevent the raising of questions that interested Kcpler and Galileo. Gesner in the sixteenth century took up the science of life where Aristotle left off with the intimate and corpuscular approach which we have characterized as Gothic. The teeming panoramas of Brueghel and Bosch represent the Gothic view on a classical scale, a reunion of classical universality through Augustine and Plato and Gothic diversity from the proto-Christian enjoyment of the smallest configurations of the natural world and indigenous northern interest in the surroundings which would lead to such works as Gilbert White's *Natural History of Selbourne* and to Izaak Walton.

The twelfth to fourteenth centuries saw a reawakening of the fear of demons. The ferment of the rediscovery of ancient knowledge and the ravages of plagues and malnutrition formed the basis for an inextricable mixture of history and mythology, as indicated, for instance, in the half-human forms in Gothic sculpture. Nicolas Pvesner in *The Leaves of Southwell King* describes the profuse evidence of new observations of the environment in the sculpturing of vegetation in the architecture of the cathedral. Walter Abell has explored the cathedral demons as evidence of a disturbed society. He concluded that the flux of abstraction and naturalism in animal representation was associated with the stability and security of people. Realistic forms expressed stability and confidence, while a shift to abstract sculpturing indicated a withdrawal toward fundamentals, away from the specific conditions of everyday life. A widespread latent natural history as well as mythology provided a wellspring for the artist and philosopher to draw from. The craftsmen in stone who created the plant and animal forms in the Gothic cathedral perhaps reflect an aspect of the prodigious revolution in sentiment and perception that accomplished the creation of the cathedral itself.

The primeval forest disappeared as the cathedrals were built. The great period of building cathedrals followed the peak of clearing forests in Europe. The "Great Mother Forest" as historian Attilo Gatti has called it, provided the motif for the architectural conception of the Mother Church. The extraordinary similarities between the interior of virgin deciduous forest and the nave of a Gothic cathedral are conspicuous. A metaphor of forms and spaces within suggests nostalgia and profound emotion linking cathedral and the post-Pleistocene primeval forest, the fears and religious insights that Germanic peoples extended from that extinct natural community. Even the mild folk tales which reach American children from Germany and England display the fineness with which the temperate humid forest was woven into the culture. This image of the cathedral has perhaps been put most eloquently by Oswald Spengler:

The character of the Faustian cathedral is that of the *forest*. The mighty elevation of the nave above the flanking isles, in contrast to the flat roof of the basilica; the transformation of the columns, which with base and capital had been as self-contained individuals in space, into pillars and clustered-pillars that grow up out of the earth and spread on high into an infinite subdivision and interlacing of lines and branches; the giant windows by which the wall is dissolved and the interior filled with mysterious light—these are the architectural actualizing of a world-feeling that had found the first of all its symbols in the high forest with its mysterious tracery, its whispering of ever-mobile foliage over men's heads, its branches straining through the trunk to be free of earth. Think of Romanesque ornamentation and its deep affinity to the sense of the woods. . . . The history of organ-building, one of the most profound and moving chapters in our musical history, is a history of longing for the forest, a longing to speak in that true temple of Western God-fearing.

The wild forest was the desert of the north, the antithesis of domesticated landscapes. There were hermits in it, but the most spectacular human occupants were simply wild— those who had fallen from grace. They heightened the effect of the wilderness by giving it human scale. The wild man in the Middle Ages, like all the rest of nature, was perceived in symbolic and allegorical terms. He was a form of disorder. "Just as the wilderness is the background against which medieval society is delineated, so wilderness in the widest sense is the background of God's lucid order of creation," says Richard Bernheimer. Connotations of wilderness widened in the Middle Ages to embrace "everything that eluded Christian norms." The wild man's counterpart was the witch. He enjoyed storms and lived in the roughest parts of the forest. As the Middle Ages waned and the primeval forest disappeared, some of his less sinful and less macabre characteristics were noticed. Where once it was right to slay or capture him, it became fashionable to "slip into the wild man's garb" as a repudiation of the hierarchic order of medieval society. And one might add to Bernheimer's observations that affirmation of the nobility of the wild man as an escape from civilized evils represented a changing attitude toward the wilderness itself.

The self-conscious enjoyment of such sublime emotions did not actually reduce the most profound human feelings and perceptions to esthetics. However vulgar, affected, foppish, and sentimental, the sublime marked a change in the relationship of man to nature, the renewal of human wonder at the natural world, a revolution which has not yet run its course. Theoretical attempts to account for man's new sensitivity were themselves part of that growing self-consciousness. After Dennis and Addison came Frances Hutcheson's *Enquiry into the Origin of Our Ideas of Beauty and Order*, which dealt with "sensations," and William Hogarth's *The Analysis of Beauty*, which also talked about persons of "sensibility." Finally, in 1757, Edmund Burke codified the effects of visible objects on the "passions" in *A Philosophical Enquiry into the Origin of Our Ideas of the Sublime and Beautiful*. He divided experience into the Sublime and the Beautiful on the basis of "subconscious" associations. The Sublime was stimulated by fear or the instinct for self-preservation; the Beautiful, by desire or the instinct for procreation. The subconscious to Burke meant temporarily latent associations by which a certain idea produced certain emotional responses. This subconscious was of course open to rational analysis. The Sublime was terrible (the ocean or snakes), obscure (as, he said, lurking druids in the dark woods), powerful (as the bull, horse, gloomy forest, or howling wilderness), deprived (darkness, solitude, and silence), vast (cliffs), magnificent (the sky), and infinite.

Burke formalized the esthetic. Walpole's Gothic novel *The Castle of Otranto* was calculated to inspire it; Dante was to be reread for this newly defined pleasure. Ann Radcliffe brought the novel of terror and the macabre to its acme near the end of the century. Like Walpole, who toured the Alps with Thomas Gray watching for appropriate scenes for Salvator Rosa, Radcliffe's characters move through a series of Rosa-like scenes in Italy. The windy solitudes in *Ossian*, a poem of 1763, provided her with ideas. In contrast to the

Italian scenery (which she had never seen), her actual land-scapes are pale and artificial. The heavy forests in her novels and the detail in which they are described are thoroughly Gothic. Later, to the German transcendentalists, as with Rad-cliffe, pictures were essential. Caspar Friedrich, the painter, went indoors with sketches, put them away, and, after a suitable wait, without again consulting his sketches, painted the landscape. A critic named Wrackenwroder is quoted as saying, "Picture galleries should be temples." The wild for-est was at the core of works by Goethe, Tieck, Wagner, and Beethoven. Their motif grew out of the association of such scenery with the early German gods, the use of the holy grove as a symbol of ritual worship, and that fantastic animation and fecund, organic nightmare of the northern forest that metamorphized into fairy tales. George Boas has written:

> The forest primeval had disappeared from the Medi-terranean basin generations before Homer. But in North Europe it still survived. Its darkness and its beasts, its wildness and mystery, were accessible to all who cared to investigate them. They were the home of the fore-bearers of Germans and Englishmen; they provided the *décor* for their rites. Consequently, if the men were to be admired so was their home. If they lived close to a state of nature, then Nature must not be the nature of Virgil and Theocritus, the smiling Sicilian fields; it must be the nature of north Germany, of Wales, of Scotland, the nature of rocky craig and tumultuous cumulus clouds, of great waterfalls; untamed by human art, raw, terri-ble, sublime.

In America the sublime was peculiarly suitable to the perception of Niagara Falls, the Hudson Valley, New Eng-land, parts of Virginia, and later the West. The vast powers of nature were apparent in America as in the Alps. Louis Hennepin, a Flemish Jesuit, visited Niagara Falls in 1678 to see the spectacle. Like Dennis in the Alps, Hennepin was elated and yet fearful. "It was a great and prodigious ca-dence of water, to which the universe does not offer a par-allel. . . . The waters which fall from this great precipice do foam and boil in a most astonishing manner, making a noise more terrible than that of thunder." There are scattered records from the following century in America that together faintly echo trends in England. Many historians have asserted that the wilderness was still too close for Americans to appreciate it in the way that it was admired in Europe. The typical gentleman was at least partly educated in Europe, and the regimen at Harvard and Yale was patterned closely after foreign schools. It was not the great abundance of wilderness in America that limited the degree to which the wilderness was admired during the nation's first two centuries, but the number of people with the suitable orientation. Mary Wolley has discovered about twenty writers who found parts of New England "romantic" before 1800, not including the many Europeans who had similar reactions.

Thomas Jefferson admired ruins while traveling in Germany, and said that Italian scenery was composed of "monuments of a war between rivers and mountains which must have shaken the earth itself to its center." He was among the first to enjoy sublime scenery in this country. In *Notes on Virginia* he wrote, "The Natural Bridge is the most sublime of nature's works. . . . If the view from the top be painful and intolerable, that from below is delightful in an equal extreme. . . . The rapture of the spectator is really indescribable."

During Jefferson's time, Ann Radcliffe's novels, especially *The Mysteries of Udolpho*, *The Italian*, and *The Romance of the Forest*, were popular in America. Typical paragraphs from the last reveal her preoccupations and her *forte*:

He entered what appeared to have been the chapel of the abbey. . . . La Motte paused a moment, for he felt a sensation of sublimity rising into terror—a suspension of mingled astonishment and awe! He surveyed the vastness of the place, and as he contemplated its ruins, fancy bore him back to past ages. "And these walls," he said, "where once superstition lurked, and austerity anticipated an earthly purgatory, now tremble over the mortal remains of the beings who reared them!". . . . Several of the pillars, which had once supported the roof, remained the proud effigies of sinking greatness, and seemed to nod at every murmur of the blast over the fragments of those that have fallen little before them. La Motte sighed. The comparison between himself and the graduation of decay, which these columns exhibited, was but too obvious and affecting. "A few years," said he, "and I shall become like the mortals on whose relics I now gaze, and like them too, I may be the subject of meditation to a succeeding generation, which shall totter but a little while over the object they contemplate, are they also sink into dust.". . .

IIis chateau stood on the borders of a small lake that was almost environed by mountains of stupendous height, which, shooting into a variety of grotesque forms, composed a scenery singularly solemn and sublime. Dark woods, intermingled with bold projections of rock, sometimes barren, and sometimes covered with the purple bloom of wild flowers, impended over the lake, and were seen in the clear mirror of its waters. The wild and alpine heights which rose above, were either crowned with perpetual snows or exhibited tremendous craigs and masses of solid rock, whose appearance was continually changing as the rays of light were variously reflected on their surface, and whose summits were often wrapt in impenetrable mists. Some cottages and hamlets, scattered on the margin of the lake, or seated in picturesque points of view on the rocks above, were the only objects that remained the beholder of humanity. . . .

"The stillness and total seclusion of this scene," said Adeline, "these stupendous mountains, the gloomy grandeur of these woods, together with that monument of faded glory, on which the hand of time is so emphatically impressed, diffuse a sacred enthusiasm over the mind, and awaken sensations truly sublime.". . . The profound stillness which reigned in these regions of solitude inspired awe, and heightened the sublimity of the scenery to an exquisite degree. "It seems," said Adeline, "as if we were walking over the ruins of the world, and were the only persons who had survived the wreck. I can scarcely persuade myself that we are not left alone on the globe." "The view of these objects," said La Luc, "lifts the soul to their great Author, and we contemplate with a feeling, almost too vast for humanity, the sublimity of his nature in the grandeur of his works." La Luc raised his eyes, filled with tears, to heaven, and was for some moments lost in silent adoration.

The relationship of man to nature in nineteenth-century America cannot be intelligently understood apart from such sentiments and the perception of wild landscapes, or indeed, of the popularity and success of Radcliffe's novels and those of her American imitator, Charles Brockden Brown. Washington Allston, the solitary, ambitious American painter whose *Storm at Sea* and *Elijah Being Fed by the Ravens* were both sublime and a new kind of achievement, greatly admired Salvator Rosa, German and English terror stories, the work of his friend Samuel Taylor Coleridge, and the books of Ann Radcliffe. He illustrated the American edition of her *The Mysteries of Udolpho* in 1795, and later painted Spalatro's vision of the bloody hand from *The Italian*. He wrote of a French castle, "It had a most picturesque appearance as the first glimpse of morning fell on its mouldering towers. It stood on the brow of a high bank of the river which glittered at its base. The description of Mrs. Radcliffe was brought immediately to my recollection." A Unitarian minister admonished his congregation to distinguish between the moral and the natural sublime, warning them to shun the latter as it appeared in Mrs. Radcliffe's scene of the bloody hand. James Thrall Soby has discovered a similarity between Catlin's descripton of the upper Missouri and the prose of Mrs. Radcliffe. William Cullen Bryant read *Romance of the Forest* while still a boy. Allston's landscape paintings, like Radcliffe's prose scenes, were constructed without field sketches. There is in both a strong visionary color. The audience for whom they wrote or painted was, on the other hand, frequently engaged in travel to wild places, such as Niagara Falls.

Niagara Falls proved to be a supreme spectacle. From the time of Hennepin spectators came in increasing numbers. An atmosphere of fanaticism and carnival stimulated daredeviltry and the sacrifice of animals in ships and rafts. Others found the experience deeply personal. The most passionate of the letters and records describing the falls were written by women. "It is now midnight," wrote one, "the roar of the waters agitates me. . . . I cannot sooth down my heart—it is kindled by deep working of the invisible. . . . My dreams are very wild here. I am not calm. A great voice seems to be calling on me. . . . I have felt a spell on my soul as if Deity stood visible there . . . I felt the moral influence of the scene acting on my spiritual nature, and while lingering at the summit alone, offered a simple prayer." Another ascribed to it a "terrible loveliness," and said, "I feel half crazy whenever I think of it." Harriet Beecher Stowe was reminded of images from Revelation and of the Great White Throne. To her, the mist seemed to be a rising soul. "I felt as if I could have *gone over* with the waters; it would be so beautiful a death; there would be no fear in it. I felt the rock tremble under me with a sort of joy; I was so maddened that I could have gone too, if it had gone." A tower was built on a small island at the lip of the falls.

The building of towers, chapels, and hotels near sites that attract travelers has been common from the earliest times. New England had no historic chapels or monasteries, but observation platforms and mountain houses appeared rapidly after 1820 near impressive scenery. Most magnificent was the Catskill Mountain House on a high cliff overlooking the Hudson Valley above Palenville, New York. Its classic facade, razed in 1956, overlooked the scene where Americans were first awakened to esthetic enjoyment of the native landscape.

The Hudson Valley was settled by the Dutch early in the seventeenth century. For eighty years its real wild men, the Indians, were dangerous. One suspects that elements of the wild-man mythology from northern Europe were transferred to this new settlement. The English succeeded the Dutch, adopting and adding to local tradition. By Washington Irving's time, the valley had a unique folklore, and this mythical and historical background opened the way for artistic and esthetic discovery of the Hudson. It is no accident that the Catskill Mountain House stood on the very spot from which James Fenimore Cooper's Leatherstocking describes the sublimity of creation. A few hundred yards away is the clove or glen in which Washington Irving settled Rip Van Winkle for his twenty-year sleep. The immediate area surrounding the Mountain House is the region referred to as "the Catskills" until after the Civil War.

Even after mid-century, Irving wrote of the Catskills as though the ghost of Ann Radcliffe were guiding his pen:

> The interior of these mountains is in the high degree wild and romantic; here are rocky precipices mantled with primeval forests; deep gorges walled in by beetling cliffs, with torrents rumbling as it were from the sky; and savage glens rarely trodden excepting by the hunter. With all this internal rudeness, the aspect of these mountains toward the Hudson at times is eminently bland and beautiful, sloping down into a country softened by cultivation, and bearing much of the rich character of Italian scenery about the skirts of the Apennines.
>
> Here are locked up mighty forests that have never been invaded by the axe; deep umbrageous valleys where the virgin soil has never been outraged by the plough; bright streams flowing in untasked idleness, unburthened by commerce, unchecked by the mill-dam.

Rising more than three thousand feet above the Hudson Valley, the Catskill escarpment is unusually abrupt and heavily forested, a contrast to the pastoral lowland. Henry T. Tuckerman, a writer, after strolling near the Mountain House, wrote: "We may imagine the effect of a lengthened sojourn in the primeval forest, upon a nature alive to its beauty, wildness and solitude; and when we add to these, the zest of adventure, the pride of discovery and that feeling of sublimity which arises from a consciousness of danger always pending, it is easy to realize in the experience of a pioneer at once the most romantic and practical elements of life."

Like many, he sensed the danger of exploration, but more important, the experience of being the first man ever to see the place. As the English vicar William Gilpin wrote in 1782, in the forest one should "suppose the country to have been unexplored." Byron put this and related ideas so well in the nineteenth century that two generations of American travelers probably quoted him more frequently in their journals than any other English poet.

> To sit on rocks, to muse o'er flood and fell,
> To slowly trace the forest's shady scene,
> Where things that own not man's dominion dwell,
> And mortal foot hath ne'er or rarely been
> To climb the trackless mountain all unseen,
> With the wild flock that never needs a fold; . . .

One of the fancied dangers of being the first into a wilderness was getting lost. The idea of the absence of landmarks and loss of orientation approaches the theme of the vision and the infinite and almost always evokes an awareness of silence. Writing for children, a nineteenth-century writer said of the Catskills, "If you were to travel among the mountains, you would sometimes meet with a farm house surrounded with meadows and wheat fields, and sometimes you would seem lost amid wild rocks, and lonely ravines, where you would hear nothing but the roar of waterfalls, cries of birds, and the voices of wild animals." (Since a noisy wilderness seemed contradictory, it was necessary to list the exceptions.)

It was not necessary actually to enter the wild forest to enjoy the possibility of getting lost. Nathaniel Hawthorne, after driving near Northampton in a coach at night, wrote, "How very desolate looks a forest when seen in this way—as if, should you venture one step within its wild, tangled, many-stemmed and dark shadowed verge, you would inevitably be lost forever."

To be actually lost was the ultimate experience. In the

Catskills this was possible in a circumscribed area, especially at night, but with near certainty of eventually reaching safety. This happened to Thomas Cole during a thunderstorm, when he found himself in one of the deep gorges:

> The truth at last crept over me. *I was lost*—lost past finding out or being found. . . . Again I tried to extricate myself from the windfall, with a desperate energy. I climbed and stooped, scrambled, crawled, and dodged. Now a limb struck me in the face, and I fell backwards among the brambles; then I made a misstep, or a rotten bough broke beneath my foot, and I plunged forward with a crash. . . . The dash of my footsteps, as I waded forward, rang strangely through the hollow cave, and I felt a wild and vivid pleasure as I advanced. I shouted, sang, whistled, for the very horror of the thing.

Charles Lanman, who admired Thomas Cole and had probably seen Cole's painting of the view from Round Top in the Catskills, went up the mountain for a night out. In the middle of the night he arose and sat upon the big rock on the summit and looked toward the Hudson in the moonlight. "Oh, how can I describe the scene that burst upon my enraptured vision? It was unlike anything I had ever seen before, creating a 'lone, lost feeling' which I suppose could only be realized by a wanderer in the heart of an uninhabited wilderness."

Thus the idea of sleeping out and of the "adventure hike" was emerging, its roots in the enigma of being, its upper branches reaching toward the dizzy jounce of the nature dabbler and tourist. But neither Thomas Cole, his colleague Thomas Doughty, nor his friend William Cullen Bryant, could be called dabblers. They were among the first to explore fully the knowledge, as Cole said, that "the most impressive characteristic of American scenery is its wilderness." Cole, English-born, was an itinerant Ohio limner before coming east. While studying in England he had copied paintings by Richard Wilson. Bryant induced him to move up the Hudson from New York City and he settled at Hudson, eight miles from Palenville and the Mountain House. From

Hudson he occasionally commuted down the river to New York to speak at the American Academy of Design, commingle with colleagues, or meet a patron. Like the painters Thomas Doughty and Asher Durand he traveled widely over New York and New England, sketching.

Cole was among those who were ruefully aware of the scarcity of ruins in America. He wrote, "We feel the want of associations such as cling to scenes in the old world. Simple nature is not quite sufficient. We want human interest, incident and action, to render the effect of landscape complete." He sought out areas such as the lower Hudson and Lake George, which were associated with long settlement and historical events. "If we were endowed with ruins we should not preserve them," complained another. "They would be pulled down to make way for some novelty. A striking instance of this tendency will be found in the fact that the last Dutch house in New York has disappeared. . . . We might have supposed that occupying so little space as they did, standing in streets with Dutch names, owned perhaps by men of Dutch descent, one, at least, of these relics of our olden time might have been preserved."

Cole may have felt that "simple nature is not quite sufficient," but a great deal of attention went into the discovery of natural ruins.

Even Indian legends could be worked into an appreciation of the time and history as a ruin, but few had been interested enough to preserve them. One writer lamented, "A scene of primeval nature and solitude . . . would that its stupendous scenery were linked with mighty incident and that its rare loveliness were clothed with the sacred vestment of traditionary lore! But alas! Its magnificent grandeur and picturesque beauty so fitted to figure in Indian romance or the settler's legend is sadly deficient in the hallowing charm of historic or poetic association!"

Less than a generation after the Presidential Range had been named in 1820, a disgruntled observer commented, "What a pity that the hills could not have kept the names which the Indian tribes gave to them . . . Webster, Clinton,

Franklin, Monroe, Washington, Clay, Jefferson, Adams, Madison. What a wretched jumble!"

A family living at Crawford Notch had been frightened from their house and killed by a rock slide during a stormy night in 1826. Their undamaged house stood unoccupied for many years, gradually falling into ruined heaps. Cole wrote,

> We now entered the Notch, and felt awe-struck as we passed between the bare and rifted mountains, rising on either hand some two thousand feet above us. With the exception of a few curling round the airy pinnacles the clouds had now dispersed, and the sun shown down brilliantly upon this scene of wild grandeur. The sight of the Wiley House, with its little patch of green in the gloomy desolation, very naturally recalled to mind the horrors of the night when the whole family perished beneath an avalanche of rocks and earth.

A visitor said of the place, "The fleetingness of human life is the reflection which focuses itself upon the mind of the traveller, as he treads the deserted chambers of that lonely house." Another added that "The furrows and ruins of a number of avalanches, too, are visible at the sides of the mountains. These possess a melancholy interest from the fact that one of them . . . swept away an entire family." Links were being forged between the architectural and the natural ruin where the two interplayed and the observer was led to an examination of the natural processes which made ruins of the mountains as well as men's works and lives.

Theodore Dwight, who traveled widely in New England as had his Uncle Timothy, looked in vain for actual remains of the Indians. In northern New England he found "mighty rocks balanced on the hills . . . apparently artificial heaps of loose stones . . . and . . . the unaccountable lines and figures traced on many rude blocks of granite." Agassiz's first visit was still twenty years away and his discovery of the ice age far in the future. Dwight was probably looking at glacial deposits and scratches—erratics, moraines, and striae. Patriotism could make men yearn for ruins. Looking at flood debris along the Saco River, Dwight added another type of natural "ruin" to the signs of the ice sheet: "We are impressed by these marks of destruction with an awful idea of the wreck we are soon to witness. . . . We find ourselves in the desolation of what was created desolate, and the rude commingling of vast objects which were before awful for size, and ranged without form or order." At the river's head he passed through Crawford Notch and down the Ammonoosuc, where there were signs of "general desolation" and the stream looked like an avenue with "impenetrable shades" on either side, arching over it like a "Gothic edifice." The debris on the flood plain looked like parts of a structure. "Ruins lie scattered and mouldering for miles down the course of the stream," he said of the trunks deposited by high water. The mist from the lake at Crawford Notch was "like Ossian's images." A burned forest resembled the masts of all of Europe's ships moored together; the rocks from the walls of the notch suggested cannon shot; and the cliffs themselves brought to mind "a palace, and yonder a whole city in ruins."

Dwight had seen Hutton's book on uniformitarianism, which said in effect that land surface is not static, and its evolution may be understood by its present processes. With Hutton's and Lyell's books, the public interest in geology erupted. Fragments of rock were recognized as products of a process and at the same time as ruins. The solution and abrasion of rocks was rapidly becoming evident, even to the layman. Of the tumbled piles of stone at the foot of the cliff faces between New Haven and Hartford, a guidebook said, "These fragments are the detritus or debris of these mountains, and everyone in the least acquainted with such countries, knows how much they always abound with similar ruins. . . . This valley is, moreover, choked in an astonishing degree with the ruins of the contiguous mountain ridge . . . piled on one another in vast confusion. . . . Leaves and other vegetable ruins have accumulated among the rocks and trees, and choked the mouths of many of the cavities among the ruins."

Organic things could also be ruins. George P. Morris's poem "Woodman, Spare That Tree" was published not long before Andrew Jackson Downing, the landscape architect, wrote, "If we have neither old castles nor old associations, we have at least, here and there, old trees that can teach us lessons of antiquity, not less instructive and poetical than the ruins of a past age." Like Irving, Bryant, and Cole, Downing was embarrassed by this national insufficiency. Some ruins were built in imitation Gothic. Irving and Cooper had their homes redone. Others followed, such as John Cruger, who built ruined arches on an island in the Hudson and scattered Mayan sculpture among them. Travelers reading European novels and poetry as they sailed up the river could see a ruined arch built on a high point near Hyde Park. Cole painted Gothic and classical fantasies, and with Downing and others, discovered substitutes. In Europe, John Ruskin spoke for all of those, including the American artists, who went as "pilgrims" on the Grand Tour to Italy: "I could not even for a couple of months live in a country so miserable as to possess no castles."

The primeval forest is a place of large trees, both living and dead. The dead trunks appealed to Cole as a form of organic ruin. Of a lake near the Catskill House, he said, "The dead trees are a striking feature in the scenery of the lake, and exceedingly picturesque—their forms rise from the margin of the deep, stretching out their contorted branches, and looking like so many genii set to protect the sacred waters. . . . What a place for music by moonlight."

The water levels of that lake had been raised slightly by the construction of a dam, thereby inundating the roots of marginal trees and killing them. Tree ruins were multiplied by man in other ways, too. Farmers girdled them, or they died from fire injury. Although there is probably no record of fires having been set to produce sublime ruins, fires were certainly lit for excitement. In this, the Americans continued the ancient pursuit of hysteria by conflagration. Charles Mason, for instance, enjoyed "the grandeur and terror of the scene" of a fire on Mt. Monadnock about 1820. "It was a beautiful spectacle and grand in itself, but rendered sublime and awful by the thought of the dread power." Some fires, like that on Monadnock, were started by hunters, others from an agricultural pretense. Panther and wolf hunts were staged in New England by large groups of armed men with packs of dogs. These chases sometimes lasted all night, or even several successive days and nights, suggesting Piero di Cosimo's fifteenth-century *Hunting Scene*, a wild melee of predatory men and animals against a background of burning forest. J. T. Headley, hiking in the Adirondacks, said that he "wanted to set fire to the trees on the summit . . . so as to present an unobstructed view," but he found the foliage too green to burn. Land clearing went on at a very rapid pace in the East during the first forty years of the nineteenth century. Travelers reported that they rode for days at a time in the smoke of burning logs. It was the traveler who recognized that as a land-use practice burning was disastrous and who could most fully lose himself in enjoyment of the world as a fiery spectacle. "We had a fearfully sublime example during the dry summer of 1864," wrote a traveler, "when the flames reached within a few feet of the outbuildings at the Mountain House . . . a view by night, of the mountains, with the flames rolling along their sides and summits, and shining forth from the trunks and tops of lofty forest trees, is a scene of exciting and appalling splendor, well nigh as great and imposing as an eruption of Vesuvius or Etna."

The frame house was a poor ruin. It decayed too rapidly, failing to signify the slow ravagement of time. However, some travelers were very determined, such as Charles Lanman, the follower of Thomas Cole. Lanman left his coach at Montpelier in 1845 and spent a morning idling in a ruined frame house, "musing upon its solemn admonition." The graveyard also offered a substitute, and with the coming of the new rural graveyards, it was possible to combine the pleasures of the pastoral imagery of the park with the sublime sense of time and the frailty of human life. Gray's *Elegy* was a specimen of the possibilities of such contemplation. But best of all were the associations derived from historical incidents. "These scenes are classic," said Cole of Lake George, thinking of the Revolution. He preferred views of the Hudson "as

seen from the rich orchards of the surrounding hills, hills that
have a legend."

West Rock at New Haven recalled "a story of trial and
fortitude, courage and magnanimity, the noblest friendship,
and a fearless adherence to political principles from religious
motives." This referred to the history of Judge's Cave on the
top of West Rock, a hideout for pre-Revolutionary rebels.

Americans were eager to enshrine their forefathers'
footprints. They doted on the Hudson with its two centuries
of history, especially its Revolutionary War episodes and its
great estates. According to a guidebook, "No place in the
Union, probably, exceeds West Point in beauty of location
and the stirring incidents connected with its early history,"
being "hallowed by the footsteps of Washington and Kos-
ciusko."

Even Niagara Falls was improved by awareness of nearby battlegrounds. "The sensibilities of my heart had been
powerfully awakened by what I had just heard of the dreadful
scenes of Chippewa and Bridgewater," wrote a traveler, "and
the roaring of the falls, which now becoming distinct, appeared like the sound of distant thunder, served to heighten
my emotions. I was all eye and ear; every moment expecting
the grand view to burst upon me." When the past failed as a
source of recorded history and when Indian legend was inadequate, there were still men creating their own legends. In a
sense, the phenomenon of American landscape painting between 1800 and 1865 was a capture of the processes of
change. The sublimity of the wheel of time and the birth of
empire crystallized in certain visible forms. The view from
West Point up the Hudson, the tombstone, the relic, the
historical marker, and the landscape painting yielded
emotional accompaniment to the contemplation of time and
God.

The terrible awe of God was made into an esthetic—or,
if you prefer, the forests and mountains of the earth came to
be revered with religious intensity. The enjoyment of primeval wilderness had not been possible before. Like other esthetic abstractions, the concept of the sublime was a portable

emotion. In America it made the discovery of magnificent scenery possible, where none was before, by discovering in natural forms and processes manifestations of the omniscient and inexorable which in Europe had been connected to mythological or historical events. The explicit focus of the sublime on virgin wilderness has created in the American character one of its few true idiosyncrasies: the emotional connection of nationalism with stupendous scenery and the phenomenon of the preservation of wilderness areas.

Chapter Six

Fellow Creatures

ALBERT SCHWEITZER declared,

> Ethics must plunge into the adventure of making its adjustment with nature philosophy. . . . Let it dare, then to accept the thought that self-devotion must stretch out not simply to mankind but to all creation, and especially to all life in the world within reach of man. Let it rise to the conception that the relation of man to man is only an expression of the relation in which he stands to all being and to the world in general.

This ethical perspective he called "Reverence for Life." [1] In several places, especially *Civilization and Ethics*, he explored our failure in the past to extend ethics to nature.

Schweitzer observed that the authors of the New Testament show little compassion for nature, compared to the Hebrews, because they expected the world to end. Although sympathy is implicit in the Christian commandment to love, Schweitzer noted that Western philosophy has followed other lines. He criticized Kant for concerning himself exclusively with man, attributing this myopic view to the influence of Descartes, who seemed to have "bewitched the whole of European philosophy with his declaration that animals were

[1] As C. H. D. Clarke has pointed out, "reverence" is a poor if not misleading translation of Schweitzer's term, "*Ehrfurcht*"— literally "honor-fear."

nothing but machines." Schweitzer compared Western philosophers to the housewife who does not want animal tracks
across her tidy floors. He observed that this dogmatic limita-
tion persists in spite of the urgings of Schopenhauer. In *Die
Weltanschaung der Indischen Denker* he contrasted this
Western hiatus to the manifold concern for living things in
Eastern religions. He acknowledged the splendid vision of the
Ahimsa commandment of Jainism against killing and its
adoption in Buddhism, indicating that it is nonetheless incomplete because of its renunciatory motives, its purely theoretical origin, and its entirely passive application.

Schweitzer clearly realized that the application of his
ethic is more difficult than its comprehension. The principle
itself is absolute. "It is easy to preach such sympathy in
general, but extraordinarily difficult to lay down rules for
making it effective." Each of us must decide for himself, he
says,

> how far he can go towards carrying out the boundless
> commandment of love without surrendering his own
> existence and must decide, too, how much of his life and
> happiness he must sacrifice to the life and happiness of
> others. . . . Not only does there come into consideration
> here the question of when the existence of the welfare of
> an animal may be sacrificed to the existence or the needs
> of man, but also the question of how we are to decide
> whether the life of well-being of one animal may be
> sacrificed to the life or well-being of another.

Schweitzer did not come to the concept of "Reverence
for Life" from the point of view of one who loves nature. To
him "the world is a cruel drama of the will-to-live divided
against itself. One existence prevails at the expense of another. . . . A longing to attain unity is not found in it. . . .
It remains a painful enigma for me that I must live with reverence for life in a world ruled by a creative will which is at the
same time a destructive will." This world is a "desert of life"
in which the practice of helping animals is "recompense for
the great misery that man inflicts upon them, and thus for a
moment we escape from the incomprehensible horror of ex-

istence." These are phrases from an essay on the ethic of "Reverence for Life" and are essential to the heart of Schweitzer's interpolation of the principle into action. To him the enormous mortality in nature is an embodiment of the evil against which the universal "will to live" struggles. He says, "The struggle for existence that takes place all around us among living creatures can never be—unless we have succumbed to thoughtlessness—a spectacle to watch with interest and delight, but always a painful one." The idea of pain here has ramifications, as he refers elsewhere to "that mysterious exaltation of the will-to-live around me." Pain, fear, and death are those realities confronted by the will and the ethic. Repeatedly, the theme of pain, suffering, and death are associated with the brutality of nature and man's cruelty. "Our own vocation," he says, "is not to acquiesce in the cruelty of nature and even join in it, but rather to set a limit to it so far as our influence reaches."

There is not much point in arguing about the existence of pain in the experience of animals. Descartes presumed that only man, with a soul, could feel pain. To a degree pain may be regarded as a very specialized phenomenon of nervous systems. The function of discomfort or pain from a biological viewpoint is survival, since it prevents the organism from allowing avoidable damage. Whether an earthworm feels what man would regard as pain is doubtful, yet it may be so, and so long as it cannot be proved otherwise Schweitzer's assumption for the purpose of his ethic is just.

Fear is an equally ambiguous term to apply to animal life. Animals flee from danger, struggle when restrained, and show the physiological flux which in man is associated with fear. But the dread of potential harm and the grim anxiety over possible oblivion require a cognition and foresight which are probably restricted at least to certain mammals if not to man alone. The natural dangers which threaten most wild animals many times a day do not disturb them for long and they quickly return to resting and feeding. Perhaps in them fear, pain, and anger are united in a single fleeting awareness which is extinguished with a behavioral response. Even so, until better communication with animals about their feelings becomes possible, it is plausible to suppose that they experience fear as well as pain. C. S. Lewis's remarkable empathy for the inner world of the bear in his novel *That Hideous Strength* suggests a "warm, trembling, iridescent pool of pre-Adamite consciousness."

But death is the crux of the matter. Schweitzer considers the Ahimsa commandment against all killing to be an ideal, its complete fulfillment impossible, and its Indian exponents therefore living an illusion. The very act of saving lives destroys and harms other lives. This is the point at which decision intrudes. The ethic of "Reverence for Life" conserves the somewhat abstract "will-to-live," but its practice is with living individuals. Each encounter with an animal is one of a lifelong chain of decisions in which the individual with an attuned sense of responsibility makes an anxious and sometimes sorrowful judgment.

The episodic, fragmental nature of this experience is fully demonstrated in Schweitzer's own African journals. Charles Jay's collection of Schweitzer's writings on African animals, *The Animal World of Albert Schweitzer*, is an appalling document. Even allowing that it covers a wide span of years and is drawn from many separate works and not written as a unit, it reveals a narrowly restricted preoccupation, almost a fixation, for certain formal relationships to animals. Description centers on hunting, control, eating, and the destruction of wild animals, their potential danger to man, the treatment of wounds caused by them, and the practical difficulties which they pose to the European in equatorial Africa.

Synoptically, the text begins with a selection on snakes. At Lambaréné these are feared, hunted, and cut to pieces on sight, regardless of species. It is said to be unthinkable to walk even in the edge of the forest without protection against them. Hunting tales follow, involving the regular eating of monkey and the danger of elephants because of the alleged increase in their numbers. Five sixths of the selections of Schweitzer's writing on elephants are on hunting it. Paragraphs on the hippopotamus are similarly intended to describe the perils of river travel, the means of hunting, and threat and injuries to people by these animals. The primates are described as ferocious, even aggressive, animals which attack man on sight. He gives a badly distorted account of the gorilla. Leopards are dealt with entirely as blood-lust killers. The tsetse fly, mosquito, and ant represent ominous and almost insurmountable barriers to life for the white man in the tropics. Even sharks and whales are discussed, the first in terms of their wolflike rapacity, the second as mammals to be hunted. The sections on tamed native animals and on imported European domestic mammals—foreigners to the African setting—are totally different in tone.

These astonishing statements of Schweitzer's are cluttered with inaccuracies, tales from doubtful sources, and conspicuous lack of interest in the animals themselves. It is almost too easy to criticize. The naïveté toward the beauty and natural history of wild animals, the omissions and misstatements are the by-products of a pursuit of an abstract harmony with nature, or, on the contrary, of a preoccupation with the fundamental moment of personal encounter—or even perhaps both together. In every instance where he feels that he can spare or aid a life Schweitzer does so. Judgment must be made in each case. In the course of the enormous effort of establishing a jungle hospital there would have been little time for first-hand scientific studies into the behavior or habits of local animals. Judgment was made on prior criteria. This fragmentary misalliance of information and hearsay represents an attempt to align the vast and formerly almost unknown fauna of Gabon with a familiar order of animal life.

This familiar order is the hierarchical tapestry of man and animal in temperate Europe. It is a blended pattern in which the human and animal spheres overlap and interact. On one hand, man may behave as a beast; he may go wild. On the other hand, the animals both coexist with and allegorically portray civilization. When a swarm of tiny ants crowded around a drop of grapefruit juice on the floor of Schweitzer's jungle office, he is reported to have exclaimed, "Look at my ants, just like cows around a pond." On another occasion army ants streaming through the settlement were hunted down with lysol. "Thousands of corpses lie in the puddles," he wrote. "Serious enemies are the traveller ants. . . . The militarism of the jungle almost bears comparison with that in Europe."

Modern Europe is composed of relatively stable biotic communities which have slowly emerged from the interaction of man and nature for more than three thousand years. This long period of settlement and pioneering in a relatively gentle and seasonal climate and fertile soil entwined the destinies of man and animal, both native and domestic. Its emerging pattern is one of change at the slow pace to its present equilibrium. Out of it came the humanized rural landscapes with their peasant *Zeitgeist*. Man and most animals survived harmoniously, each, to varying degrees, a permanent factor in the other's life.

Animals are classified by man in this tradition in several ways. Every kind is either domestic, tame, or wild. Equally important, every animal is either a predator or a prey. Here the parallelism with militarism is suggested, for these relationships are seen as analogous to those of human social relationships. The barnyard and village is the nucleus of successive zones of life. Innermost are the village and its immediate cohabitants. The gardens and fields are dominated by domestic plants and animals. Beyond them the land use is more extensive with more or less tame wildlife. Outermost are the plants and animals of the wilderness. The boundaries are constantly being crossed in both directions. Man is predatory on plant and animal life and competes with animal predators; he occasionally hunts in their domain and they in his. The nature philosophy of the European peasant is traditionally an extension of the ethics of this system, the relationships of the immediate barnyard community and the man-dominated community to the peripheral wilderness with its supposed dangers and lurking beasts. Moreover, the animals of the barnyard and fields—wild and domestic—are perceived as an allegory on the human group. Besides being a source of occasional food, animals have assumed roles and values as symbols of human personality, occupational specialties, or roles in the society. The connotations are so finely embedded that cultural stability—or inertia—prevents a deeper appreciation of their natural life. The images of wolf and bear, pig and duck have a supra-biological place in mythology. In folk art these allegories provide the prototype by which children in this tradition learn the lessons of social existence, within the human group as well as in rural nature.

The man-nature world of Mother Goose is dominated by magic, where men may be cast in the forms of animals and where animals speak. It is as old as Aesop and as new as Donald Duck. The characters in Mother Goose personify human situations, scheme, build, plant, harvest, and sometimes inflict or suffer brutality. The cast are fitted with personalities determined by their status as predator or prey, wild or domestic, and their zone of operations. Rewards and punishments keep foxes and hens in rigid order. Not only does this system dramatize human society, but also it predisposes judgment on all members of the community, from the barnyard to the forest. The predator is occasionally admired for his cunning, but in the end he is sunk in the stream or burned in the kettle. The general antipathy felt by people of this civilization for wild predators—eagles, owls, wolves, foxes, snakes, bears, and the wild cats—and their repugnance for parasites—worms, fleas, lice, and flies—is part of an ethos. The parallel between war and predation is based on the mutual factors of aggression, mortality, and injury to man and his domestic community.

This is the rural setting from which Schweitzer came—a landscape of agricultural and pastoral enterprises, diversity, and self-sufficiency. To this imagery the peoples of the West remain sentimentally and spiritually, if not economically, devoted. Schweitzer's boyhood ambition was to be a swineherd. Appropriately enough, among the most cherished pets at Lambaréné was Josephine, a tame native boar. With dogs, chickens, and goats it wandered freely at the station, even into the church. In time Josephine became a nuisance, and Schweitzer writes, "I proposed to the missionary who was in charge of the station that because of all this I should kill her." Shortly thereafter, the boar killed five hens and "was enticed into the hospital, tied up, and expeditiously and artistically slaughtered." This satisfaction in artistic slaughter is a part of the pattern of peasant life, something which may be done skillfully or poorly, a part of the orderly pattern of the European view of animals in the service of man.

Schweitzer was not bound by the peasant perspective on life, but he came from that ethos and his philosophy was conditioned by a barnyard view of animals. Frederick Franck writes in *Days with Albert Schweitzer*, "To me Albert Schweitzer of Lambaréné is what in German is called a 'Groszbauer' (great-peasant) and his hospital is his farm. This kind of peasant is not just a farmer, he is a European phenomenon, a man rooted in his soil and living in a very special relationship to it. His farm is his kingdom; he rules over his farm hands and maids with paternal authority." Out of his own vast energy he wills upon his environment a form, creating a community with the materials and skillful techniques of tradition.

Wherever they have gone in the world, Europeans have taken with them plant and animal associates, with varying degrees of success. Schweitzer imported goats and chickens, writing, "I used to cherish the hope that the natives would little by little come to raise milk goats in their villages," but the obstacles of climate, disease, and apathy were too great. The immediate area of the hospital had already been cleared and planted to European trees and other plants by missionaries, and it is evident that Schweitzer felt strongly the necessity of perpetual struggle against nature to keep the bridgehead of the European man-animal-plant community intact.

Schweitzer had spontaneous affection for domestic animals. With some reservations, as in the case of the boar, he cherished also the tame and captive native species. These birds and mammals roamed about or were kept in cages. His great satisfaction in their beauty and grace and constant concern for their well-being was an avocation. Wild animals, on the other hand, evoked just as spontaneously the stern voice of judgment. The wild forms were not molested unless they threatened—upon which they were destroyed. The exercise of ethics in these situations is primarily an extension rather than an enlargement. "Ethics, therefore, consists in this: I feel a compulsion to extend to all the world around me the same reverence for life that I extend to my own. . . . The relation of man to man is only an expression of the relation in which he stands to all being and to the world in general." Therefore, when he said, "It is good to maintain life and to promote life; it is evil to destroy life and restrict life," Schweitzer apparently did not mean promotion or destruction of life only by man but the regulation of killing by other animals as well. This axiom is not only an admonition against unnecessary killing but is the basis upon which man decides which living things and natural circumstances are good and which are evil, with the obligation of protecting some and destroying others. This philosophy projects human interpersonal ethics, as defined in Europe and extended to animal life there, to landscapes and their inhabitants everywhere. This is essentially the Judeo-Greek position that man is here to impose his order on the natural world, but expressed in activist Christianity.

Schweitzer has said that the ethic of "Reverence for Life" must be distinguished from nature philosophy and that, "willingly or unwillingly, ethics must plunge into the adventure of making its adjustment with nature philosophy, the outcome of which cannot be anticipated." The mode of this distinction and adjustment is not shown but may be inferred from his essays and descriptions of animal life. It is indicative that he used the term "protection" and contributed to publications of animal protective associations rather than those dedicated to the preservation of animals. This seemingly slight difference reflects a fundamental disparity in approach. The question must be raised as to whether the ethic can achieve an adjustment with nature philosophy on the basis of the attitude and approach of the protectionist.

The phrase "Reverence for Life" occurred to Schweitzer a half-century ago as he stood on the deck of a steamer plowing slowly up the Ogowe River. Since then there has been much new study of the interrelationships of organisms and dynamics of their populations. The web-like structure of their interdependencies, the contributory role of death, and the concept of the on-going mosaic community are regarded as fundamental to the order of nature. The well-being of any animal in these intricate patterns is inseparably linked to that of the whole community. Predatory forms, disease organisms, and microbes of decay are necessary to the mosaic. Over the centuries man has fought nature for a toehold in this scheme. Now, with success at the push of a button, he finds that too much control is self-defeating, that the eradication of predators releases a swarm of their prey who consume the habitat and die in a ruined environment. No clear line can be drawn between the good and bad which a predator brings to its prey. What had seemed in the backlash of the Darwinian revolution to be illimitable cruelty and bloodletting in nature is no longer accountable merely in those terms, for cooperation and links of dependence extending in every direction are equally important.

In this connection, tropical Africa has offered some important object lessons in recent years. The English peanut scheme for East Africa was a notable failure because of a lack of preliminary study of the soil and its biotic and chemical components. Too many goats and cattle have plunged local communities into a downward spiral of poverty, disease, soil erosion, and habitat destruction. A futile effort to control sleeping sickness by the destruction of antelopes and other large mammals was undertaken in the early 1950's, its aim to reduce the nonhuman reservoir of disease. Thousands of animals were slaughtered on the veldt in this fiasco in the name of public health, the only result the further decimation of a magnificent heritage of animal life. Everywhere that medicine reduced human mortality and populations exploded, people have changed from hunting and transient agriculture to sedentary farming, which in the humid tropical environment brings new problems.

Difficulties of these kinds may be inevitable effects of the impingement of civilization upon Africa and its political awakening. The ideological stigma of the zoo image to new nationalists may result in repudiation of the wild heritage in Africa. The price of such change is frequently held to be the destruction of animal life. Civilization and wildlife are considered by some as mutually exclusive. As Waitari, the European-educated native politician in Romain Gary's *The Roots of Heaven*, says, "Africa will never awaken to her destiny until she has stopped being the world's zoo. America emerged from limbo with the disappearance of the bison; as long as wolves pursued the sledges on the Russian steppes, the Russian peasant died of squalor and ignorance; and the day when there are no more lions or elephants in Africa there will be a people master at least of its own destiny." The idea that civilization is such an either-or choice is deep in the traditional attitude of the West, hence a legacy of colonialism.

The transplantation of the barnyard scheme to tropical Africa is more severe than shifting it to America. There it means a substitution of whole groups of plants and animals, the disruption, reduction, and even extinction of native species. In America there has been considerable integration. Some stockmen in Wyoming, Colorado, and Montana have learned to encourage the coyote as a desirable predator on rodents which compete with livestock for grass. The imposition of a European small-farm association upon a tropical humid area is much more drastic, and so is the judgment on various native species. The great difference in seasons, climatic pattern, and abundance of life work against the wholesale importation of bio-cultural habits. Ultimately there must be a compromise between native wildlife, including its pests and predators, and the imported domestic organisms. Medicine and politics are bringing revolution to Africa, both superimposing upon environments to which they must adjust or which they may destroy. Revolutionaries tend to overlook intrinsic patterns and to sacrifice indigenous values.

R. A. Piddington has itemized the danger of extinction to many species of African wildlife, in *The Limits of Man-*

kind. While some African animals must be reduced in number and distribution, there is a genuine ethical and moral question of man's right to usurp space entirely or to exterminate. These animals live as populations, social groups, and species as well as individuals, and their survival ultimately depends upon what happens to populations, not to individuals. While these plural entities are perhaps less lovable and more abstract than individuals, they hold the fate of the individual locked in their destinies.

The Indian Jainists, who influenced Schweitzer, live in a profoundly altered and adjusted environment where humanity presses hard against the land. They avoid harm to each bit of life they encounter. It is possible in this dignified and intimate situation to succeed in the immediate ethic while the biological mosaic collapses. The same theory plus a more positive approach, with its preoccupation for the particular encounter and its abstraction from life of a will-to-live, is essentially "Reverence for Life." The ethic imposes an obligation to extend sympathy and help to life, and with Schweitzer it is further bound by a contingency of judgment based on a balance of good and evil, so that it is sometimes necessary out of the motive of reverence to destroy the organism.

It is not the decision to destroy which poses the problem, but the criteria for the decision. A half-century ago there was little but traditional prejudice. The focus on individual death must be shifted to the web of life. The natural community is a system of energy and material flow, as well as an association of plants, animals, microbes, and men. Death is part of its life transformation. The sensitive man projects his own perceptions and fear of death into his assumptions about other living things; but it could become the emotional basis for a broader and healthier concern. The death of the individual is not insignificant, but the death of a population or species is far more serious, for it reduces the richness and stability of all surviving life and the biosphere itself.

The difference between protection and preservation is the difference between individual and population. Attitudes toward hunting exemplify the contrast. Schweitzer opposed hunting as unnecessary infliction of pain, suffering, cruelty, and death. In an article on falconry he objected to hunting as a sport: "Is there a friend of nature who really finds pleasure in the tragic spectacle of the abuse and killing of a weak bird by a strong one, and who, by training birds of prey, takes pains to see that this spectacle shall be offered him as frequently as possible?" Yet captive gazelles were confined near Schweitzer's living quarters at Lambaréné in a small enclosure. Like falcons, gazelles are wide-ranging, mobile, superlative examples of fleetness and beauty. Who can say what suffering the captive gazelle knows?

Wanton destruction is always inexcusable, but hunting can be defended as a special kind of contact with the natural world in a reverent way which I will elucidate further along in this chapter. Many of the great conservationists in Europe and America have been sportsmen. The point is that preservation addresses itself to an equilibrium between man and animals in a world where both have rights to survive and where survival is mutually dependent. The idea of protection does not ensure survival, however, since it is concerned not with the organization of nature but with an extension of man-to-man ethics applied in an atomized fashion.

"Reverence for Life" has never dressed itself as an inductively derived scientific hypothesis. It is essentially a matter of faith, not wholly subject to natural history. As a religious conviction, it is in a sense outside scientific criticism. But the Judeo-Christian tradition behind Schweitzer's basic outlook does not wholly separate nature and spirit, faith and experience. This very aspect of Schweitzer's concept of Christianity is, in fact, a part of his explication of the difficult ground between ethical doctrine and the world in which we find ourselves. Science is one of many human activities which may be called upon to inform both faith and theology. Schweitzer accepted it as such, as indicated in *Out of My Life and Thought*, when he says,

The study of the natural sciences brought me even more than the increase of knowledge I had longed for. It was to me a spiritual experience. I had all along felt it to be psychically a danger that in the so-called Humanities with which I had been concerned hitherto, there is no truth which affirms itself as self-evident, but that a mere opinion can, by the way in which it deals with the subject matter, obtain recognition as true. The search for truth in the domains of history and philosophy is carried on in constantly repeated endless duels between the sense of reality of the one and the inventive imagination power of the other. The argument from facts is never able to obtain a definite victory over the skillfully produced opinion. How often does what is reckoned as progress consist in a skillfully argued opinion putting real insight out of action for a long time!

He observed that "Reverence for Life" has a religious character that is essentially Christian and that it is an error for Christianity to withdraw from the rational thought of the times. He was dedicated to independent, elemental, Stoic thought, based on the truth as perceived and on the "results of epistemology, of logical speculation, of natural science, of psychology, of sociology," and in man's relation to the world.

In addition to opposing mindlessness and the abdication of intelligence, his ethical mysticism, then, is willing to appropriate available information when, in applying the ethic, each man "makes distinctions only as each case comes before him, and under the pressure of necessity, as, for example, when it falls to him to decide which of two lives he must sacrifice in order to preserve the other. But all through this series of decisions he is conscious of acting on subjective grounds and arbitrarily, and knows that he bears the responsibility for the life which is sacrificed."

"Reverence for Life" is distinguished from various Eastern ideals of similar intent by its strong element of positive action as opposed to the principle of nonactivity and the latter's limited exercise of compassion by not-doing. It expresses the world-and-life-affirmation of the ethic opposed to escapism and passive, expiatory asceticism. The ethic emphasizes a universal brotherhood in all life in that each has a will-to-live. In man this is manifest as self-devotion, and the energy of this devotion is obligated by the ethic to promote all life.

When Schweitzer says of the ethic, "With its will to work, it can leave aside all the problems concerning the result of its work," he is speaking of the application of reverence to an endless chain of discrete encounters or of programming the ethic for protection. If the result of application were a sweeping destruction of life, then it would have to concern itself with the broad context: and there is nothing in the principle itself which prevents it from being destructive.

In the modern world of chemical sprays and violent poisons, of the manipulation of whole watersheds and forests, the worldwide transport of disease microorganisms, proposals to artificially illuminate the night sky or to melt polar ice caps, and of giant earth-moving machinery, there is evidence of mindlessness in spite of all of its genius and determination for progress. These inventions even make possible a Schweitzerian judgment on the destruction of single lives, for men pressing buttons to explode bombs or to dump pesticides from an aircraft may never see the animals whose existence is threatened. Purposely or inadvertently, because of the vast texture of life, it may be impossible for them to know the effects of their actions.

Schweitzer's worldwide plea to stop the testing of atomic weapons indicated a shift to include the preservation as well as the protection of life. Our dealings with other living things at the individual level remain ethically important, but every year become a smaller part of the total transaction between man and nature. As the individual cells in the human body are continually dying and being replaced, they are transcended by their respective and separate will-to-live in the interest of the whole organism, whose continued existence is thereby promoted. In nature the individual is incomplete when abstracted from its environment and will not survive the destruction of its habitat. The tropical forest is an organism whose identity demands ethical treatment. Its health depends upon the continued existence through cycles of life and death of its components. Man has become a parasite upon the body of this forest just as have the protozoa causing sleeping sickness upon the bodies of Schweitzer's patients. The protection of the forest and respect for its unity is also an extension of self-devotion; but in this case man may be the worst enemy of the forest, and predators on man and his livestock may have to be preserved in order to save it; the human population may even have to be limited to do so. Judgment in this complicated situation must not be derived only from an extension of ethics formerly relating man to man, or even man to his barnyard community. It should take cognizance of the integrity of the natural community, both for its entirety and for the individual microbes, plants, and animals, which, with their inorganic surroundings, form a continuum. In the long view, there is no other way to protect the individual organism than to preserve its natural habitat.

Today science alone cannot demand or impose an ethic directed to the protection of life in its mosaic setting. Indeed, science progresses faster in the production of weapons of control than in discovering how man is dependent upon patterns and interdependencies in nature. Only an ethic religiously conceived can do this, and the only one clearly visible in the Western world is Schweitzer's "Reverence for Life." [2]

Killing animals for the meat industry or for scientific research can be rationalized to the satisfaction of all but a few, but hunting for sport is frequently regarded as morally indefensible. Some of my acquaintances class hunting with war and murder. They are humane and humanist, with broad literary knowledge, articulate and very keen, as it were, in the slaughter of the advocates of hunting. In a debate in *The Saturday Review*, for instance, Joseph Wood Krutch carved up his hunter opponent and served him to the readers, steaming in his own juices.

[2] I first wrote these criticisms of Schweitzer in 1956, some years before the groundswell of negative comment that appeared in print about the time of his death, much of which is a nay-saying with which I do not agree. He remains unquestionably the most sensitive conscience of our time on this matter.

Hunting has been defended by the fiction that sporting activity in the field somehow prepared a young man for a higher plane of conduct in human affairs. But whatever validity this idea had became obsolete with the end of aristocratic social structure. It has been held that the hunt promotes character, self-reliance, and initiative—an untenable Theodore Roosevelt belief. The development of leadership does not depend on killing. Assertions are sometimes made about instinctive needs and vague primitive satisfactions and psychological benefits, but the sharpest opponents of hunting appear simply not to have forgiven Darwin and Freud to begin with. To suggest that hunting has psychic or evolutionary values only infuriates. Others claim that the hunter is really attempting to escape the roar and friction of civilization, to squeeze out of society's trammels for a few hours of recuperation. The outraged response is, of course, that hunting with a camera is equally rewarding and more uplifting. According to the Faulkner and Hemingway interpretation, hunting is a manipulation of symbols for proving one's virility or otherwise coping with the erosion of the human personality and the decadence of civilization.

Opposition to hunting for sport has its accusing finger on the act of killing. Determinism gives no out. We cannot plead that we are bipedal carnivorous mammals and damned to kill. We must discover what it means to search for an equilibrium between the polarities of nature and God. We find that to share in life is to participate in a traffic of energy and materials, the ultimate origin of which is a mystery, but which has its immediate source in the bodies of plants and other animals. As a society, we may be in danger of losing sight of this fact, kept vividly before us in hunting.

The condemnation of killing wild animals assumes that death is the worst of natural events, that order in nature is epitomized by living objects rather than the complex flow patterns of which objects are temporary formations. The implication is that carnivorous predation as a whole is evil. The anti-hunters face a paradox of their own making. Dr. Schweitzer, who did not believe in hunting for sport, sprinkled his jungle writings with accounts of righteous killing of predators. Europeans and Americans in the same *Zeitgeist* have always destroyed predators, the big cats, eagles, wolves, bears, and pests such as rodents, insects, and birds.

Joseph Wood Krutch condemns the hunter for killing, claiming that the distinction between life and death is one of the most absolute boundaries which we know. But this is not so. Life has atomic as well as planetary dimensions. The most satisfactory definitions and descriptions of life are in physical and chemical terms of events and processes which, occurring in a certain harmony, produce what we call life. The organic and the inorganic are mingled inextricably in the living body.

The traditional insistence upon the overwhelmingly tragic and unequivocal nature of death ignores the adaptive role of early death in most animal populations. It presumes that the landscape is a collection of *things.* In this view the dissolution of body and personality are always tragic and disruptive, and do not contribute to the perfection of an intelligible world. But death, as transformation in a larger system, is an essential aspect of elegant patterns which are orderly as well as beautiful: without death growth could not occur, energy could not flow beyond plants, nutrient substances would be trapped forever. Without death the pond, the forest, the prairie, the city could not exist. The extremely complicated structure of living communities has yet to be fully explored, but constitutes a field pattern. Plants and animals participate in them without question in an attitude of acceptance which in human terms would be called faith.

The unfortunate social and economic misapplication of Darwin's theory in the late nineteenth century can still be seen in reluctance to accept evolution as a significant factor in man's highest as well as his more primitive activities. Evolutionary theory also had the curious effect on some people of making nature seem more chaotic instead of less. Evolution is unrelated to the fate of individuals. We have projected our notions of ethics and our terror of death into our perception of all life. Animals die before they have lived out their potential life span; that is characteristic of the natural world and essential to our understanding of it.

A moral criterion is sometimes offered for killing limited to the necessity for food and defense. This logically opposes the sportsman and approves of the slaughterhouse. Under primitive conditions killing meant something quite different than it does in the modern slaughterhouse or by the broad-scale application of chemical pesticides. The events of daily life in a hunting society are permeated with universal significance immediate to every individual. No activity of life is regarded as "merely" physical, but always related to a whole, partly unseen. We cannot now adopt animistic superstition nor regain that kind of consciousness, but we admire the poignant sense of the interpenetration of man and nature which primitive life ritualizes and we may seek its results. Primitive ways are nearly gone but we acknowledge that such reverence for life is more reverent and is better ecology than a fanatic emphasis on fear of death and the attempt at godship by judging all instances and causes of death among animals. To our repugnance for soil (dirt), parasitism (disease), and decay (slime) we add predation. We condemn it as though it were murder, and extend "justice" into biotic realms where it is meaningless, incorporating democracy with its protection of the "weak" and containment of the "strong." Man dominates some parts of nature, but there is no process known by which this vindicates extending his social ethics, his democracy, or any other ideological or moral system into the adaptations of populations or the interrelations of species.

Does the hunter not interfere in natural patterns and upset nature's balance? Yes and no. Man is not a demigod operating above and outside nature. But nature is in him as well as he in it. Nature's balance is always slightly upset.

Individuals are important. The taking of a life, so evanescent in a cosmic scheme, is nonetheless profoundly moving to us as individuals. Killing an animal probably obliterates an awareness somewhat similar to our own consciousness. As sympathetic and vulnerable humans, we are confronted with mystery by the death of any creature. This is why the tension over killing is so incisive and urgent. Our sympathy for a fellow creature is felt intensely at the crucial moment of death. Yet that emotion fulfills a cultural and personal necessity for evidence of our connection to large-scale processes in a moment of profound intensity. If the death is so experienced our response may be regarded as a form of behavior which unites men with nature rather than alienating them.

Mental well-being is defined by a mode of cultural behavior. Culture is an interface between man and his environment. Collective dreams and myths, apprehended symbolically, change slowly with the healthy functioning of society and the psychic security of its members. There is in literary and pictorial arts an iconography of hunting. With its artistic heritage, hunting is much more than a wanton vestige of barbarism. It is intimately associated with social order and with love. "Venery" is an archaic term meaning both sexual pursuit and hunting game—the foundation of love. The origins of human compassion belong to the hunters of old.

Hunting may be an inherent behavior, but it is not *only* an instinct. It is a framework of organization which acknowledges an extra-human context. Killing is not justified simply as indigenous or venerable. But it is a historical part of the activity of a people. It has a place in the total fabric of what they have become, a mode of their relationship to nature. For perhaps 95 percent of their history men and "near-men" have been hunters. Primitive peoples ritualize hunting except where hunting societies and the technological world have collided, where cultural deterioration has reduced customary inhibition to wanton killing.

Probably the richest collection of the ceremonies of propitiation of wild spirits by hunters is Sir James G. Frazer's *The Golden Bough*. If anthropologically obsolete, Frazer's perspective and genius for collecting remain nonetheless monumental. To judge from *The Golden Bough*, hunting has been universally bound by ceremonial preparation and epilogue. When British Columbian Lillooet Indians dispose of the bones of their kill in a certain way, saying, "See! I treat you respectfully. Nothing shall defile you! May I be successful in hunting and trapping!" they are not only seeking to perpetuate their food supply. They do more than solicit success and spiritual acquiescence. Their ceremony makes less distinction between subject and object than we assume in the orthodox sense of magic. Even Frazer's view of ritual as coercive and petitionary was perhaps too restrictive. The ceremony is also an affirmation and participation, not only manipulative but attuning, assimilative, and confrontative. Imitative magic is prototechnological and prescientific, but that part emphasizing "we-hood" and the participating in a larger whole are religious.

Both magic and religion in primitive ritual reveal fundamental components of the hunter's attitude. The organized ceremony simultaneously serves a magic and a religious purpose, and ecological and social functions as well. The ceremony is aimed at maintaining equilibrium in the total situation. The whole of life, corporeal and spiritual, is affected. The prey, or parts of it, are killed ritually and eaten sacramentally. By following the prescribed style the hunters sacrifice the prey in evocation of events too profound for conscious understanding. By its own self-imposed limitations the ritual hunt renounces further killing in favor of a larger context of interrelationship. If the preliminary solicitation is effective and the traditional procedure is followed, the hunt is successful. Unlike farmers who must labor in the fields and who earn by their sweat a grudging security within nature, the primitive hunter gets "something for nothing." The kill is a gift. Its bestowal depends on the conduct of the hunters. Without this gift the hunter will die. As Malinowski says, "food is the main link between man and his surroundings" and "by receiving it he feels the forces of destiny and providence." Of all foods meat is the gift *par excellence* because shortage of protein, not shortage of food *per se*, is the essence of starvation. The elusiveness of the quarry explicitly symbolizes the continuing dependence of human life on powers beyond human control. Hunting provides the logical nucleus for the evolution of communal life with its celebrations of a biosocial participation mystique and the sharing of the kill.

What do the hunt and kill actually do for the hunter? They confirm his continuity with the dynamic life of animal populations, his role in the complicated cycles of elements, his sharing in the sweep of evolution, and his place in the patterns of the flow of energy and in the web of his own society.

It may at first seem irrelevant to seek present values for us in the strongly schematized hunting behavior of primitive man. But "our deepest experience, needs, and aspirations are the same, as surely as the crucial biological and psychic transitions occur in the life of every human being and force culture to take account of them in aesthetic forms," says Richard V. Chase. Many anthropologists report that there is widespread belief in the immortality of the spirits of all living things, a point of view which we may be too barbaric to share. Frazer wrote, about the time Schweitzer was conceiving of "Reverence for Life," "If I am right in thus interpreting the thought of primitive man, the savage view of the nature of life singularly resembles the modern scientific doctrine of the conservation of energy." The idea of organic interrelationship which ecologists explore may spring not from inductive science at all, but from a rather fundamental human attitude toward the landscape. In these terms, the hunt is a singular expression of our identity with natural processes and is carried on with veneration appropriate to the mystery of those events.

This concept transcends particular economic situations. Men in all sorts of societies—primitive, pastoral, agricultural, and technical—continue to hunt fervently. The hunt has ceased to be the main source of food, but remains the ritual symbol of a larger transaction. The prey represents all that is received, whether from a host of animal gods, an arbitrary god, or from the law of probability.

It is sometimes said that hunters are cruel, insensitive, and barbaric. In fact, however, the hunter may experience life and death deeply. In a poem called "Castles and Distances" Richard Wilbur writes:

Oh, it is hunters alone
Regret the beastly pain, it is they who love the foe

That quarries out their force, and every arrow
Is feathered soft with wishes to atone;
   Even the surest sword in sorrow
    Bleeds for its spoiling blow.

   Sometimes, as one can see
Carved at Amboise in a high relief, on the lintel stone
Of the castle chapel, hunters have strangely come
To a mild close of the chase, bending the knee
   Instead of the bow, struck sweetly dumb
    To see from the brow bone

   Of the hounded stag a cross
Grown, and the eyes clear with grace. . . .

In urban and technological situations hunting continues to put us in close touch with nature, to provoke the study of natural history, and to nourish the idea of conservation. Even royalty is subject to the uncertainty of the gift. From the Middle Ages we have numerous examples of the values of the hunt. Its forms coincided with social structure in complex royal households and its practice stimulated first-hand observation at a time when hearsay and past authority were the main sources of information. The unique work of Frederick II in thirteenth-century ornithology is an example, an advance in the understanding of birds gathered during hunting trips afield. A more recent example is the work of the late Aldo Leopold. A hunter and a forester, his career was a living documentation of the slow sensitizing of a man to his environment through the medium of gun and dog. In postulating a "split rail value" for hunting, Leopold observed that hunting is a reenactment of a historically important activity when contact with the natural environment and the virtues of this contact were less obscured by modern urban life.

Civilization extends the means of food and energy distribution and of storage against lean years. The ultimate origin of food in the soil is no longer apparent to the average person, as even agriculture is a closed industrial process. In this engineered and insulated atmosphere the natural world has become a peripheral relic, a strange, sometimes entertaining, sometimes frightening curiosity. What has become of *the gift?* It has receded from view except for those who seek it. They may be found in the open country trying their luck. By various arbitrary limitations, both behavioral and mechanical, the hunter curbs his technological advantage. This peculiar assemblage of legal, ethical, and physical restraints consti-tutes sportsmanship, a contemporary ritual. The hunt is ar-bitrarily limited. The hunter brings to focus his whole physical and spiritual attention on the moment of the kill. He expects to eat the quarry, even though economically it is dietetically irrelevant. Yet he will cook and eat it in a mood of thoughtful celebration known only to hunters.

It follows that hunting is not just an excuse to get out of doors. Killing and eating the prey are the most important things that hunters do. The successful hunt is a solemn and yet glad event. It places man for a moment in vital rapport with a universe from which civilization tends to separate him by its fostering of an illusion of superiority and independence. The natural environment will always be mysterious, evoking an awe to be shared among all men who take the trouble to see it. If modern sportsmanship is a shallow substitute for the complex mythology or unifying ceremony of other cultures, we must acknowledge that only a part of the society hunts, that ritual forms of this technological era are still young and poorly defined, and that we are part of an age which may be said to be living on the accumulated capital—cultural and biological—of a million years of hardship, death, effort, and invention. Given a hard-earned margin magnified by ma-chines, human society may behave irresponsibly for a time and forget the ties that bind it to the world.

Regardless of technological advance, man remains part of and dependent upon nature. The necessity of signifying and recognizing this relationship remains, though it may not seem so. The hunter is our agent of awareness. He is not only an observer but a participant and receiver. He knows that man is a member of a natural community and that the proc-esses of nature will never become so well understood or con-trolled that faith will cease to be important.

Chapter Seven

Varieties of
Nature Hating

NEARLY EVERYBODY knows that this is an era of the ravagement of nature. It is one of those aspects of the times
which we deplore, such as mass culture or a high incidence of
crime. We put the problem in care of public agencies and
interest groups, thereby organizing and delegating it. Occasionally it erupts into our lives as smog or water rationing
or the difficulty of finding a fish to catch, but what are these
compared to our personal problems?

In truth, delegation is only what seems to be happening.
The machinery for pigeon-holing the ravagement of nature is
itself part of the process. We treat nature as though it were
something out there, separate from ourselves, which we can
turn over to a bureaucracy. It is convenient to blame the
destruction of nature on impersonal, inexorable, collective
forces incidental to progress, technology, or civilization. We
can rise even to evangelical indignation against waste and
greed. But what is commonly called the conservation movement, the political and educational form of this indignation, is
only the inside of the skin of the hairy monster of destruction.

And what is the monster himself if he is not simply

cupidity and wastefulness? What is personality? What is culture? We are like blind men exploring, not parts of an elephant, but the root system of a forest, the eddies of an estuary. The only certainty we have is that it is *our* monster; it is us. If we are interested in placing blame then we must go beyond blaming the tools we use; the monster is not a rabbit who happens to have big teeth. The feces it flings, its trumpetings in the midst of our angry accusation, its earth-shaking footsteps are not the monster either, only its smeary disorder in our landscape.

Like any good natural history, the life cycle of this beast has a time and place. It is part of a history of people perceiving their environment and formulating ideas of it upon which to act, ideas which haven't a chance of being completely right. Its genesis is a brew of images, ideas, and dreams working against the surface of reality, like the chemical mish-mash brewing the first life on the soupy shallow bank of an archacozoic sea. Then the unfit molecules simply failed to survive; now we thrust our moribund notions upon the world and hold them stubbornly there. They become part of belief and tradition for reasons other than viability: their apparent harmony with some abstract convictions, their esthetic fit in a philosophic system, or as a convenient disguise of some truth which we fear.

One of these truths, for example, is the inevitability of disease and mortality. Life is given only to be snatched away. Even our brief sojourn is fraught with pain and disorder. Suffering and death surround us. We fight disease, not only as individuals with our own antibodies and white blood cells, but as society—which is as it should be. Unfortunately the mythology available to organized medicine from its primitive prototypes associated sickness with demons. This was not properly an antinature attitude in a nontechnological society which did not conceive of itself outside nature. But when demons were given the Judeo-Christian twist, with its medieval delight in the corruption of the body and the association of the body with nature, the body became something base even in good health. The Western world is scarred by pathophilia, a puritanical obsession with wounds and deformity. Miracle healing remains at the heart of fundamentalist preoccupation with the flesh, a long, sordid history of masochism, sadism, and fanatical hordes of pilgrims in search of divine cures. This emphasis on the flesh, and on the springs and caves and rivers where cures were supposed to be found, has been negative. Not that cures haven't occurred, but the image of nature in such a tradition is not sweet. The body is not only the gross husk to which the real self seems shackled in life, but a very dirty trick, first because it dies so soon and second because it sickens or malfunctions. If this body is our personal collection of the physical stuff of which the rest of nature is made then how gross and defective must all the landscape be.

By the mid-twentieth century it had become possible to pursue an ideal of perfect vigor—that is, to engage in keeping the demons at bay even though well—via nutritional adjuncts and sanitation and preventive medicine. Cleanliness has become attached to this medical fanaticism, first because there is a real connection, but foremost because the soap and perfume and cosmetic industries have exploited and exaggerated the fears of social opprobrium. The microscope has magnified, given more explicit form to, and confirmed our conception of unseen demons. We need not wait until some physical or social disaster befalls to exorcise them with a miracle lather.

What has this to do with nature as a whole? It is from dirt that the germ-demons come, and the world is covered with dirt. To make it acceptable, to make it healthy, it needs what we need: to be cleansed. Yet we cannot accomplish this. Decay, manure, the gases of fermentation, mud and ooze, blood and death and disease are everywhere.

This leads us to another of those truths which we would rather not confront: the implication of evolution. The problem is not the conventional one of man-the-quasi-ape or even man-the-animal (which most educated people think they have assimilated, although no one knows what being an animal means). No, an equally profound implication has to do with the necessity of disease and death, of parasites and predators, even in human life. Man's animality is not only a vertical historical connection, but a horizontal present one. I do not mean only that he depends on plants and some animals for his food; I mean the thousand connections of the web of life— which includes all those squirting, palpitating, secretory, carnivorous convulsions of life. I am speaking of his connection with the biosphere, the whole shell of life on earth, the massive organic system of quivering protoplasm, organized at innumerable levels, infinitely more complex, more elegant, and more durable than we know. Dr. Schweitzer would disinfect this whole *ensemble* if he could, out of love of it and us. Such is the Darwinian vista which we have failed to apprehend: a physiology of the whole resembling that within the cell, where membranes are continuously formed and dissolved, molecules shifted to and fro, broken down, new ones synthesized, pulsations, regulatory removals, the end of structures and forms which are replaced by new ones. It is as though we would go into the cell and halt all the breakdown processes, the secretions and excretions, the phagocytic activities, the smelly decompositions. The holy war against swamps, fens, heaths, deserts, jungles, snakes, leopards, spiders, brush, weeds, bacteria, fungi, worms, and all the other ecological equivalents of the cell's organs of catabolism is the fanatic scorn for organic nature coupled with a fixation on the runny blemishes and the awful odors to which we, as mammals, are so sensitive and so attracted.

The smell of nature is one of its most ambivalent qualities for man. He is a member of a class of animals many of which communicate by means of secretions and excretions and most of whom are keenly interested in the olfactory universe. I was reminded of this by one of the modern French writers, who are so preoccupied with the rottenness of man, who was lamenting as he rode in a horse-drawn carriage in Paris how inferior man is to the horse with its neat, aromatic defecation. One fancies that there may be a ranked series of domestic animal turd smells, a scale upon which pigs and chickens and man rate at the bottom. This is one argument for vegetarianism, that is, herbivorousness, not made much of. Nonetheless, infants and psychotics and barbarians all show that our mammalian positive thinking on this subject still lurks just below consciousness. It has been suggested that our repugnance for human odor originated with primate nesting habits, if, like the gorillas, the human ancestor soiled his nest every night. The problem became intensified when pre-men and men took to permanent domiciles in caves. A selective pressure working against our older mammalian pleasure in the smell of feces might have been related to the spread of certain internal parasites, carried like hookworm in dung. The move into caves created not only the first insistence upon sanitation, but possibly the first sense of guilt—the kind imposed on our child minds by bowel and bladder control—the real basis of sin.

And so we have the dilemma of smell: perfume is made from the musk of skunks. It is hardly one of the world's great problems, but a perfect miniature of the duality of health and sickness, of the Western medieval repudiation of the body coupled with an inordinate fascination for its excretions, the utter disregard of the ascetic for his bodily well-being against the pilgrim's frenetic pursuit of a cure, the deliberate maltreatment of self contrasted to pep pills and the fads of super-health. The same society is despoiling part of its natural environment as though waging war against it and preserving other parts as the world's first inviolate sanctuaries against any material use whatsoever.

There are other contributions of early man to the modern psyche, though the very existence of a collective unconscious bearing a burden of ancient attitudes and imagery is impossible to prove and meets scorn from those ideologically committed to a dogma of unlimited individual freedom, to the infant mind as a *tabula rasa*. Work in the biochemistry of memory will probably uncover soon a biological basis for what some psychologists and psychiatrists, anthropologists, students of mythology, of the history of art, and of animal behavior have already seen in man. If there is a mutual substratum of proto-ideas, the experience over a million years of struggle and aggression in a world where the margin of survival was nearly always narrow may well have left its mark. What would such a mark be? Perhaps it is embodied in all those hideous monsters and threatening forms shadowed forth in dreams and mirrored in legends. Or perhaps the constant vigilance and maneuvering to secure a place in the world—strategy which at best permitted men and society little more than a fingerhold—would now manifest itself as opposition to nature. Such an attitude might have been a great advantage in circumstances where aggressive initiative and determination meant survival instead of death. Even in times of well-being, such a drive would send men into new lands, across difficult passes and water barriers and deserts to places where the human niche in nature was unfilled. The impulses to explore and emigrate had to be stronger than the many social and ecological advantages of remaining, even against the instinct for the home territory and the security of the known world. The tension upon our psyches of breaking the bonds of place is still apparent around us, sometimes working creatively in increased sensitivity and perception, but more often breaking custom, losing awe of and respect for the world, making places at best interchangeable and alike. Rootlessness is often held to be a source of individual and social ills, and the ecological truth is that ills of this kind are inseparable from the context of man in nature and from the hostility he feels for his natural environment. It is as though he has a vast reservoir of struggles in his past which can be drawn upon as creative inspiration or which can give him motive for a war against nature—which he at first seems to win, using the tools invented since the domestication of animals.

There is a sense in terms of modern self-consciousness in which it would be easy to misunderstand the primitive struggle in nature. Indeed, I do not wish to imply that we have an ancient tradition of hostility to nature as we ourselves understand it, only that struggle itself has produced a temperament which can be usurped by the modern ego and used toward its own much more explicit idea and means of conflict, separation from and denial of the world. The discontinuity which we feel is relatively new. It culminates in the existential view—the philosophical attitude of technological man insofar as he is indifferent to the destruction of the natural world. But to blame technology for such destruction is much too simple. We cannot, in fact, explain nature hating very well, only follow some of those threads which seem to exemplify or illuminate it.

It is also too easy to blame Christianity. Both transcendental romanticism and ecology, the two most potent forces for the preservation of nature, are products of a Christian culture. Even so, nature hating *is* intimately connected to the Judeo-Christian root system. The orthodox medieval Christian attitude toward nature is derived essentially from the prejudices and pride of men engaged in equatorial pastoralism and trade. The Persian duality of light and dark, of good and evil, of sky and earth are central dichotomies in Christian thought. St. Paul described the fall and subsequent curse of man and the earth because of Adam's sin. The Christian fathers were revolted by our mammalian physiques. Man's birth *inter feces et urinam*, so disgusting to Tertullian, was a defilement. The world according to Augustine was *massa perditionis*. Man was the only spiritual creature on earth, an angel slipped from grace.

The Greeks and Hebrews had invented the linear perspective of time. Their new historical awareness attributed to time a beginning and end, to the world a creation and a doomsday. As the Christians came to entertain this idea, finite nature was symbolic of a greater universal history. The obligation of the human individual was to prepare himself for judgment elsewhere, to be preceded in time by another coming of the Messiah. The belief in an immanent apocalypse could scarcely enhance any hope for a harmonious future in nature for mankind. Such a formal, dogmatic view renders the natural world soulless, uninteresting, and more or less invisible if not downright evil. By the end of the fifth century the division between sacred and profane was emphatic. The world had become essentially an examination hall with emblems, signs, and symbols of other-worldly truths. To St. Jerome the landscape was enigmatic, dangerous, animated by demons. Even St. Francis's plea for kindness toward animals was a patronizing condescension which distinguished between their soulless state and that of man.

All of these negative aspects of nature in a Christian world may be collectively called the "Messiah complex," but it is neither limited to Christianity nor does it date only from Christ. It is at the heart of the Western attitude, its foundations spread over the ancient Near East, the Mediterranean World, and western Europe. It could be epitomized in medieval Christianity because a heritage of nature hating was already available to draw upon. Christianity is the most urban of the great religions. Its early sects were country dwellers or "pagans" only so long as they had to be. The city, as man's creation, comes nearer to being a kingdom not of this world and, being a product of mind, is nearer the supernatural as we imagine it than the natural. Hermitic and monastic retreat to the wilderness was less to seek the virtues of the country than because the city, although the center of iniquity and sin, was the corruption of the best into the worst. In both the temple and monastery the Word was more important to those men than experience of nature. Their deep alienation from nature contrasted to the sense of unity and harmony found in naturalistic philosophies which develop an acceptance of natural events; from the emerging beliefs and self-consciousness of three thousand years of civilization, Christianity selected hopes and rationalizations against natural events. This side of Christianity appears to have grown from a system of concepts poorly related to the realities of the natural environment. An eloquent and succinct statement of this emphasis on the discontinuity between man and nature in Christianity is given by Alan Watts in *Nature, Man and Woman:*

> We begin, then, to discern the reasons why Christianity as we have known it differs so profoundly in style from the natural universe. To a large extent it is a construction of ideas or concepts playing together on their own, without adequate relation to that world of

nature which ideas represent. . . . May it not be, then, that many of the central ideas of Christianity are creative inventions, like the cities in which they were nurtured? . . . In Christianity, however, the stress is upon belief rather than experience, and immense importance has always been attached to an acceptance of the correct formulation of a dogma, doctrine, or rite. Early in its history Christianity rejected *gnosis*, or direct experience of God, in favor of *pistis*, or the trust of the will in certain revealed propositions about God.

Spirit, then, is distinguished from nature as the abstract from the concrete, and the things of the spirit are identified with the things of the mind—with the world of words and thought-symbols—which are then seen, not as representing the concrete world, but as underlying it. . . . Thus the realm of concepts acquires not only an independent life of its own, but a life more real and more fundamental than that of non-verbal nature. Ideas do not represent nature, but nature represents ideas in the clogging vesture of material stuff. . . . The form of Christianity differs from the form of nature because in the church and in its spiritual atmosphere we are in a universe that has been *made*. Outside the church we are in a universe that has *grown*. Thus the God who made the world stands outside it as the carpenter stands outside his artifacts . . . In practice it is his transcendence, his otherness, which is always stressed. . . . Conceiving, then, man and the universe as made, the Western and Christian mind endeavors to interpret them mechanically —and this is at once its genius and its blindness. It is an *idée fixe* that the universe consists of distinct things or entities, which are precisely the structural parts of artifacts. . . . Furthermore, the workings of the natural universe are understood in terms of logical laws—the mechanical order of things viewed as a linear series of causes and effects, under the limitations of a consciousness which takes them in and symbolizes them one at a time, piece by piece. . . . It appears that nature is a mechanism because such a mentality can grasp only as much of nature as it can fit into some mechanical or mathematical analogy.

If there is truth in Immanuel Velikovsky's theory (the near collision of Venus and the earth as the cause of the Biblical catastrophes) there is good reason for the Christian and pre-Christian apocalyptic frame of mind. Watts's idea of a mechanical world as part of a Christian culture is actually a recent development. The precarious ecological (and possibly geological) situation in which history emerged is and was fraught with floods, invasions of locusts, epidemic disease, tempestuous storms of dust and sand, as well as wind and rain, and always the narrow margin between desert and fruitful land, famine and plenty. Natural disasters are the avenging strokes of angry and jealous gods, not of the whirring of a machine. The apparent antithesis between the arbitrary god and mindless machinations of natural laws does not constitute a contradiction in Western thinking, however, so much as the poles between which that thinking has moved.

The absolute creator god who stands apart from nature is drawn from the Hebrew Yahweh, who in turn descended from more primitive concepts of Sumerians, Babylonians, and Phoenicians. As elsewhere in the world the creation myth is fundamental to culture itself. Among agricultural peoples, creation involves a male and female, who, by a metamorphosis from the spirits of stone, tree, and animal, assume human form. Their myths include, beyond the creation, a struggle between the divine hero and his enemies, his death and resurrection, a sacred marriage between the hero god and the Mother Goddess, and a triumphant procession. In the myth from which Genesis is partly derived, Yahweh, in the garden, created man and then woman from his rib. The world outside was arid and barren. E. C. Rust, in *Nature and Man in Biblical Thought*, says:

> Although in later days the Israelites of the Puritanic type looked back to the desert wanderings and upheld the desert ideal, the ordinary sojourner in the "promised land" regarded the arid wastes of the desert as places to be avoided. They were the home of the curse and the abiding place of the wilderness demons. Indeed in three passages the wilderness is described by the word *tohu*,

the very word which in the later record of creation is used to describe the primeval chaos out of which the world was made. Thus in the primitive mind, fresh from the great deliverance under Moses, the desert rather than the flood waters of the Mesopotamian Valleys may well have been the primeval chaos out of which the inhabited world was made.

A later and more sophisticated form of the myth placed Yahweh at a distance, operating through the spoken word, and includes the sun, moon, and stars in the creative act. The Book of Psalms is the most ecstatic statement of this in the Old Testament. Rust continues:

> We have seen the pagan creation myths with their naturalistic setting drawn up into the covenant-faith of Israel and transformed to become the media of a lofty creation-faith. No longer have we a demi-urge who along with His creatures belong to the primeval form-less matter. Chaos remains, but Yahweh stands over against it, moulding it that it may give birth to the orderly setting and life of nature. God is supreme, majestic in His creating and unlimited in His power. The whole creation is dependent upon Him and is re-lated to Him in its creatureliness, waxing old like a garment, whilst His glory is from everlasting.

Even so, every aspect of the creation was evidence of His wisdom and majesty to the Hebrew. The orderliness of the world was a source of constant wonder. It was this won-der which the Christians discarded for arguments from design or immortality, preferring theism and abstractions. To the Christian the Church offered doctrine and proof which became more important than the personal experience or the awe of creation. The binding of the Hebrew soul to that of the land, of the covenant as the marriage of Yahweh to the land in which they were the agents, the psychic bond between land and people so profound that when Adam sins the ground is also cursed, the division of nature into a hierarchical order, each level with some degree of independence and freedom, the livingness of nature, capable of sympathy with man and of response to the rule of the Creator—these the Christians abjured in favor of Manichaean dualism, the disobedience and sinfulness of man, sacrifice, puritanism, and the shift of emphasis in behavior and belief from this world to another.

The idea of a "wonder" to the Hebrews of the Old Testament was that of everyday perception. All nature was supernatural, though not part of the divine being, not pantheistic. A wonder was not a break in a natural law; it was a particularly evident divine activity, and in this sense there was no distinction between a natural and a supernatural explanation of any event, such as the crossing of the Red Sea. Man was regarded as an epitome of natural order. But he was a custodian, not an owner. Yahweh represented the culmination of an evolution away from the theophanies of storm and fire to a moral god imposing his will through history. According to the Hebrew view, man was more than part of the natural order, but also his body was more than a prison for a fallen soul; the body was not a seat of lust, as St. Paul declared, or the site for war between flesh and spirit, but flesh plus the vitalizing *ruach* of God. The Hebrew attitude shared with, or brought to, Christianity, however, a lack of humanitarian feeling for animals, as all were judged in relation to man and none had a right to live outside man's rule. Job indicated that one can sin against the land but not against the animals.

The Christians de-emphasized the divinity of nature and, with St. Paul, identified the flesh as merely physical, earthly, natural, visible, external, and weak. The flesh was condemned to sin, influenced by the lodgement there of evil. One of the great problems and, indeed, misconceptions, which has plagued Christian thinkers from St. Paul to Schweitzer is that of carnivorousness. Rust says:

> St. Paul is strangely conscious of the problem that so easily vexes our modern mind. The great wastage in which the generative powers of nature seem involved, the internecine warfare in which nature seeems red in tooth and claw, the seemingly meaningless and even evil forms of organic life which the process of nature has

produced, the unending struggle for existence which underlies the whole natural order. . . . The whole process of nature seemed subject to emptiness, futility.

Death and predation are evils which did not exist in paradise and which would again be done away with. The nearly fanatic zeal for curbing natural predation and predators has deeply marked Christian nature hating and in modern times has caused untold harm to biological systems by well-meaning meddlers.

Another of the themes nurtured by the Church which denigrated nature came from later Greek thought, which has produced the modern rational mind. Abstract Greek philosophy, puritanical Christianity, and modern industry may seem far apart, but are alike in their dependence upon abstractions. The application of physics and chemistry to the transformation of nature involves chemical reactions, molecules, atoms, and various forms of energy which are themselves invisible. The barbaric, organic, mystic, poetic, and inductive character of modern biology would not be puzzling to a Chinese Buddhist, but its deductive formulations would be. The Greeks deduced from Euclidian propositions a small number of axioms and relations as a modus for knowing nature experimentally. This creation of intellectually constructed entities disavows the importance of the senses, just as did the puritanical Christians on different grounds.

This confluence of ideas from anastomosing historical streams coincided with a profound change in the character of human consciousness. One aspect was a shifting of equilibrium in "the great enigma of the duality of the sexes" toward the dominance of the male, to male values and phallic primacy. In *Phallic Wounds*, Bruno Bettelheim says, "In a patriarchical society in which the procreational ability of women gave them a relatively more important role, men may at first go far in asserting their superiority." The modern use of gadgets, Bettelheim says, may be related to passing beyond a "passive giving one's self up"; that is, living beyond what nature provides.

Only with phallic psychology did aggressive manipulation of nature by means of technological inventions become possible. . . . One might even speculate as to
whether men did not create the larger forms of society
after they despaired of being able, by magic manipulation of their genitals, to bear children . . . The failure
of autoplastic manipulation to give men powers equal to
women's in procreation may have been the cause of their
turning to alloplastic manipulation of the natural
world.

Rudolf Steiner, the anthroposophist, and his disciple
Owen Barfield envisaged this evolution of consciousness in
non-Freudian terms. Steiner believed that the human self-
consciousness has become progressively acute, detaching
people first from the natural world and then by degrees individuals from each other and even from words and thoughts.
He saw this growing separation as the unique heritage of modern man, increasingly and terrifyingly isolating him from
communication, understanding, and continuity with the rest
of creation, making him hopelessly incapable of knowing, perceiving meaning, or loving. The existentialist dilemma is not
so much a form of nature hatred as despair. The individual
nourished only by attention to himself is a deformity far more
hideous than the Christian hatred of the world. After all, the
orthodox Christian position was one pole of the feeling for the
environment. If Steiner was correct, the varying degrees of
self-consciousness and separation are an irrevocable evolution
of the mind because of its own activity. But this evolution did
not appear until profound social and ecological changes occurred recently in the span of man. I think these changes are
part of cultural evolution beginning with the domestication of
plants and animals. The rift did not grow inevitably from leisure or art or the mind of man, all of which have been highly
developed for hundreds of millennia. The ecological virginity
of man belongs to his hunting days, then and now. This virtuous existence ends with the "control" of organisms in pastorality and farming. The gods, concepts, values, images, and
myths feeding into the abyss between Western man and his

natural environment all grew from agriculture and pastorality, and the urban life they supported. Part of the urban mythology, even today, is the ideal of the natural nobility and virtue of the farmer and shepherd. But this idea is only a retrospective response to the harmonious ecology of rural Europe for the past five centuries. It also conceives of an innocence which is only relative to that of urban life. By urban I do not mean merely living in a city, but the physical and spatial separation from the organic world, exaggerated ideas of man's control of his world, extreme verbalization and abstraction, the existence of architectural manifestations of enduring institutions, and the persistent environment of geometrically created space.

John Dewey wrote an admirable essay on this subject called "Antinaturalism in Extremis." He traces to Aristotle and Plato the hierarchical conception of reality with the physical at the bottom and the intellectual at the top. But he notes that there is a vast distance between what the Greeks meant by "matter" and its current meaning. Moreover, Greek thought came to us processed by medieval metamorphosis at the hands of Christian theologians, with the result that Aristotle became the Church's official philosopher and, with Plato, the founder of spiritualistic antinaturalistic philosophy. The Pauline and Augustinian interpretation of Greek ideas tailored them to fit a philosophy of bodily corruption and carnal flesh. Likewise a modern nonspiritualistic antinaturalistic philosopher such as Kant regarded the old, "natural" Adam as less than the "spiritualistic" Adam. Hence, says Dewey, there have been two antinaturalistic schools: first the supernaturalistic and second its rationalistic philosophical derivative. Both identified naturalism with materialism and reductionism, which destroy logical, esthetic, moral, and other human values. The weight of this antinaturalism in the past millennium has penetrated our very languages, profoundly influencing the meanings of words, incorporating assumptions of the depravity of man and corruption of nature into thinking, alleging that naturalism leads to a philosophy of government by force, preventing scientific methods in inquiry into the social sciences, and attacking philosophical idealism and transcendental romanticism.

That romanticism supports nature and classicism opposes it is a general misconception, nowadays spread by exponents of development and progress who use "romantic" as a
derogatory term for a nature lover. There is a modern romanticism which can be traced to the philosopher Immanuel Kant
and which became the basis of cults of personality, individuality, and personal freedom, which are highly esteemed by the
contemporary mind. Nature was denied by him and his followers, particularly among German poets, as a source of truth
or criteria, knowledge or guidance for man. This view was
extremely romantic in that it opened to man a possible romance of being and becoming unrestrained by natural process
or causality—romantic, but diametrically opposed to transcen-
dentalism, for it separated men historically and organically
from nature and led to the rejection of responsibility for
human action upon a world considered unknowable, incoherent, and alien.

There is hardly a faculty of philosophy at a major university whose thought is not dominated by either rationalistic
or supernatural antinaturalism. The extraordinary characteristic of antinaturalism is its lack of philosophy; that is, its
assumptions about the nature and value of philosophy that
cause it to omit serious discussion or reflection of the ethical,
moral, religious, and esthetic relationships of man to nature.
It is not that philosophy wastes much time condemning the
"merely material"—that assault is past—but damns by omission, an omission so profound that many young doctoral grad-
uates in philosophy do not apprehend the scope of their own
antinaturalism because of their narrowed understanding of
the philosophical endeavor.

The evolution of consciousness that imparted a new
sense of separateness from nature, the Christian hierarchic
view of man at the apex of a pyramid with nature at his feet,
the Persian dualism, the Greek abstract thinking which projects the abstraction back upon natural reality—these are
perhaps only occasions in the inevitable calamity of minded-
ness in which the overspecialized brain ultimately destroys
itself, like any other evolutionary fixation that goes too far.
They are instances of the effect of civilization and the destiny

of consciousness. Let us turn to concrete effects of this change
as it effects the control of nature, first as landowning.

The settled farmer claimed an ownership in land, unlike
the primitive hunter or nomadic planter-gatherer. Yet all
were territorial. The robin defending its acre of lawn in the
spring suggests ownership. It is doubtful that the robin enter-
tains such an abstract concept, but a kinship is there, and all
the accusations of humanizing and anthropomorphizing are
useless against it. We are amused to see the robin acting as
though he owns the yard, because we know that we own it.

By social ritual, ownership is now sealed by franchise,
and space is represented as property. Property in turn consists of a bundle of rights, neither more nor fewer than law
permits, custom decrees, and neighbors tolerate.

Landowning attitudes determine the tenacity with
which the property is held and facility with which it is bar-
tered away. The attitude is composed of territorial feelings,
previous experience on the land, what has been planted or
built, the relationship between the place and the individual's
image of himself, and so on. The rights granted by society
may be outside this patchwork of feelings, having no influence in what is most important in ownership. Like the robin,
the individual participates in events which are not fully understood concerning a particular place.

The historical beginnings of the official concept of property are unknown. It probably started with a clan territory,
but there were always special places to which it did not refer:
burial grounds and other sacred places, springs, and sites of
certain minerals. The amount of land owned as a unit changes
with the economy, extensive where land is poor, reduced
where crops grow well. Property rights come more sharply
into focus in settled agriculture than in pastoralism or hunting.

Our modern rights in law are derived from Roman and
feudal backgrounds. From at least the time of imperial Rome
individual freedom and landowning have been related. The
slave could not own land. Land has signified social status,
political prestige, and power. Landowners were traditionally

voters and controllers even in democratic systems. The stair-step order of the feudal domain was a division of rights in the land, all of which belonged to the sovereign. These rights and obligations descended through classes to the serf. The author-ity over land use and the proceeds from it were divided accordingly. The scenery created by this arrangement, the feudal Dorf, remained geographically predominant well into the present century. The settled, man-nature fabric of north-western Europe was the legacy of this venerable system.

The obligations of stewardship in the manorial system grew from this division of a bundle of rights in which no one class assumed absolute power of disposition. Its weakness was that improvement of fields was undermined by occasional reassignment among the peasants and by the lack of pride in ownership. The system is looked upon as having been inefficient and static. But the inefficiency was itself a buffer, as the untapped resources were available for intensified utili-zation, allowing a margin of safety. In the face of modest agricultural demands, the soil remained stable enough to endure climatic variations and human requirements, evolving into a harmonious interpenetration of man and environment, a beautiful habitat unusually steady in a world of man-dominated deteriorating habitats.

Outright land ownership has been identified with modern capitalism, accused by its critics of denying non-landowners their share of a "universal" heritage. A communistic system of state-owned lands has not, however, guaranteed the shared sense of responsibility springing from the feudal structure. On the contrary, the absence of personal rights in land may discourage individual responsibility toward it. In any case, the attitude of farmer and pastoralist does not descend from an ideology but emerges from a host of personal and social ex-periences.

In the manorial system, peasant use of the fields and forests was based on shares and on easement and servitude. With some exceptions, entail and primogeniture kept the estate together in the name of the oldest son. The land could not be bought and sold. Then, with the usurpation and enclosure of commons and the rise of industry, modifications in the legal status of property exposed land to exchange. It is little more than two centuries since the rights to land and its fixtures became an estate, and tenancy agreements a lesser estate, which could be held in fee simple and so bought and sold. As money rents appeared and fee proprietorship gave the user almost unlimited rights, land units were marketed according to a two-dimensional surface measurement carrying those rights certain distances into the air above and the earth below. Land's most unique characteristic as property is its immobility, making it "realty," or "real" as opposed to "personal" property. Realty is legally "a tangible commodity not created by man."

The shedding of tradition and rise of urban life in the United States separated the American from the soil more completely than the citizen of any other nation. This transition was illustrated by John B. Jackson, the editor of *Landscape* magazine, by comparing the American farmer of the seventeenth-century New England nuclear village to the nineteenth-century farmer in Illinois and to the Texas farmer-rancher in 1950.

To the New England Puritan, the farm and family were part of a hierarchic structure, with God at the top and the natural world at the bottom. The stone fences and permanent fields were a monotonous, familiar fragment of creation, part of the trial of this world in preparation for a better one. Although nature was more or less hostile to the Puritan exile, its onerous demands were merely the inflexible price of security and holiness. The farm was static and poor compared to an Illinois farm two centuries later. The self-sufficient prairie settler of the nineteenth century regarded his farm as an expanding organism through which he was related to all nature, loving and yet conquering it. He regarded the outdoors as both church and recreation, the family rather than the town his social unit. He bought his land from a speculator and his grandson would sell it. He grew a cash crop as well as necessities, using mechanical tools, and spent his money for goods made elsewhere. His fencing was more flexible, his practices subject to improvement and change. With a large garden and lawn and a sense of being part of nature, he had a stronger idea of a beneficent creation than his ancestor in New England, but the flexibility of the farming pattern and his growing dependence on manufactured goods and a cash market were a wedge between him and the environment, foreshadowing utter dependence on a distant technology by his Texas grandson in 1950.

The Texan did not live on the farm nor keep a garden. He lived in town in a cement-block house which was a convenient social and nutritional "transformer," rather than a family center as in 1850 or a protective extension of the church as in 1650. The ranch-farm was a matrix for converting energy into money. It was held on credit, irrigated, its fields and crops manipulated according to an interconversion of work, time, money, and the machinations of the market. A graduate of an agricultural college, the Texan used many power-tools, some rented and some owned, and purchased all his goods and food. At any time he might sell out and go into some other business.

The Texas farmer was more like his distant Puritan ancestor than like the Midwesterner in his aggressiveness and lack of sentiment toward the environment. To some extent this similarity merely delimited the beginning and end of the era of transcendental romanticism. But the similarity is due in some part to the difficulty of making land yield in a rugged, fringe environment. New England was looked upon as a howling wilderness; parts of Texas were a desert.

As we have seen, the desert is much more than a climate or soilless landform; it is a constellation of values and images, closely related to the ideas of wilderness and of paradise. These stereotypes have risen again and again in attempts of Western men to perceive their relationship to nature. In answer to the question "What is the place like?" which was to be so often asked from the time of Marco Polo on, an answer in terms of fixed images conveyed far more than ordinary speech.

Such stereotypes close the eyes of subsequent travelers or settlers, releasing them from the trauma of confronting the unknown. There is another stereotyping instrument of the explorer, indeed, of the organized political state, and that is the map. With the division of the circle into degrees and minutes the map became possible as a mathematical representation. Its beginnings were probably Babylonian, but in the Nile Valley it was associated with the collection of taxes. In this vast flood plain landmarks were sparse. As early as Ramses II (1300–1233 B.C.) a national land survey was conducted. Boundaries on maps represented demarcations of the earth. The Greeks, with their concept of the spherical earth, projections, parallels, and meridians, made a culmination of those Ptolemaic beginnings. The Romans and Middle Ages Europeans were indifferent to mathematical geography, but it was revived in the fifteenth century. Three centuries later the French began the first national survey, using an astronomically determined base line for triangulation. The Americans adopted such a rectangular system in 1784, replacing the New England system of "meets and bounds" or description of property by natural objects. The base line was usually a parallel of latitude from which townships were numbered, while ranges east or west were counted from principal meridians. As new land, such as the Midwest, was surveyed before or at the time of settlement, county boundaries coincided with survey boundaries and roads were laid out on section lines.

Perhaps no other abstraction about nature has been so dramatically and literally projected back upon the earth. In a sense the history of Topophobia began with the creation of abstractions to organize perception, and has moved to the substitution of abstraction for perception. Next to the emergence of the formal garden (model landscapes resulting from this symbolizing of an abstract mathematical image of the universe), the American land survey was the world's most extensive example of the rationalized landscape. Insofar as the system was based on cartographic lines and points, its orientations were ultimately celestial. It was a projection upon the earth's surface of a uniform, mechanical treatment of the universe, or, rather, that aspect of the universe which may be treated so. Though based on curved orbits and the surfaces of spheres, it is experienced as straight lines. The rectangles it imposes can be infinitely divided and so brought to the scale of human activity and mobility—or expanded to the scale of machines. They are rigid and inorganic. To me they represent the outstanding illustration of the human nervous system imposing conditions on the natural environment which work ultimately to its own destruction. The grid survey operates as a cybernetic system, confirming and emphasizing one aspect of the perception of nature at the expense of others.

Such a vision of "improved" nature is the common feature of powerful, autonomous engineering cultures or agencies, part of advanced technological societies. It is an ecological disaster because it identifies order with a limited kind of regularity with effects which are more far-reaching than mapping. It seems to provide a rationale and justification for the control of nature that aims to improve it but sanctions the destruction and removal of any elements which do not seem to fit the pattern. It is not surprising that this is epitomized in a militaristic age, because it is a kind of war against selected objects, species, processes, and forms in the landscape. Engineers, builders, and planners, much alike in their mentality, apply the products of mathematicians and physicists willing to pollute the world with radioactive residues and chemists who abjure responsibility for poisoning the environment deliberately with biocides and industrial and automotive wastes. It takes much nature hating to do these things, though none of these people nor the public whom they "serve" would ever think of themselves in such terms. They mask themselves consciously through public relations and unconsciously through all the philosophic, political, and psychological justifications we have mentioned.

For ages the transformation of elements into foods and other compounds usable by man was accomplished solely by plants and animals. Primitive technology and the domestication of organisms—the so-called agricultural revolution—modified that situation only in efficiency. But with storable grain the commodity made its appearance, the first step toward treating the world as stuff with no greater relevance. The full flower of this attitude awaited industrial synthetic processes, the creation artificially of wants and waste through mass communication and industrial specialization, the complex of modern civilization as a predator and parasite on nature. Until recently the struggle to exploit was limited only by the empirical wisdom of custom and the obstacles presented by nature itself. At first man utilized only a few plants, animals, and minerals. But they were not resources in the modern abstract sense. The explosion of the number of such usable substances and the invention of new ones and new combinations chemically extended the part of the environment convertible to usable materials. In recent decades we have rapidly approached the point at which any or all the stuff of the earth, sea, and air become grist, and the poisonous, "useless" residues of these conversions accumulate proportionately. Until recently the abstraction "resource" could be distinguished from the nonusable or sometimes esthetic portion of the natural environment—the concept of a detached resource dates only from the eighteenth century. But as we approach the capacity to use all the elements, minerals, and compounds, resourcism expands its meaning from a limited portion of nature to a proto-philosophy of man and nature. At first it would seem that since resources are "conserved" because they are useful this would lead to the conservation of all nature. Indeed it may eventually do so when our "use" and "needs" are better understood. But in the meantime the pace of technological change is so little synchronized with the rhythms of natural adjustment and equilibrium that its shifting, atomistic levy disrupts the loom of the world. By striking inadvertently at intangible patterns and organizations, technology gives us objects and substances of a highly improbable and sometimes exquisite kind; it also advances disorder in the world. Resourcism is the most insidious form of nature hating because it poses as a virtue, as prudent, foreseeing, and unselfish. It destroys the world and ourselves in spite of the altruism of its protagonists because they no longer operate as a face-to-face social or economic entity; while as components of corporations, governments, or other agencies they do not touch the world with their own hands. There is no blood on their fingers, but no blood in them either.

The outward effects of treating the world industrially or as the dead inert stuff of a commodity, as convertible energy, as the equivalent of money, appear confirmed by success. The conservationists who fragment the world into resources have tricked themselves into believing that an either-or situation exists, by which the technological exploitation of the land-scape in the past has some unfortunate aspects but is the price we must pay for a better, longer life. They pretend that the alternative is to go back to nature, to become savages. Nature control by engineering is presented as an inextricable part of modern medicine, and anyone who would speak against its good effects would murder babies.

Hence the current forms of nature hating carry all the energies of prudery, religious zeal, patriotism, humanitarian-ism, and the aggressive pursuit of comfort and things. They are cloaked in good intentions and altruistic goals. They are not a choice of evil over good as we think of that choice in a free society. It has taken four thousand years of struggle to "lift" man "above" nature. In the course of that struggle language and thought and behavior in the West have lapsed into a two-simple framework of discontinuity and opposition: spirit and body, mind and matter, earth and heaven, man and nature, good and evil. It is not an insoluble dilemma, but it is far more dangerous than we permit ourselves to know.

Chapter Eight

The American West

The Plains

PERHAPS THERE IS no better example of the evocative power of natural landscapes than the response of westering pioneers to novel erosional remnants and angular cliffs. To many of the thousands who followed the Oregon Trail before 1850, the escarpments and sedimentary bluffs along the Platte River in western Nebraska were the structures of a ghostly architecture. The Reverend Samuel Parker wrote in his diary in 1835:

> Encamped today near what I shall call the old castle, which is a great natural curiosity . . . [it has] the appearance of an old enormous building, somewhat dilapidated; but still you see the standing walls, the roof, the turrets, embrasures, the dome, and almost the very windows; and the guard houses, large, and standing some rods in front of the main building. You unconsciously look around for the enclosures but they are all swept away by the lapse of time—for the inhabitants, but they have disappeared; all is silent and solitary . . .

These speculations were more than the whimsy of a saddlesore preacher. The journals of mountain men, farmers, speculators, and soldiers are replete with similar comparisons. Their wonder is directed towards "rocks" called Steamboat, Table, Castle, Smokestack, Roundhouse, Courthouse, Jail, and Chimney. Why should these particular rocks have looked more like buildings than any back East? And why should they have made such an indelible impression on the traveler? These are problems in human ecology, of the formation of attitudes toward the landscape; of the fusion of an experience in nature with historical ideas of process and natural change; and they reveal a projection into new situations of values evolved in an old, familiar, and different environment.

Proceeding northwest along the terraced banks of the Platte at a longitude just beyond 103 degrees, a few minutes south of the 42nd parallel, the traveler was about six weeks out of Independence, Missouri. After crossing the upland between the Platte forks, he had followed for almost two weeks the "shores" of what Washington Irving described as the "most beautiful and least useful" river in America. Because the Platte was a kind of linear oasis the itinerant was scarcely aware of the progressive alteration in vegetation and land forms. The travelers hailed from several states, particularly Eastern and Midwestern. They were heterogeneous groups, numbering sometimes in the thousands. They were alike insofar as they shared the geological provincialism of men reared in the sub-humid forest landscapes of America and Europe. They shared also the historical background and values of Protestant Yankees and Hoosiers of the 1830's and 1840's.

At Scott's Bluff the itinerant had climbed more than three thousand feet above Independence. He had traversed the northern high plains from the oak-hickory forest to the margin of semiarid highlands, from regions of more than thirty inches of rainfall annually to under fifteen. Leaving the savannahs of the western boundaries of the forests, he had crossed the tall-grass prairies and the shorter mixed grasses, to the place where the upland vegetational cover ceased to be continuous—a significant point in the vegetational influence on the geomorphic processes of weathering and mass wasting. The traveler had also entered a region of greater daily temperature range, more numerous cyclonic storms, and less relative humidity, with their varied and subtle effects on human perception and response.

Plodding up the valley of the Platte, with its arm of forest, meadow, and savannah, the traveler penetrated unaware new biotic and geomorphic surroundings. Shortly after he had entered what is now Scott's Bluff County, Jailhouse Rock and Courthouse Rock appeared on the left horizon some fifteen miles away. As the column passed slowly to the right of these structures, more came into view, finally an escarpment parallel to the trail about five miles from the river. This mountain, Wildcat Ridge on present maps, is more than thirty miles long and sends three spurs north almost to the river's edge, the westernmost being Scott's Bluff.

The first fifteen miles or so produced a galvanizing impact on the observer. There had been intimations of things to come, such as buffalo trails that looked to one pioneer "like the once oft-trodden streets of some deserted city." The valley with its pleasant greenery had itself been suggestive; Rufus B. Sage observed that "everything had more the appearance of civilization than anything that I have seen for many days, the trees, the shrubs and bushes, grapevines, the grass—resembling blue grass—the singing of the birds in the trees, the sound of the ax cutting wood for breakfast . . ." Then, as the westbound party drew abreast of the bluffs, a wave of astonishment swept through it. John Bidwell wrote in 1841, "the scenery of the surrounding country became beautifully grand and picturesque—they were worn in such a manner by the storm of unnumbered seasons, that they really counterfeited the lofty spires, towering edifices, spacious domes, and in fine all the beautiful mansions of cities."

Numerous observers discovered lighthouses, brick kilns, the Capitol of Washington, Beacon Hill, shot towers, churches, spires, cupolas, streets, workshops, stores, warehouses, parks, squares, pyramids, castles, forts, pillars, domes, minarets, temples, Gothic castles, "modern" fortifications, French cathedrals, Rhineland castles, towers, tunnels, hallways, mausoleums, a Temple of Belus, and hanging gardens which were "in a tolerable state of preservation, and showing in many places hardy shrubs that, having sent down their long roots into partial openings of the supporting arches, still smiled in beautiful green, amid general desolation," according to J. Quinn Thornton. Taken at a glance the rocks "had the appearance of Cities, Temples, Castles, Towers, Palaces, and every variety of great and magnificent structures . . . splendid edifices, like beautiful white marble, fashioned in the style of every age and country," reported Overton Johnston and William Winter. Where more palpably than in America could such a jumble of architecture actually look like a city?

Here were the minarets of a castle; there the loopholes of bastions of a fort; again the frescoes of a huge temple; there the doors, windows, chimneys, and the columns of immense buildings appeared in view, with all the solemn grandeur of an ancient, yet deserted city, while at other points Chinese temples, dilapidated by time, broken chimneys, rocks in miniature made it appear as if by some supernatural cause we had been dropped in the suburbs of a mighty city—for miles around the basin this view extended, and we looked across the barren plain at the display of Almighty power, with wonder and astonishment. [A. Delano]

But the cities were not often American. What cities came to mind?

The mind was filled with strange images and impressions. The silence of death reigned over a once populous city, which had been a nursery of the arts and sciences, and the seat of a grand inland commerce. It was a Tadmore of the desert in ruins. [J. Q. Thornton]

What people had lived there?

No effort of the imagination is required to suppose ourselves encamped in the vicinity of the ruins of some vast city erected by a race of giants, contemporaries of the Megatherii and Icthyosaurii. [Edwin Bryant]

Noble castles with turrets, embrasures, and loopholes, with draw-bridge in front and the moat surrounding it; behind, the humble cottages of the subservient peasantry and all the varied concomitants of such a scene, are so strikingly evident to the view, that it required but little stretch of fancy to imagine that a race of antediluvian giants may have here swayed their iron sceptre, and left behind the crumbling palace and the tower, to all of their departed glory. [John K. Townsend]

What had happened to them? There was a room, suggested J. Q. Thornton, where "that monarch might have sat upon his throne, surrounded by obsequious courtiers and servile slaves, while the lifeblood of men better than himself was being shed to make him a holiday." Perhaps because of this degeneracy the city had been overwhelmed. Another suggested that it had been occupied by "a people who had perhaps gone down into the vortex of revolutions . . . leaving no trace of their existence, save those remains of architectural grandeur and magnificence." From the position of the ruins some travelers reconstructed the probable course of the catastrophe, a series of pitched battles, slaughter, pillage, fire, and the "bodies in promiscuous piles about the gates."

The illusion was so difficult to resist that a present reader of these journals discriminates with difficulty between a speculative visual play on forms and their animation by ghosts from the European and Biblical past. The mirage "would deceive the most practiced eye were it not known that it is situated in a wilderness hundreds of miles from any habitation." There was a continual protestation of bemusement and flashes of embarrassed self-consciousness. The Reverend Sam Parker declared that "one can hardly believe that they are not the work of art. Although you correct your imagination, and call to remembrance, that you are beholding the work of nature, yet before you are aware, the illusion takes you again, and again your curiosity is excited to know who built this fabric, and what has become of the bygone generations." Israel Hale rode twelve miles to inspect the incredible Chimney Rock:

I could not help imagining that it might be the work of some generation long extinct and that it was erected in commemoration of some glorious battle or in memory of some noble chieftain. But on arriving at the spot I could discover no marks of hammer, ax, or chisel, no cemented joints by which it should be cemented in one solid mass.

The first half of the nineteenth century had been an era of geological discovery. The impact of this science was felt by many who had little education but for one reason or another were interested in minerals and rocks. Among them, and certainly among the more educated groups, geology was providing exciting new vistas of the earth's surface and the origin of land forms. By 1835 anyone who thought about the new geological information at all was aware, however vaguely, of the process of change. It was a time of tension at the popular level between an old assumption of a created static world and the discovery of a new one in which time and nature seemed to carve the landscape.

Geology strongly influenced certain esthetic ideas and objects, particularly the picturesque and sublime ruin. The ruin has a respectable and venerable iconography. It had, for instance, Christian and pre-Christian symbolism. With the Renaissance and its new veneration for classical antiquity, and the emergence of nationalism with its celebration of the indigenous past, the ruin became enmeshed in several historical strands. Perhaps the ruin's most provocative effect was as testimony to the ravages of time. It is unfortunate that, while most esthetic histories probe the importance of the ruin in the eighteenth and nineteenth centuries, there has been very little study of its ecological context.

The Chimney, noted William Watson, "is composed of soft sandstone; and like the surrounding bluffs, is in a state of decay; and nothing that I saw on the route put me so strongly in mind of my approaching dissolution." There is no question that the city in Wildcat Ridge was in ruins. One rock had "the appearance of a vast edifice, with its roof fallen in, the great doorways partially obstructed, and many of the arches broken and fallen." The structures were all magnificent, "but now lift up their heads amid surrounding desolation; befitting monuments of man's passing glory, and of the vanity of his hopes," sighed J. Q. Thornton. The description of the cycle of empire which is postulated by several itinerants was exactly the view of cyclic history that Thomas Cole, the landscape painter, had impressively depicted in his five large paintings of *The Course of Empire*.

Perhaps no aspect of the pioneer experience at Scott's Bluff was more cogent than the combination of geomorphic circumstances. The arm of the familiar deciduous forest community that follows the Platte may, as already suggested, have masked the transition into a novel environment. But the geomorphic situation was suddenly evident. Because of its cut-and-fill nature, much of the Platte Valley is without bluffs; in Scott's Bluff County the river has not only cut bluffs, but they are sufficiently distant from the trail to be seen as a whole. Semiarid climatic conditions begin to prevail at about this longitude, and there seem to be fundamental changes in the relationship of mass-wasting or erosion factors. Debris is rapidly removed. Plants and their acid secretions do not gently round off the hilltops. The result is that the forms of the hills are no longer curved and their slopes lose the S-shaped profile characteristic of a humid climate. A theoretical line, the critical slope, is much decreased with the result that, with the passage of time, the mountains retreat as cliffs rather than lose height and steepness.

The peculiar situation in Scott's Bluff County is partly due to the location and direction of a tributary called Pumpkin Creek, which flows east into the North Platte. For some distance it parallels the larger stream and like it has cut deeply into the conglomerates, sandstone, and compacted alluvium of various sizes and resistances. Wildcat Ridge is a neck of upland towering between the two valleys. Regressive erosion into this ridge has separated it in several places, leaving isolated outlying remnants and sculpturing it with the aid of other climatic agencies into a maze of forms that show the differential erosion of the various materials. Architecturally, a single cliff is only a facade, a bas-relief, compared to the fully sculptured three-dimensional forms cut from the rock between these two streams.

The clear air and absence of trees made perspective exceedingly difficult for men whose visual habits had developed with the size and distance clues of a humid landscape. The three long dissected spurs running north from the ridge lend additional depth to the scene, creating the impression upon an observer of standing in the city rather than looking at a flat picture. The box canyons into which he looked, Horseshoe Flat and Cedar Valley, contained nothing to dispel the architectural image, their floors neatly terraced by the stream.

In this way the ceaseless process of geomorphic change had staged a scene which caught the imagination. The architectural forms in the distance seemed to belong to an esthetic developed around ruins, and perceptual experience may have been heightened by novel physical circumstances. But alone these do not account for the extravagant response of plains-weary pioneers any more than they explain the modern traveler who is drawn to those same rocks today by subtle forces which he cannot identify. There was more to the experience than contemporary esthetics. It seems possible that Wildcat Ridge and Scott's Bluff and other cliffs along the Green, Snake, Missouri, or Platte Rivers operate as signs in part of the biological syndrome associated with "imprinting." When a gosling just from the egg attaches itself for life to the first-large-object-moving-away as its "mother" it is imprinted for life. This is the fixing of associations at a crucial period in the developing brain. Rocks of certain angular shapes may always mean "man-made structure" to European-Americans because of an indelible association of form with human works perceived at a crucial moment in mental development. A somewhat similar phenomenon is the interior of the forest as a temple, of which there are many examples in literature. J. Z. Young has suggested that large structures, notably cathedrals, are, because of their permanence, ultimate symbols of the most human of qualities—the striving for perfection and permanence of communication. It is interesting to note that thousands of people moving up the Platte in the 1840s left their names, destination, and the date carved and written on every available surface along the Oregon Trail.

The illusion of architecture associates these structures with nobility and with a violent destruction. Revolution against autocracy and despotism, the American Revolution particularly, was fresh in mind and yet distant enough to be part of history. Although professing opposition, then as now, Americans seemed strangely receptive to external forms and appurtenances of aristocracy. Other cultural archetypes of the European background were the images from the forest myths of the children's stories and the architectural fantasies of the Gothic novel, filling the American cultural vacuum of old, familiar forms. In addition, the Mediterranean and Near Eastern heritage of classical history was associated with architecture. Archaeology created the notion of the Cycle of Empire, a cherished view of history in the eighteenth and nineteenth centuries. A pre-Biblical myth involved the rebuilding of ruined cities in the desert by heroic measures. W. H. Auden probed the idea briefly in *The Enchafèd Flood* and indicated the effects of its imagery on the literate mind of the nineteenth century. The mystery of the Lost Tribes was a living issue. Here is a coincidence for further historical study. To what extent and in what ways did the expressions of human experience in the American West fall back on the imagery which had originally come from the deserts of Transjordan, Asia Minor, and the Nile fringes? It is a factor in the inception and pursuit of our national concept of reclamation and the fanatic idea that only good can come of unlimited irrigating, reclaiming, and populating the deserts of America. No complete explanation of the formation of the American's ideas of their West could afford to omit the significance of desert or semiarid land forms as a compelling force.

The Parks

On Sunday evening, August 21, 1870, Lieutenant Gustavus C. Doane, U.S. Second Cavalry, stationed at Fort Ellis,

Montana, received orders to choose a sergeant and four privates for a mission of "important military necessity," and to prepare to depart the following morning. A perceptive and vigorous man of thirty, Doane was soon to discover that his mission had no more military significance than protection from Indians of a half-dozen sight-seeing tourists.

The party which left Bozeman at 11:00 a.m. on the 22nd was an exceptional group. General Henry D. Washburn, its leader, had prevailed upon General Phil Sheridan to order the escort, over the objection of the Fort Ellis commander that his troops were already too widely scattered fighting Indians for the safety of the fort. A veteran of the Civil War, Washburn was then Montana's surveyor-general. With him was Nathaniel Pitt Langford, President Andrew Johnson's territorial governor-appointee and U.S. Collector of Internal Revenue. Langford, who later became famous as a vigilante, a describer of nature in Victorian euphemisms, chronicled the enterprise that was to become known as the Washburn-Langford-Doane Expedition. Its objective was to explore the upper Yellowstone River and to verify or discredit a half-century's accumulation of rumors about fantastic rainbow-colored hot springs where it was possible to hook a trout in one shimmering pool and flip it into a boiling pink and yellow caldron to cook it, a forest of geysers, and huge waterfalls.

With Washburn also came Probate Court Judge Cornelius Hedges, the party's most truly literate member. A New Englander (Yale '53), Hedges had taught school and practiced law and was destined to prominence for forty years in the public affairs of Montana. His daily experiences went into a diary with a poetic flourish and reference to the Lake Poets, Poe, or classical literature. There was also Truman C. Everts, state assessor of internal revenue; Lyman Trumbull, assistant assessor and son of an Illinois Senator; Samuel T. Hauser, president of the Helena First National Bank and later state governor (who kept a diary of the expedition, too, written rapidly with a soft lead pencil in a miniature pocket journal); and Warren C. Gillette and Benjamin Stickney, two prominent merchants of Helena, where most of the party lived. At the last minute a ne'er-do-well named Jake Smith enrolled. It turned out that Jake cheated at cards, slept on guard, and generally proved the habitual foil to his upright companions.

All were keen outdoorsmen except Everts, the assessor, who allowed his horse to stray, became befuddled and separated from the party while it was enroute through a pine forest near Yellowstone Lake, and was lost for thirty-seven days. His horse stampeded when he dismounted to look for tracks, and with it went his gun. He accidentally broke his glasses. Nearsighted, he stumbled through snowstorms and lived on roots in an area where Jim Bridger had reported that even the crows carried provisions. Everts discovered after two desperate weeks that he could make fire with his field glasses. Weakening, he was stalked by a mountain lion and was incoherent when two trappers finally found him. Meantime, the expedition had become history and returned to Helena with its entourage of cooks and packers after delaying to search for the assessor. Everts soon became something of a national hero and wrote a book about his adventure.

The loss and rescue of Everts caught public interest, which was further fired by articles by Langford and Hedges. A tale of wonders from such reputable citizens could not be ignored. The Honorable David E. Folsom, a wealthy rancher who had come west with Langford, declined to accompany the Washburn Expedition in 1870 because he had seen Yellowstone the previous year. His descriptions were so incredible that he had ceased talking publicly for fear of being permanently labeled a liar. An article he and a companion had written about the geysers was rejected as fiction by a national magazine, although it found a publisher elsewhere.

Near the end of the expedition Hedges had proposed that the area should be preserved as a public park. All but Smith enthusiastically concurred, and the party returned from the wilderness determined to get Congressional action. General Washburn went to Washington and Langford toured the eastern lyceum circuit in the winter of '70 and '71.

Their efforts resulted in the government's Hayden Expedition the following summer. This was an official party, ponderous with scientific talent, and included the photographer J. B. Jackson and the painter Thomas Moran. Moran's huge panoramas of the Yellowstone Valley overwhelmed spectators, including Congressmen, and the government eventually paid him $10,000 for two of them (one now hangs in the Secretary of the Interior's Conference Room and the other in the Smithsonian Institution). By act of Congress, Yellowstone became the world's first national park in 1872.

This extraordinary event occurred when Indians were still a danger in Yellowstone. The general atmosphere was one of gold-hunting, root-hog-or-die, cut-out-and-get-out, where wilderness seemed to be civilization's worst enemy; of a national orgy of westering, land speculation, and claim-staking. In Yellowstone a huge piece of wilderness was preserved by Congress, two thousand miles away, with no means of enforcing such preservation except by appointing Langford park superintendent without funds or help. What were the rationalizations for reserving a slice of the unlimited green cheese which to some seemed as remote as the moon?

There was awareness in 1872 that natural resources were wasting—the last great herd of buffalo was already tottering and industrial logging had moved into the South—but not even the most altruistic or simple Congressmen assumed that sealing off the Yellowstone Plateau from claims would help diminishing resources. The act had something to do with vague qualities compounded of admiration for scenery and morality, as well as indifference and apathy (the vote was along party lines, the Republicans winning). In short, the National Park Act had the insubstantial and obscure reference of an act of faith without apparent theology.

The gentlemen on the Washburn Expedition and their counterparts with Hayden are the key to the existence of the national parks. Their diaries of the trip reveal the themes on which they became arbiters of American nature esthetics. The account by Lieutenant Doane, who commanded the military escort, is sensitive, even brilliant. He rejoiced in the distant views and natural curiosities. He was the party's most indefatigable hunter and explorer. His sparkling report, long since buried in the Army's morgue of official papers, comes through even today with good sense and the freshness of discovery. Part of it was written in spite of the agony of an infected thumb which had so drained his resources that he slept solidly for thirty-six hours after Langford lanced it with a pocket knife.

The image of the Yellowstone compounded by the men with Hayden and with Washburn, by Folsom, by one William Lacy, a Virginia planter who was there in 1863, and perhaps a few others, was a different Yellowstone than that seen by scores of men who had been there before them. Mountain men like Jim Bridger, John Coulter (who was there in 1806), and Joseph Meek lived on the edge of danger with a casual humor almost unknown today; to them Yellowstone was a great natural joke, a campfire tale come true. The fumaroles looked like the chimneys of Pittsburgh. To unnumbered and unnamed bands of trappers and gold seekers it was merely a passing curiosity. The relatively unique vision of the men with Washburn had to do with contemporary esthetics and an acquired virtuosity. As a contemporary writer said of the western mountains, "One must carry something of culture to them, to receive all the benefits they can bestow in return." This requisite cultural baggage, laboriously transported into virgin territory, produced the first national park.

Langford published his journal as *The Discovery of Yellowstone National Park*. That is, the area contained features that seemed like a park and worth preserving to him and his companions, if not, for instance, to the fifty or so trappers who were there with Bridger in 1846. It did not need to be constructed, as did Central Park. The secret was that to Langford the landscape looked anything but wild. This was due mostly to coincidence. The natural land forms and vegetation of Yellowstone resembled certain humanized landscapes plus objects that were considered an improvement on wilderness, such as ruins.

On the surface, any reference to ruins reflected the social status of the class which indulged in art collecting. Ruins were evidence of the great wheel of time, invoking images of classical antiquity, and confronted human consciousness with a time stream of sublime cyclic flow in which empires grew, flourished, and decayed. From the time of the Italian Renaissance this esthetic reflection on time had captured the modern mind and it was further stimulated by new approaches to the study of history in the eighteenth century. For all their protestations against aristocratic postures, clichés on independence, and disavowals of the physical artifacts of a class society, Americans never seriously questioned the social value of national tangible evidence of history.

Writers, then painters and poets, had injected the image of the ruin into general Western cultural heritage. The eighteenth-century English had discovered their own ruined abbeys, walls, and relics, and built fabrications in their estate pleasuring grounds. Well-to-do Americans toured Europe's great ruins and returned home to lament that "we have neither old castles nor old associations." Why should I visit America, asked John Ruskin, where there are no castles. Patriotism wanted suitable icons. George Washington had not slept in enough places to go around, or in the kind of places that became durable ruins. Meantime, exploration in South America, Africa, and the South Pacific, as well as the United States, showed that ruins were where you found them. The Washburn party in the upper Yellowstone canyon observed rock formations that were geologically novel, and more important, architecturally suggestive. Their resemblance to buildings was so insistent that the educated imagination needed little prompting. As it was, they welcomed the ruins along the Yellowstone with passion, with all the momentum of American tourists unleashed in Rome or the Rhineland. While Hudson Valley aristocrats were copying old Gothic or wishing they could import Scottish castles intact, Langford, Hedges, and Doane were discovering an unchartered heritage of castles, fortresses, and ramparts already in the American landscape. Minarets, watchtowers, and turrets lined the canyon of the Yellowstone where Folsom, silenced by fear or embarrassment for the extravagance of his fantasies, confided to his diary "a huge rock that bore resemblance to an old castle; rampart and bulwark were slowly yielding to the ravages of time, but the old turret stood out in bold relief against the sky. . . . We could almost imagine that it was the stronghold of some baron of feudal time and that we were his retainers returning laden with the spoils of a successful foray." The geysers were fountains, and the terraced hot springs were exactly the kind of adjunct that one might expect in a villa garden.

The geology of these natural ruins was new to men from a humid environment. The climatic forces that sculpture rocks architecturally are characteristic of the continental interior of the American West and have to do with the forms assumed by certain mineralogy in a particular climate and the equilibrium between rock decay and removal of the resulting debris. While pictures of the geysers of New Zealand and Iceland had appeared in popular literature, and everyone "knew" what a desert or mountain range looked like, the western European esthetic of natural beauty nonetheless contained little imagery of angular desert geology. Perhaps this element of novelty rendered it easy to perceive a rectangular block or wall-like cliff as an edifice. It may be asked whether any cultural conditioning would be necessary to combine the human inclination for geometric architecture and the impression that natural rectilinear forms are somehow associated with an intelligent builder. In any case, the journals of the Doane Expedition leave no doubt that the haunting architecture of the Yellowstone's filagreed cliffs delighted Americans who were wistfully conscious of a national cultural shortcoming. Entertaining the pleasant illusion that the rocks were the ruins of buildings led to an equally gratifying dream that the area had formerly been inhabited by a highly civilized and artistic people who, like the ancient Greeks and Romans, had vanished, leaving their works to the amazement of future generations. At the same time, these gentlemen were interested in the rock itself. American geology had outstanding professionals, like John Wesley Powell, who was busy in the Colorado gorge, and good amateurs as well. The men of the Washburn party knew that these rocks were ruins in their own right. Looking out from Mt. Washburn, Doane grasped at once that the whole plateau was a complex volcano. Chemical and mineralogical observation occupied much of their time.

The architectural qualities of Yellowstone's rocks added dimension to their geology. The same processes that sheared fragments from the Pantheon fractured the canyon walls. Natural ruins and man's ruins met in the same arena of time, victims together of weather and climate, so that the American West could display as much evidence of time's wheel as could Europe. Together, the architectural and geological curiosities formed a basis for literary and pictorial description of great empires, which centered on the imagery of the ruin.

There was also a moral and allegorical aspect of the ruin in the wilderness. In the mythology of the ruined city, where man's evil had brought the retribution of decay, a hero appears to build a new and better society. The Washburn party arrived at Yellowstone in a spirit of evangelical fervor. But the "City" could not be rebuilt because the values of the myth had been rearranged. In the nineteenth century the city had become itself the symbol of man's depravity, whereas in the classical view of life it had been the normal arena of life. One no longer went into the wilderness penitently, for meditation and self-denial, but to immerse oneself in untarnished creation and to confront the sanctity of a virgin. Since the ruin had come to be seen as both a natural curiosity and a picturesque monument, this conflicting heritage of ideas could be resolved: in preserving Yellowstone park it was implicit that reclamation must follow, but the public was not to come as settlers and builders. The wilderness must remain wilderness, and the ruins forever ruins. It was the character of the pilgrims themselves that was to be reconstructed.

Natural ruins do not wholly account for the popularity of Yellowstone, since the West is full of rectangular erosion. It was a novel visual experience. The vertical dimensions of the landscape were very great and the local relief on an enormous scale. From high points the landscape was most impressive; any mountain looks bigger from the top of another mountain. The horizontal scale was also unusually great. It is associated with the transparency of the dry air. In a combination of these situations the novelty to an Easterner is likely to be emotionally dazzling. The experience takes on mystic overtones; it becomes an encounter with cosmic forces. Such a view permitted sweeping observations and composition of verbal panoramas, counterparts to the pictures being painted by Frederick Church and Albert Bierstadt. While comparable scenery was found in certain parts of the eastern United States and in Europe, Yellowstone's fame suggests that release from the limits of the customary horizons prepared the tourist for transcendental amazement in the West.

Reaction to the "wonder" did not require the educated eye and was more common than the baggage of the educated gentlemen. Geysers, falls, lakes, and canyons were Yellowstone's wonders. Falls have been primary tourist attractions for a thousand years. Their peculiar fascination is not associated with fashions in esthetics or refined tastes. The awe with which they are regarded is not and perhaps cannot be intellectualized. Falls are as fundamental to the wonder of nature as the spontaneous belief that there is a spirit in things with motion. Falls belong to a category which includes fire, clouds, and even trees tossing in the wind.

A second group of natural wonders is composed of forms which do not move, but in which vitality is immanent, for they suggest the human body. Mountains, forests, large rivers, lakes, caves, and geysers are anatomical. Such wonders partly account for the curiosity that lures tourists into the landscape and especially to the national parks.

The spiritual impact of these wonders elicited Biblical quotations by the men with Washburn, including a psalm by the taciturn leader himself. As the group sat around the campfire, Washburn intoned, "When I behold the work of Thy hands, what is man that Thou are mindful of him!" Having looked at the lower falls all day, Langford wrote, "I realize my own littleness, my helplessness, my dread exposure to destruction, my inability to cope with or even comprehend the mighty architecture of nature. . . . We are all overwhelmed with astonishment and wonder at what we have seen, and we feel that we have been near the very presence of the Almighty."

Here are clearly better than ordinary grounds for preservation. There were, according to Langford, "exhibitions which suggest no other fancy than that which our good grandmothers have painted on our boyish imaginations as a destined future abode." "The beauty . . . is overpowering," wrote Doane, "transcending the visions of the Moslem's Paradise." The image of paradise involves the Garden of Eden and the garden to nineteenth-century English and Americans meant the landscape park, a descendant of the paradise garden by way of the classical pastoral and the village green. The "natural" garden or "park" was the estate grounds, landscaped to blend into the rural countryside. The park was a particular association—planned randomness—of scattered trees, lawn, and winding streams connecting lakes. It looked somewhat like paintings of Arcadia or of paradise. It was both an abstraction from nature and a figment of human experience, roughly equivalent to the pastoral landscape of mixed forest and meadow from which modern European man emerged. The English landscape park was not properly a wonder, although it inherited an artificial mount, or even a grotto; not a ruin, although ruins were constructed to add to the effect; nor yet merely panoramic, although the views were sweeping and extensive.

As a symbol of refinement and well-being the park became important to Americans who were eager to keep up with their English cousins. With the professional aid of Andrew Jackson Downing, the Hudson River estates developed "pleasuring grounds" on the English model. Nor was the gentleman's park limited to the wealthy; Frederick Law Olmsted's Central Park proved in 1858 that in America every man could have his park. Thousands picnicked in similarly planned pastoral grounds in the new rural cemeteries near

Boston and Philadelphia. Although considered "natural," these parks were carefully planned, planted, and manicured. They were far from the original wilderness which the pioneers had to invade, cut down, and humanize in order to establish agriculture.

This was the visual surprise of the Western wilderness: truly wild places that resembled civilization's most ornamental achievement—the estate park—which was, in turn, linked with an image of paradise. William Gilpin's *The Parks of Colorado*, published in 1866, was a description of genuine wilderness, although a park had never been wilderness in Europe.

The association of park landscape and paradise is apparent in landscape paintings of the time like Thomas Cole's *The Expulsion from Eden*. Members of the Washburn expedition wrote about paradise with its fountains. They found in Yellowstone "innumerable groves and sparkling waters, a variegated landscape of surpassing beauty." Standing on the lake shore with its grassy meadows, it seemed to the observer "almost incredible that so tame and so quiet a scene could be found in the midst of a region usually so wild and terrible." Nearby there was a "beautiful park of firs with a broad meadow just in front. No artificial arrangement of trees could have been more perfect." It was the sort of landscape that Constable had painted at Vivenhoe Park, a grassy retreat insulated from the outer world by distant groves, a solitude where cattle or deer munched the turf and gracefully composed themselves into groups.

The explanation of the existence of the natural park in America, like that of the architectural land forms, resides ultimately in unique climatic areas, usually at altitudes of at least four thousand feet. Where a region of natural grasslands, prairie, tundra, or marsh adjoins a forested area, there is usually a transition zone in which there are scattered trees with grassy areas between them. More often in the Rocky Mountains, open areas with scattered aspens succeed the destruction of the forest by fire, and there were many natural fires even before white men appeared. At higher elevations where forests approach the limits of their range regrowth after a fire may be slow and spotty, with lichens, grasses, and flowering herbs filling in the open places. Sometimes the high meadows have the environmental conditions of tundra, and elsewhere the vicissitudes of soil moisture prevent forest growth by providing too little or too much soil water during the growing season. In the valleys, which are often surrounded by dense forest, there may be open meadows with scattered deciduous and evergreen trees which most nearly approximate the lawn park. Usually the meadow is on flat, poorly drained ground. Many of these flats are beaver meadows (former beaver ponds that have been filled with organic material and alluvium). Like the higher areas, these natural parks usually have low soil temperatures and pockets of water-saturated soil. The grazing animals that substitute for cows or sheep of the English park are the elk and mule deer, which have the assistance of many minor lawn mowers in numerous rodents and rabbits. Only in midsummer are the parks comfortably warm for people; at that time the parks are green, flowery, and virginal. They are seen mainly by tourists who come from lower elevations and the altitude probably contributes subtly to the observer's sense of exhilaration.

Similar parks exist in the Cascade and Sierra Mountains. Yosemite Valley offers precisely the same combination of major features: the unusual visual experience, the natural wonders, the waterfalls, the architectural geology, and the natural paradise or garden park. Yosemite was withdrawn from homesteading and reserved as a park eight years before Yellowstone, but instead of becoming a national park at that time, it was ceded to California on the condition that it be preserved and became a national park in 1890. The history of its esthetic discovery is a remarkable parallel to that of Yellowstone. The gentlemen who "discovered" its natural beauty were a minority of all who saw it first in 1851 and 1852, but they brought "something of culture" to the valley, and their almost unbelievable reports stirred men of similar enthusiasm who in turn exerted their influence on Congress. It is significant that Frederick Law Olmsted, who was professionally weaned on the parks of Europe and who helped design Central Park, had a hand in preserving Yosemite.

In the case of both parks, their establishment came about at the end of an era in which nature had been philosophically regarded as benign and beneficent. It was the time of the omniscient naturalist, unlimited natural bounty, and an agrarian national orientation. After Yellowstone it was nearly twenty years before a second national park was established, then with a new social and scientific justification. The wonder, the ruin, and the natural park were a creative combination in the era of nature love; a combination discovered during the exploration of the West where unique geomorphic forms and vegetational communities combined cultural images and natural pride. Civilization and wealth traditionally coincided with the architecture and parks. It took educated tourists to recognize these similarities, men who wished that America were more embellished.

Failures of the New Parks

The sublime wonder, ruin, and English-type lawns in remote places were the component images which made Yellowstone and Yosemite seem worth preserving. What can be said of the system of national parks today? Together with national monuments, there are now more than two hundred. (A national monument is proclaimed by the President; a national park is established by Congress.) An integrated system with a philosophy of administration came when Stephen Mather organized the Park Service in 1916. Four fifths of its areas have been added to the system since then. The high proportion that fail to meet the criterion of looking domesticated or improved is striking. The newest are desert, swamp, or dense forest with few of the traditional esthetic qualifications except that they are wonders. They are not even that in the usual sense of a visible object; they are abstract wonders. The whole swamp (as in the Everglades) or forest (as in the Olympic Rain Forest) is conceptualized as a wonder. The totality has become the wonder rather than any object in it. Some of these newer parks are not even visible panoramically, which would have been a sin against nineteenth-century esthetics of the sublime.

This evolution of wilderness esthetics began with a few individuals far back in the nineteenth century, such as William Cullen Bryant, George Catlin, Henry Thoreau, and Thomas Cole, who urged public preservation of natural relics. At that time it was perhaps too improbable and unexciting— even against progress—to get much public support. Yet, it has never died. Professional and amateur naturalists have continued to espouse it. Their argument is an intellectual complement to the emotional appeal of wonder preservation. Yellowstone provided the political machinery and the precedent for reserving other areas. Surprisingly few scenically undesirable areas got into the system by public or political pressures. Many members of the National Park Service are naturalists, and a philosophy of supreme sample relic preservation has marked the thinking of that agency and its supporters. But there is a great difference between the concept of pictorial beauty based on paradise and scientific arguments for preserving relic samples of wilderness. It takes a great deal of argument to persuade an American to *resist* the exploitation of natural resources in the name of progress. A combination of deeply set cultural images could persuade him in the Yellowstone, but where no such images exist the proposal loses its immediate self-evident justification.

In spite of the strategic role of the desert in our religious history, the relatively new desert parks have not been esthetically assimilated. Although there has always been some pressure to open the parks to commercial exploitation, those pressures are directed to the unparklike parks. Dinosaur National Monument, a desert park, was considered a weak link if not an Achilles' heel in the park system, by the purest school of commercial developers. Presumably, the legal establishment of water, timber, or mineral use in one park would open up the others by precedent. In a five-year struggle between developers and preservers in the 1950's, the fundamental question

was whether or not the monument actually contained a
sufficiently spectacular synthesis of the traditional park landscape—although it was never put in these words. The
preservers published photographs of vast panoramas, architectural rocks, and a rippling river. The developers concentrated on pictures of arid "waste" and the lake they wished to
create—the latter having its own wonder value. More recently
the attack was turned on the Grand Canyon. For closely
similar reasons it is not surprising that the tropical marshes
of the Everglades National Park and the rain forest of the
Olympic National Park are two of the most embattled areas in
the system. Both contain desirable material resources, and
neither are conventional parks. The symbolism of well-being
and wealth of estate-pleasuring grounds does not entirely
account for our parks. The green or commons is a country
cousin of the park concept. Central Park was originally conceived as a kind of large estate ground for the opulent villas
that would surround it, but at the same time it was to be a
congenial space for popular outings and thus fulfill a social
necessity. But there seems to be no natural place for a picnic
in the heart of the Everglades, among the dripping ferns of
the rain forest, or on the Grand Canyon's rocky perimeter.
These are not conventional pastoral settings. Moreover, the
outing has taken on a new and nationally economically sanctioned and commercialized recreational dimension; the parks
have emerged in its vernacular as playgrounds for the millions. Present-day recreation, which is often defined nega-
tively as escape from an unpleasant environment or boring
routine, is replacing the pilgrimage which had natural wonders as its objective. This new version of the national park is
only another form of material exploitation, not because of its
motives, but because people so motivated require so many
props, machines, and controls on nature. The original park,
which in Europe was a humanized landscape in harmony with
intense human pressures, could, like Central Park, sustain
heavy traffic without deterioration. The American national
parks of the original type, like Yellowstone and Yosemite, are
by comparison extremely fragile, because however much they

resemble the gentleman's park superficially, they have reached their lawn-tree state in the relative absence of human tread. Even so, they are more resilient in the face of an onslaught by tourists than unparklike parks. Lawn and trees are hardy associates of human activity, but not so the environments where living things endure on a more tenuous and less recuperable basis, as in the desert or cold forest, or even in the rich subtropical places of superabundance, where the pattern is small numbers of many kinds of organisms in a competitive balance which man joggles easily. In such places popular use depends on renovating and artificializing. No "national playground" is consistent with the outdoor museum, wilderness relic, or natural shrine in environments that cannot stand much tampering.

The natural museum is an intellectual counterpart to the sensory catharsis of natural parks. The outdoor museum has a patriotic-historical value insofar as it involves the preservation of native life and original landscapes, although this, strangely, does not seem to be a particularly cherished idea. There is more enthusiasm for the preservation of natural areas for scientific research on the nature of natural processes, study of systems too elaborate to be mocked-up in the laboratory.

Its value is potentially very great to a technological society which periodically gets itself into dust bowls, floods, and other catastrophes. Natural relic preservation may prove to have value also as a storehouse of plant and animal species which are otherwise becoming extinct, and which at any time may become useful in medicine, industry, or agriculture. The fungi that produce antibiotics are just such organisms, many of them living in only undisturbed forest. In addition, there are numerous educational uses of such natural areas. To an open-minded and reasonably intelligent observer the various scientific needs of outdoor museums and natural areas are reasonably convincing: proponents, even if romantic, scarcely give the impression of being harebrained. Yet, a very small number of people are directly involved. Just as it was a small number of people who established the first parks, on the basis

of a refined nature esthetic. There was an equalitarian yearning for such upper-class tastes. The public and its Congress
knew what a "temple of nature" a "natural Wonder" or a
"gentlemen's park" might be; but a forest which is a "natural community representing the bio-ecological climax" is apt
to get the axe as soon as it can be converted into card-
board at a profit.

While the natural area idea finds its way into wider
awareness and public acceptance, there is also some new
esthetic appreciation of the lawnless parks. As the artist races
forward with new visual abstraction, the casual tourist follows his cold trail. If the desert is not a garden in the usual
sense, it does have color, and Americans have discovered
color fairly recently. A rather wide public enjoyment of Bryce
and Zion National Parks is not based entirely on architectural
fantasy. The Painted Desert was added to the Petrified Forest
National Monument in 1932—twenty-six years after the
Monument was established. The impressionist spectrum in
painting quickened by the invention of color film has finally
enabled large numbers of people to achieve or retain the
pleasure inherent in color vision. This is, perhaps, the most
recent general step in the appreciation of natural scenery.
Possibly the abstract form is next, and we may hope to attain
the sophisticated level enjoyed by the Navajos in this respect.
On the other hand, there may be limits to the rate at which
the public will accept abstractions by art in its dominion over
the beauty of nature. Friends of the parks may hope that there
will never be an epitaph for an exploited Everglades reading
"When Nature Failed to Copy Art."

Whether the parks can survive the interval before the
emergence of suitable public esthetic is uncertain. There are
two ways in which a continuation of conflict could be averted.
The first would be to give up the controversial areas in the
face of growing commercial demands and economic pressures, and retreat to the conventional parks for a concerted
defense. This would consolidate the park system and enable a
society with rather specific esthetics to preserve the whole
system. An example of one of the first parks to be sacrificed

would be the Rain Forest of the Olympic Peninsula, most of
the Olympic National Park. Nearby chambers of commerce
would enjoy a brief burst of progress, parts of a local economy would boom temporarily, a few thousand more homes
would be built faster (but not at a lowered cost), a lumber
company or two would be appeased politically, and the only
forest of its kind would vanish without a chance of returning.
Desert parks, in much the same fashion, might eventually
produce sugar beets under irrigation or become practice
ranges for new weapons.

An alternative would be the playground policy, taking
all comers whatever their motives and desires. This is the
route along which the park service is apparently being im
pelled. There is a certain amount of education available to the
park visitor, but not toward new esthetic desires and satisfactions. The major effect is instead to whittle the wilderness to
fit the pastoral playground picture—an undertaking that,
incidentally, would be much less expensive in some mountain
and forest areas outside the parks proper. With the wilderness squeezed into the recreational mold, only the most overwhelming wonders will rear their heads beyond the facade.
Many tourists do not get beyond the engineering. The veneer
of comfort and excitement has been well built. The tourist
may never suspect that he is not getting all nature has to
offer.

Amiable diversions for all comers are popular with the
public. The diversions are swimming pools, beauty parlors,
bars, dance floors, gift shops, movies, and other entertain-
ments to shake off the horrors of the highway. Perhaps scattered lawns and trees will be built into the Everglades, Death
Valley, and the Olympic Forest. By clearing a few extra feet
of mangrove, cactus, or hemlock, it would be possible to
surround the playground with the necessities of life, not perhaps on the scale that Central Park is circumscribed, but
ultimately approximating a refined, though busy, midway.

James P. Gilligan, a professional in forestry and recreation, observed more than a decade ago that this kind of
democratization was destroying the wilderness. Urged to build

more and more facilities, the Park Service is merely applying the philosophy that as many people as possible should use these areas, even though finally there is little left of the original landscape. "Americans will continue to saturate choice recreation sites opened to motorized entry," Gilligan said, "and then complain because everyone else is also present. The real democratic significance of our parks may not be in providing access and accommodations to everyone, but in holding a few undeveloped areas where high quality recreation benefits can still be obtained by those willing to make the effort." Gilligan concluded that "most endeavors to retain such areas for a relatively small number gradually yield before the demands of an eager traveling public, which has not yet grasped the full significance of our national park system."

There is also an unexplored possibility that many of the traveling public could learn that their sought-for pleasures are not to be found in the parks, and they might voluntarily go elsewhere. The usual traveler can engage in contemplation of a geyser only so long. If the Park Service were not to divert the traveler with entertainment he might move on to complementary activity elsewhere and his hotel room and his standing space would be available for someone else. He might discover that he actually prefers the race track or Hoover Dam and go there next year instead. It seems possible that much of the present tourist pressure on the parks is not so much an expression of a desire to see certain wonders as it is a function of a footloose population, high-speed automobiles, convenient highways, and the new abstract tourism discussed in Chapter Four.

Except for this unlikely educational development, it appears that mass use may be an obliterative process, a choice even worse than giving away the lawless parks.

The case seems dark for Mr. Gilligan's suggestion of holding undeveloped areas for the peculiar wilderness values. Since we are not likely to give away any of the areas, they must all stand by the weakest member or fall. The parks may dissolve into playgrounds for mass use. This would save the newer parks from the clutches of the developers if dismemberment by the construction of semi-amusement facilities could be called saving. A few years ago the Park Service undertook a ten-year building program. All the conservationist friends of the parks worked for greater appropriations from Congress on the erroneous assumption that they were helping to preserve the parks. Many national park areas have remained pristine because the Park Service has been too poor to build roads into them. The back country represents administrative poverty. Now the agency is affluent. The wilderness enthusiasts should seek: (1) reduced appropriations to starve out the new building programs and (2) policies limiting the number of park visitors. If the first is suggested tongue-in-cheek, the second is seriously intended. If the number of visits were limited, the parks might survive and serve their purpose. Admittedly, this policy would leave the newer parks at least as vulnerable as they are today to those who insist that the enjoyment of nature is a romantic dream that should not stand in the way of progress, that "use" of the parks should include the harvest and development of timber, water, mineral, and other material resources. In pseudo-professional jargon such opportunists aver that material resources are "locked up" in the parks. Obviously, what they want would destroy the unique quality of the wild places even faster than commercialized recreation.

The dilemma would seem to be almost beyond solution, although an answer presumably lies somewhere between opening the parks to material exploitation or, in order to perpetuate politically a "preservation" policy, holding perpetual open house for an endless thundering herd. The Park Service may be too retiring or too hot on the scent of power and empire in the bureaucratic jungle to try rationing the use of wilderness parks. Its civil servants give out the impression that there would be rioting in the streets or, worse, in the House. No one has taken the trouble to learn what it is about the wilderness, besides stereotyped imagery, that draws people. No one has expressed surprise that Dinosaur National Monument was saved from progress by thousands of people who never saw that Monument and probably never will. Yet, that is the most illuminating aspect of the whole episode.

Those citizens aimed tons of mail at their Congressmen, but not to save Dinosaur for science, not to spite Utahans, not even to preserve a place for their next summer's vacation. The wilderness evidently has value beyond such motivations. The exploiters' schemes for the unparklike parks carried the assumption that these are less defensible—that is, these lack the association of cherished images and their despoilation in the name of development and improvement would be unopposed. The events proved that this hunch was wrong. The public reaction was a slowly augmenting, enormous cry of protest, climaxed by a national uproar which drew the critical examination of relatively uninterested politicians and economists. The economics of the whole Upper Colorado River Project, of which the Echo Park Dam in Dinosaur was only a small part, was impugned. The anguished cry for values that were intangible nearly swept away the whole scheme. To salvage the huge project, President Eisenhower, Secretary of the Interior Douglas McKay, the state governors, and the dignitaries of the Upper Colorado River Development Commission withdrew their support of the dam in Dinosaur. Theirs was a political reaction. But the tide of protests against dams in the park had not to do with politics or economics.

What the conservationists apparently wished to save was a fragment of the earth's primeval wilderness big enough and genuine enough to influence the imagination, particularly the urban mind. A large part of the public accurately sensed and shared this objective. It is neither wholly an intellectual nor wholly a cultural matter, but partly the expression of an impulse to hold on to an aspect of the environment that has always been real to humanity: the uninhabited place and the reality of wildness and danger.

There is more to it than place. It is wilderness from which we, as living things, have come, and represents the wild landscape with its creatures which has surrounded the habitations of men for millennia. It extends to individual species in that wild community. For example, a part of the same emotion was directed toward saving the "vanishing" whooping crane. People worked to save the last thirty-odd whooping cranes, irrespective of the fact that they had no more idea of ever seeing a wild whooping crane than they did of camping at Dinosaur. Both are symbols foolish to ignore, and yet we pass over this strange behavior as though we had every intention of saving the cranes in order to make them into hats. There are numerous other animals whose survival is cherished for similarly symbolic reasons.

As for the landscape itself, however much it resembles Arcadia, paradise, or the ruins of Greece, and whatever vast, nervous body of recreationists go to the parks for want of somewhere better to go, it seems apparent that the response is to the lure of far-off unknown places, to the eternal challenge and enigma of forest and desert, the spirit of danger, and the promise of the not yet domesticated lands. It would be surprising indeed if the wilderness which surrounded man so long did not occupy a place in the process of thought itself. Fears have in a sense become needs. Until recently there have always been unexplored regions relatively near at hand. Dinosaur National Monument is as near today to New York as the Catskill escarpment wilderness was a century ago.

The desert, swamp, and rain-forest parks are conspicuously unlike traditional pleasure grounds. The unparklike parks fail as public commons because they have a unique function of their own which playground use will destroy. Perhaps we could survive without that function, though we may not survive without the kind of concern of which wilderness preservation is an example.

It is fair to ask at this point why in a general consideration of man and nature we have examined the beginnings of Yellowstone and Yosemite and the recent parks in detail. The answer is that they are, or were, the world's most extraordinary examples of the preservation of whole landscapes, or segments of nature. It is important to ask what those responsible thought they were doing. In large part we have seen that they thought they were perpetuating something resembling fine English estates, or perhaps we should simply say, ideal scenery. But in effect that was not all they did. They were involved in an experience that had been recognized for more than two centuries as "sublime" and which had been reduced by vulgar imitation to sentimentality and damned by literary critics as affectation.

I do not wish here to attempt to defend the sublime, but rather to say something further about preservation. Among those professionals in the modern world who stand between ourselves and nature, who are our agents, as it were—the agricultural engineers, hydrologists, farmers, foresters, mining engineers, public land agencies, contractors, and planners of various sorts—there is a generally held distinction between *conservation* and *preservation*, and there is a common misunderstanding about them. To them the first means proper use, and naturally, with the vast needs of humanity, includes an ideal dispensation of most of the world. The latter means a special type of land reservation for esthetics, recreation, or science. One is, to them, a general philosophy, the other a very specialized form of land use. All of these "resource" people, especially the foresters, are at pains to remind the public of this distinction, lest a groundswell among gardeners, bird watchers, and other "nature nuts" against the devastation of the world environment take the form of more preservation. Technical foresters have been making this point now for so long that they are always ready with outrage against any such attempts. They learn in college an indignation and righteous humanitarian horror of "locking up" the raw materials used by our civilization. They have not been above showing that preservation is immoral and un-American, since it "wastes" those resources we could otherwise use. The posture is completed, of course, by their magnanimous agreement that we may properly have a little bit of preservation, as they know that man has emotions and does not live by bread alone. Certainly it will chagrin many of them to hear such generosity and common sense called an exploiter's game. But the error in their view can be demonstrated in a five-minute lesson in biology. We must first dispose of the alternatives— conservation ("wise use") and preservation—which they offer, and look at all human activity in nature as falling along a graded scale of environmental modification. There is a polarity indeed in land use, but the actual events always fall in the tension zone between them and never at the extremes. Something is preserved and something used in every situation. The thing kept or lost is always a species of organism. I shall take, somewhat arbitarily, five examples of use intensity and try to show how and why preservation is the dominant element in each, in all land use.

I. The conventional idea of preservation is setting apart an area with a minimum of human intervention, at least by agricultural and technological man. Such a landscape is protected from change by man in its growth and reproduction, and from interference in its catastrophes as well. Forests may be blown about by storms or knocked down by slides, or live out their lives in a process of gradual replacement. Invasion by and extinction of organisms tend to be very slow. The area remains an essential expression of geological, climatic, and evolutionary processes acting on a biota. This is preservation *sui generis*. Its protection from modern man extends even to the *individual* organism. It is most commonly practiced in scientific natural areas where men come as students and witnesses.

Our natural parks are not so protected. The National Park Service traditionally fights fires and insect epidemics and is increasingly occupied with providing visitor facilities. Ecologically, the Park Service is committed to the perpetuation of things-as-they-are, or, biological climax communities. This policy is due to the peculiar esthetic presumptions of the originators of the park system, of some Congressmen, and of a group of people—largely Easterners—who might be collectively described as members of the National Geographic Society before 1936.

II. The second example is the protection of species or their niches. The individual organisms are not sacrosanct, but populations of indigenous organisms and the place which they occupy in nature are. The soil and the particular structure of the natural community with its populations of native organisms are preserved. The size of the populations may be manipulated and harvest made by man. Modest alterations in food chains are made without otherwise changing the qualitative aspects of the system. As hunter, forester, or gatherer, men impinge mainly quantitatively on the system. Though men drain off substance and energy they preserve the stability and productivity of the community. The great majority of biotic interrelationships and dependencies remain intact, for only in their preservation is an enduring harvest of the native species insured. By focusing on the harvest component of the infinitely complex metabolic system, one may be misled into speaking of "use" as opposed to preservation. But the overriding essential is that the community is preserved as a group of populations or a taxonomic mosaic.

III. More intense use occurs at a third level of preservation. Here the basic energy flow structure is preserved, but substitutions are made in the food webs. These substitutions are both intentional and incidental. Individual organisms are not protected; indeed, whole populations may be manipulated, even extinguished or added. The additions are mostly domestic or "camp follower" or pest species. In admitting domestic plants and livestock, their parasites and symbionts are admitted as well. In some pastoral economies these introductions have been made so gradually that the underlying energy pattern or *ecosystems* have been stably sustained; these attenuated natural communities continue without breakdown. A preponderance of native forms—plants, birds, reptiles, especially invertebrates and soil microbes—are merely adjusted quantitatively.

The visible scene seems utterly transformed. This is due to the scope of human vision and our preoccupation with domestic species. We see the landscape, the mesocosm. We do not see an environment or a community, but a field with its orchards or cattle. These few species, because of their size, give a distorted impression of the amount of modification. It is important to remember that at this *trophic* level of preservation thousands of native species continue to share space and support each other, to interact among themselves and with introduced species in transferring nutrients and energy. Except for competitors with man at the peak of the ecological pyramid, even the vertebrate components of these systems, the rabbits, squirrels, and moles, are preserved.

IV. At a further degree of modification new plants are introduced which dominate the energy-fixing process. Competitors and parasites are combatted at all levels. There is a gross rearrangement of the community, with large amounts of life removed, as in truck farming and other agricultural crop production. Yet, even though the principal consumer is man or domestic animals, all breakdown, decay, and other transformation processes are carried on by wild organisms. The actions of other invertebrates are also utilized in the preservation of the soil. In effect, this preserves the complex of biogeochemical cycles characteristic of the area. These are the fundamental ties of unity. The removed materials must be replaced with other organic and chemical equivalents, but the nature of these patterns is still determined by the climate and geology of the area, and sustained by bacteria.

The increasingly demanding routine of modern agriculture—rotation; cultivation; fertilization; weed, pest, and disease control; hormone applications; harvest techniques; seed and plant treatment—is the price paid for the preservation of the element cycles. Even the most intensive irrigation vegetable farming depends essentially on the preservation of a natural exchange soil system about which relatively little is actually known except that its details are formidably complex and obscure, and dependent upon hundreds of kinds of microbes which must be preserved.

V. The preceding type grades off through hydroponics to a final type which is included primarily for reasons of symmetry. This assumes an ultimate ability to control or dispense with the ecosystem, to undertake at a physiological level only the preservation of energy capture, transfer, and amino-acid synthesis. Individuals, species, populations, food webs, trophic pyramids, and even the nutrient cycles would be abandoned. There are some people who neither want a world occupied exclusively by a single multicellular species (man) nor believe it possible. With it comes artificial photosynthesis, *in vitro* tissue culture, genetic control, and the pursuit of the synthetic protein. The question could be raised for this category as well as any of the others, whether man can be psychologically healthy in it.

Even in such a world, however, the fixation of energy would be contingent upon chemical and thermodynamic factors operating now in nature. These determine all transfer and are governed by the laws of thermodynamics and the operation of biochemistry and biophysics. These processes are coextensive with the life of cells, which in turn form organisms and populations. Even if man were to extend his protoplasm so that it occupied a large fraction of the solar system he would be dependent upon stable systems described by cellular and solar physics, a relationship constituting a sort of cosmic ecology whose integrity would have to be preserved.

The following table summarizes the various levels of nature preservation:

TYPE	PRESERVED	TYPICAL HUMAN ACTIVITY	USED
I *sui generis*	forests, lakes, deserts	observing	space, air
II niche	population	hunting, gathering, forestry	some individual organisms
III trophic	food chains	pastoralism	domestic animals
IV ecosystemic	biogeochemical cycle	agriculture	domestic plants
V thermodynamic	cellular organization	bio-engineering	elements, energy

From this series it may be seen that the preserved component is far more basic and more massive than the harvestable or modified component and that the stability of the system is more important than its manipulation. The absence of man in the food chains does not necessarily render a type worthless; it may be particularly important in the study of natural processes critical to the other types. For man's economics the efficiencies of types II, III, and IV are probably low compared to that conceivable in V. Insofar as resource use is successful and enduring (*i.e.*, there is conservation) at each level, there must be a clear understanding of what must be preserved. This has not always been the case because of the exaggerated importance of the directly usable forms and materials.

Historically it appears that the world is moving in both directions from III. In one direction, lands formerly used extensively for grazing and forestry are converted into agriculture. Agriculture itself increases in intensity, approaching the laboratory conditions of V. In the opposite direction, lands used for hunting and forestry are more explicitly designated. Activities not compatible with them are given over to parks and nature reserves. The amount of land committed to type I continues to increase. This need not be alarming because the effectiveness of IV and V will not be measured by the acre, and as they become more efficient there will be more land available—at least until the bulk of humanity spills over into them.

At all levels how much is harvested is less important than the preservation of a stable continuum. The different levels have different proper rates of human use. Type III imposes, for instance, a pace harmonious with the characteristic rate of population adjustment, soil formation, and food-chain stabilization. The tempo in IV may be faster, limited by rates of carbon and nitrogen fixation, other oxidations, the addition of chemical substrate, and the flow of gases and fluids at various temperatures. The tempo innate to each type is enormously important and often overlooked. Indeed, the rate at which significant change occurs in I coincides with climatic change, continental uplift and erosion, and organic evolution and is fast becoming the only place where these tempos can be seen manifested in the landscape by the sensitive observer.

The appreciation of preservation as the essential transaction puts conservation, resource use, and the man-nature relationship itself in a new and somewhat unfamiliar light. Henry Thoreau's famous statement that "in wildness is the preservation of the world" ceases to be ambiguous and inoperable in the modern world when wilderness, as the collective of wild things, is seen to be an epitomization, indeed an abstraction, like mankind or truth. But it also has biological reality. In wilderness are preserved *all* kinds of plants and animals, *all* those interconnecting events which are the physiology of life. We ourselves do not need all of them to live (for example, the lion catching the deer), but their loss is a diminution of the whole for which there is no remaining equivalent, like a small amputation. When we cease to preserve a predatory relationship, such as the lion and deer, by allowing the destruction of its participants, we have paid a price for some "necessary" advance in our civilization. The price is an increment of death. Such increments are cumulative, like the effects on the body of ionizing radiation. The irony is that well-being does not demand the sacrifice of the beauty of the world, which is the esthetic experience of its physiology. The real distinction between type I and the others is that there is nothing unique to types II to V, nothing which is not found in I. As we have seen, II–V are conversions, deletions, and substitutions, largely rearrangements of the patterns of I. There is nothing wrong with any of these preservation-use intensities; no human experiment in the use of nature is immoral. But nature is events, not stuff. The wilderness is like a great river of events, diverted by men into this or that irrigation ditch. Any number of patterns of ditches are possible—as long as the river flows.

ఴ ఴ

Sources and References

Chapter One   THE EYE

Arnheim, Rudolf: *Art and Visual Perception.* Berkeley, Calif.: University of California Press; 1954.

Bartholomew, George A., Jr., and Joseph B. Birdsell: "Ecology and the Protohominids," *American Anthropologist,* LV: 481 (1953).

Berrill, N. J.: *Man's Emerging Mind.* New York: Dodd, Mead; 1955.

Boulding, Kenneth: *The Image.* Ann Arbor, Mich.: University of Michigan Press; 1956.

Clark, J. G. D.: *Prehistoric Europe, the Economic Basis.* London: Pleiades Books; 1948.

Cobb, Edith: "The Ecology of Imagination in Childhood," *Daedalus,* Summer 1959.

Comfort, Alex: *Darwin and the Naked Lady, Discursive Essays on Biology and Art.* London: Routledge & Kegan Paul; 1961.

Corner, E. J. H.: "The Evolution of Tropical Forests," in Julian Huxley et al.: *Evolution as a Process.* London: Allen and Unwin; 1954.

Cornish, Vaughn: *Scenery and the Sense of Sight.* Cambridge: The University Press; 1935.

de la Mare, Walter: *Desert Islands and Robinson Crusoe.* New York: Holt; 1930.

East, W. G.: *An Historical Geography of Europe.* New York: Dutton; 1943.

Ellis, Havelock: "Mescal, a New Artificial Paradise," *Annual Report, Smithsonian Institution,* 1: 537 (1897).

Fiske, Donald W.: "Effects of Monotonous and Restricted Stimulation," *Functions of Varied Experience.* Homewood, Ill.: Dorsey Press; 1961.

Frankfort, H. and H. A.: *The Intellectual Adventure of Ancient Man.* Chicago: University of Chicago Press; 1946.

Fry, Roger: *Vision and Design.* London: Chatto and Windus; 1920.

Gibson, J. J.: *The Perception of the Visual World.* Boston: Houghton Mifflin; 1950.

————: *The Senses as Perceptual Systems*. Boston: Houghton Mifflin; 1966.
Gombrich, E. H.: *Art and Illusion: A Study in the Psychology of Pictorial Representation*. New York: Pantheon; 1960.
Hallowell, Alfred I.: *Culture and Experience*. Philadelphia: University of Pennsylvania Press; 1955.
Hawkridge, Emma: *The Wisdom Tree*. Boston: Houghton Mifflin; 1945.
Hjort, Johan: *The Human Value of Biology*. Cambridge, Mass.: Harvard University Press; 1938.
Hockett, Charles F., and Robert Ascher: "The Human Revolution," *American Scientist*, LII: 70 (1964).
Howell, F. Clark: *Early Man*. New York: Time Inc.; 1965.
Huxley, Aldous: *The Doors of Perception*. New York: Harper; 1954.
————: *Heaven and Hell*. New York: Harper; 1955.
————: *Tomorrow and Tomorrow and Tomorrow*. New York: Harper; 1952.
Kliver, Heinrich: *Mescal, the Divine Plant and Its Psychological Effects*. London: Routledge & Kegan Paul; 1928.
Koffka, Kurt: *Principles of Gestalt Psychology*. New York: Harcourt, Brace; 1935.
LaBarre, Weston: *The Human Animal*. Chicago: University of Chicago Press; 1954.
Laughlin, William S.: "Acquisition of Anatomical Knowledge by Ancient Man," in Sherwood L. Washburn, ed.: *The Social Life of Early Man*. Chicago: Aldine; 1961.
Malinowski, Bronislaw: *Magic, Science and Religion*. New York: The Free Press; 1948.
Minnaert, M.: *The Nature of Light and Color in the Open Air*. New York: Dover; 1954.
Mitchell, S. Weir: "Remarks on the Effects of *Anhelonium Lewinii* (the Mescal Button)," *British Medical Journal*, Vol. II (1896).
Ogle, Kenneth N.: "The Visual Space Sense," *Science*, CXXXV: 763 (1962).
Patch, Howard Rollin: *The Other World According to Descriptions in Medieval Literature*. Cambridge, Mass.: Harvard University Press; 1950.
Pevsner, Nikolaus: "Constable and the Pursuit of Nature," *The Listener*, Nov. 24, 1955.
Polyak, S. L.: *The Vertebrate Visual System, its Origin, Structure and Function and its Manifestations in Disease with an Analysis of its Role in the Life of Animals and in the Origin of Man, Preceded by a Historical Review of Investigations of the Eye, and of the Visual Pathways and Centers of the Brain*. Chicago: University of Chicago Press; 1957.

Portmann, Adolf: "The Seeing Eye," *Landscape*, IX: 1 (1959).
Roheim, Geza: *The Gates of the Dream*. New York: International Universities Press; 1953.
Ruskin, John: *Modern Painters*. Vol. III. New York: Wiley; 1878.
Ryan, T. A.: "Geographic Orientation," *American Journal of Psychology*, LIII: 204 (1940).
Scott, John P.: "Critical Periods in Behavioral Development," *Science*, CXXXVIII: 949 (1962).
Shepard, Paul: "The Arboreal Eye," *School Science and Mathematics*, December 1964.
Smythes, John: *The Analysis of Perception*. London: Routledge & Kegan Paul; 1956.
Soloman, Philip, et al.: *Sensory Deprivation*. Cambridge, Mass.: Harvard University Press; 1961.
Vernon, M. C.: *Visual Perception*. Cambridge: The University Press; 1937.
————: *A Further Study of Visual Perception*. Cambridge: The University Press; 1952.
Von Senden, M.: *Space and Sight*. London: Methuen; 1960.
Walls, Gordon L.: *The Vertebrate Eye*. Bloomfield Hills, Mich.: Cranbrook Institute of Science Bulletin, No. 19, 1942.
Wasson, Valentina P. and R. Gordon: *Mushrooms, Russia and History*. New York: Pantheon; 1957
Werner, Heinz: *Comparative Psychology of Mental Development*. New York: Harper; 1940.
Whorf, Benjamin Lee: *Language, Thought and Reality*. New York: Wiley; 1956.
Young, J. Z.: *Doubt and Certainty in Science*. London: Oxford; 1950.

Chapter Two THE SENSE OF PLACE

Adler, B. F.: "Maps of Primitive People," *Bulletin of American Geographical Society*, No. 43, 1911.
Aiken, Conrad: *A Letter from Li Po and Other Poems*. New York: Oxford; 1955.
Ardrey, Robert: *African Genesis, a Personal Investigation into the Animal Origins and Nature of Man*. New York: Atheneum; 1961.
————: *The Territorial Imperative*. New York: Atheneum; 1966.
Bachelard, Gaston: *The Poetics of Space*. New York: Orion; 1964.

Briggs, Asa: "The Sense of Place," in *The Quality of Man's Environment*. Washington, D.C.: Smithsonian Institution; 1967.

Campbell, Joseph: *The Masks of God: Primitive Mythology*. New York: Viking; 1959.

Clay, Grady: "Remembered Landscapes," *Landscape*, VII: 2 (1957–8).

Eliade, Mircea: *The Sacred and the Profane, the Nature of Religion*. New York: Harcourt, Brace; 1962.

Gottman, Jean: "Locale and Architecture," *Landscape*, VII: 1 (1957).

Hall, Edward T.: *The Silent Language*. New York: Doubleday; 1959.

———: "The Language of Space," *Landscape*, X: 1 (1960).

———: "The Maddening Crowd," *Landscape*, XII: 1 (1962).

Hawkes, Jacquetta: *A Land*. New York: Random House; 1952.

Hediger, P.: "The Evolution of Territorial Behavior," in Sherwood L. Washburn, ed.: *The Social Life of Early Man*. Chicago: Aldine; 1961.

Hoijer, Harry, ed.: *Language in Culture*. Chicago: University of Chicago Press; 1954.

Isaac, Erich: "Religion, Landscape and Space," *Landscape*, IX: 2 (1959–60).

———: "God's Acre," *Landscape*, XIV: 2 (1965).

Levy, Gertrude: *The Gate of Horn; A Study of the Religious Conceptions of the Stone Age and their Influence Upon European Thought*. London: Faber; 1948.

Peattie, Roderick: *Geography in Human Destiny*. New York: George W. Stewart; 1940.

Van Gennep, Arnold: *Rites of Passage*. Chicago: University of Chicago Press; 1960.

West, Rebecca: Preface, *Selected Poems of Carl Sandburg*. New York: Harcourt, Brace; 1926.

Chapter Three   THE IMAGE OF THE GARDEN

Allen, B. Sprague: *Tides in English Taste*. Cambridge, Mass.: Harvard University Press; 1937.

Addison, Joseph: *Remarks on Italy*. New York: G. P. Putnam's Sons; 1854 (1703).

Barto, Philip Stephan: *Tannhauser and the Mountain of Venus, a Study in the Legend of the Germanic Paradise*. New York: Oxford; 1916.

Bidwell, Percy W.: "The Agricultural Revolution in New England," *American Historical Review*, XXVI: 4 (1921).

Black, John Donald: *Rural Economy of New England*. Cambridge, Mass.: Harvard University Press; 1950.

Blunt, Anthony: "The Heroic and the Ideal Landscape in the Work of Nicolas Poussin," *Journal of the Warburg and Courtauld Institutes*, VII: 154 (1944).

Boas, George: *Essays on Primitivism and Related Ideas in the Middle Ages*. Baltimore: Johns Hopkins Press; 1935.

Burckhardt, Jakob: *The Civilization of the Renaissance in Italy*. London: Harrap; 1929.

Carleton, Lieutenant James Henry: *The Prairie Logbooks* [1844–5], ed. Louis Pelzer. Chicago: The Caxton Club; 1943.

Clark, H. F.: *The English Landscape Garden*. London: Pleiades Books; 1948.

Clark, Kenneth: *Landscape into Art*. London: J. Murray; 1949.

Crisp, Sir Frank, ed.: *Medieval Gardens*. London: John Kanc; 1924.

Darling, Frank Frazer: "Man's Ecological Dominance Through Domesticated Animals on Wild Lands," in William L. Thomas, ed.: *Man's Role in Changing the Face of the Earth*. Chicago: University of Chicago Press; 1956.

de Beauvoir, Simone: *The Second Sex*. New York: Alfred A. Knopf; 1953.

Downing, Andrew Jackson: *A Treatise on the Theory and Practice of Landscape Gardening*. New York: Wiley and Putnam; 1844.

Eckstein, R., and Elane Caruth: "From Eden to Utopia," *American Imago*, XXII: 1–2 (1965).

Eliade, Mircea: "The Yearning for Paradise in Primitive Tradition," *Daedalus*, Summer 1953.

Fierz-David, Linda: *The Dream of Poliphilo*. New York: Pantheon; 1950.

Fisher, Seymour, and Sidney E. Cleveland: *Body Image and Personality*. New York: Van Nostrand; 1958.

Forde, C. D.: *Habitat, Economy and Society; A Geographical Introduction to Ethnology*. New York: Dutton; 1950.

Frankfort, Henri: "The Archetype in Analytical Psychology and the History of Religion," *Journal of the Warburg and Courtauld Institutes*. XXI: 166 (1958).

———: *The Birth of Civilization in the Near East*. Bloomington, Ind.: University of Indiana Press; 1951.

Freud, Sigmund: *A General Introduction to Psychoanalysis*. Garden City, N.Y.: Doubleday; 1952.

Gothein, Marie Luise: *A History of Garden Art*, ed. Walter P. Wright. New York: Dutton; 1928.

Graham, Edward H.: *Natural Principles of Land Use*. New York: Oxford; 1944.

Greg, Walter W.: *Pastoral Poetry and Pastoral Drama; A Literary Inquiry with Special Reference to the Pre-Restoration Stage in England.* London: A. H. Bullen; 1906.

Grigson, Geoffrey: "The Room Outdoors," *Landscape*, IV: 2 (1954–5).

Harrison, Jane Ellen: *Mythology.* Boston: Jones; 1924.

Harrison, Thomas P.: *The Pastoral Elegy.* Austin, Tex.: University of Texas Press; 1939.

Huizinga, J.: *The Waning of the Middle Ages, A Study of the Forms of Life, Thought and Art in France and the Netherlands in the Dawn of the Renaissance.* London: St. Martin's; 1924.

Hutchinson, G. E.: "The Gothic Attitude to Natural History," in *The Itinerant Ivory Tower.* New Haven: Yale University Press; 1953.

Jackson, J. B.: "Ghosts at the Door," *Landscape*, I: 2 (1951).

Lewis, C. S.: *The Allegory of Love.* Oxford: Oxford; 1936.

Manwaring, Elizabeth Wheeler: *Italian Landscape in Eighteenth Century England; A Study Chiefly of the Influence of Claude Lorraine and Salvator Rosa on English Taste, 1700–1800.* New York: Oxford; 1925.

Marx, Leo: *The Machine in the Garden.* New York: Oxford; 1964.

McGuire, Dian K.: "An Italian Garden of Love," *Landscape*, XIII: 2 (1963–4).

Mikesell, Marvin W.: "Deforestation in Northern Morocco," *Science*, CXXXII: 441 (1960).

Olmsted, Frederick Law, and Theodora Kimball: *Forty Years of Landscape Architecture, Being the Professional Papers of Frederick Law Olmsted.* New York: G. P. Putnam's Sons; 1922.

Price, Uvedale: *Essays on the Picturesque.* London; 1810.

Priestley, J. B., and Jacquetta Hawkes: *Journey Down a Rainbow.* New York: Harper; 1955.

Quigley, Hugh: *The Land of the Rhone.* Boston: Houghton Mifflin; 1927.

Rank-Sachs, Otto: "The Unconscious and Its Forms of Expression," *American Imago*, XXI: 1–2 (1964).

Schum, Paul B.: "The Central Park of New York City," *Landscape Architecture*, XXVII: 3 (1937).

Scully, Vincent: *The Earth, the Temple and the Gods.* New Haven: Yale University Press; 1962.

Sears, Paul B.: *Ecology of Man.* Eugene, Or.: Oregon State System of Higher Education; 1957.

Shepard, Paul: "The Cross Valley Syndrome," *Landscape*, X: 3 (1961).

Stambler, Bernard: *Dante's Other World; the Purgatorio as*

Guide to the Divine Comedy. New York: New York University Press; 1957.
Stern, Karl: *The Flight from Woman.* New York: Farrar, Straus; 1965.
Stroud, Dorothy: "Our Landscape's Debt to the Eighteenth Century," *Geographical Magazine,* XXV: 1 (1952).
———: *Capability Brown.* London: *Country Life;* 1950.
Topitsch, E.: "World Interpretation and Self-Interpretation, Some Basic Patterns," *Daedalus,* Spring 1959.
Tunnard, Christopher: *Gardens in the Modern Landscape.* New York: Scribner; 1948.
Valency, Maurice: *In Praise of Love.* New York: Macmillan; 1958.
Ville, Egbert L.: *First Annual Report on the Improvement of Central Park,* City of New York, 1857.
Von Neumann, Eric: *The Great Mother.* New York. Panthoon; 1955.
Warner, W. Lloyd: *The Living and the Dead, A Study of the Symbolic Life of the Americans.* New Haven: Yale University Press; 1959.
West, Rebecca: *The Strange Necessity.* New York: Doubleday; 1928.
———: "Whittaker Chambers," *The Atlantic,* May 1952.
Wright, John K., ed.: *New England's Prospect: 1933. American Geographical Society Special Publication No. 16,* 1933.

Chapter Four   THE ITINERANT EYE

Anderson, Edgar: "Horse-and-Buggy Countryside," *Landscape,* IV: 3 (1955).
Anonymous: *The Scenery of the United States.* New York: D. Appleton and Co.; 1855.
Atwood, Wallace W.: *The Physiographic Provinces of North America.* Boston: Ginn; 1940.
Auden, W. H.: *The Enchafèd Flood.* New York: Random House; 1950.
Bates, E. S.: *Touring in 1600.* Boston: Houghton Mifflin; 1947.
Bevan, Edwyn: *Holy Images.* London: Allen and Unwin; 1940.
Brooks, Van Wyck: *The World of Washington Irving.* New York: Dutton; 1944.
Coates, Reynell: "Rural Scenery Near Philadelphia," *Sartain's Magazine,* IX: 226 (1851).
Cole, Thomas: "Essay on American Scenery," *The American Monthly Magazine,* I, New Series, January 1836.

Cranch, Christopher P.: "The Painter in the Woods," *Sartain's Magazine*, X: 43 (1852).

Curtis, George William: *Lotus Eating*. New York: Dix, Edwards & Co.; 1856.

Davis, William Morris: "The Physical Features of New England," in Sam. H. Scudder: *Introduction to the Butterflies of New England*. Cambridge, Mass.: Harvard University Press; 1888.

Dow, Charles Mason, ed.: *Anthology and Bibliography of Niagara Falls*. Albany, N.Y.: State of New York; 1921.

Dwight, Theodore, Jr.: *Sketches of Scenery and Manners in the United States*. New York: A. T. Goodrich; 1829.

———: *Things as They Are, or Notes of a Traveller Through Some of the Middle and Northern States*. New York: Harper; 1834.

Gilpin, William: *Remarks on Forest Scenery, and Other Woodland Views (Relative Chiefly to Picturesque Beauty)*. London: R. Blamire; 1791.

———: *Three Essays: on Picturesque Beauty, on Picturesque Travel, and on Sketching Landscape, to Which is Added a Poem on Landscape Painting*. London: R. Blamire; 1792.

Goodrich, Samuel: *Peter Parley's Tales About the State and City of New York*. New York: Pendleton and Hill; 1832.

Hammerton, Philip Gilbert: *Landscape*. London; 1885.

Howard, Claire: *English Travellers of the Renaissance*. New York: John Land; 1914.

Howitt, William: "The Rural Life of England," *The New York Review*, XI: 170 (1839).

Hussey, Christopher: *The Picturesque; Studies in a Point of View*. New York: G. P. Putnam's Sons; 1927.

Huth, Hans: *Nature and the American, Three Centuries of Changing Attitudes*. Berkeley, Calif.: University of California Press; 1957.

Jackson, J. B.: "The Abstract World of the Hot Rodder," *Landscape*, V: 1 (1955).

Keyserling, Count Hermann: *The Travel Diary of a Philosopher*. New York: Harcourt, Brace; 1925.

King, Thomas Starr: *The White Hills*. New York: Hurd and Houghton; 1870 (1859).

Klingender, Francis D.: *Art and the Industrial Revolution*. London: Noel Carrington; 1947.

Lanman, Charles: *Letters from a Landscape Painter*. Boston: J. Munroe & Co.; 1845.

Lassels, Richard: *The Voyage of Italy, or a Compleat Journey Through Italy*. London; 1686.

Lillard, Richard D.: *The Great Forest*. New York: Alfred A. Knopf; 1947.

Maugham, H. Neville: *The Book of Italian Travel* (*1580–1900*). London: Grant Richards; 1903.

Newcomb, Robert: "Beckett's Road," *Landscape*, XIII: 1 (1963).

Newton, Arthur Percival: *Travel and Travellers of the Middle Ages*. London: Routledge & Kegan Paul; 1926.

Noble, Louis L.: *The Course of Empire*. New York; 1853.

Ogden, H. V. S. and M. S.: *English Taste in Landscape in the Seventeenth Century*. Ann Arbor, Mich.: University of Michigan Press; 1956.

Pacht, Otto: "Early Italian Nature Studies," *Journal of the Warburg and Courtauld Institutes*, XIII: 1 (1950).

Panofsky, Erwin: *Early Netherlandish Painting: Its Origins and Character*. Oxford: Oxford; 1954.

Peckham, Harry Houston: *Gotham Yankee*. New York: Vantage Press; 1950.

Phelps, Elmira H. L.: *Caroline Westerley, or the Young Traveller from Ohio, Containing the Letters of a Young Lady of Seventeen Written to her Sister*. New York: J. J. Harper; 1833.

Pieper, Josef: *Leisure, the Basis of Culture*. New York: Pantheon; 1952.

Richards, T. Addison: *American Landscape Annual, American Scenery Illustrated*. New York: Leavitt and Allen Bros.; 1854.

Robertson, Andrew: *Elementary and Practical Hints as to the Perception and Enjoyment of the Beautiful in Nature and the Fine Arts* [1836], ed. Emily Robertson. London: Eyre and Spottiswood; 1896.

Rockwell, Rev. Charles: *The Catskill Mountains and the Region Around*. New York: Taintor Bros.; 1867.

Seznec, J.: *The Survival of the Pagan Gods; the Mythological Tradition and Its Place in Renaissance Humanism and Art*. New York: Pantheon; 1953.

Shelton, Rev. F. W.: "Ascent in 1858 of Mt. Mansfield," *Knickerbocker*, LV: 4:353 (1860).

Shepard, Paul: "The Nature of Tourism," *Landscape*, V: 1 (1955).

Smallwood, William Martin: *Natural History and the American Mind*. New York: Columbia University Press; 1941.

Smith, S. C. Karnes: *Crome*. London: P. Allen; 1923.

Stephens, Leslie: *Men, Books and Mountains*. Minneapolis: University of Minnesota Press; 1956 (1869).

Sweet, Frederick A.: *The Hudson River School and the Early American Landscape Tradition*. Chicago: Art Institute; 1945.

Taylor, Bayard: *Views A-Foot*. New York: G. P. Putnam; 1855.

Von Humboldt, Alexander: *Cosmos*. New York: Harper; 1850.
Whitcomb, S. L.: "Nature in Early American Literature," *The Sewanee Review*, V: 2 (1897).
White, Lynn, Jr.: "Natural Science and Naturalistic Art in the Middle Ages," *American Historical Review*, LII: 3 (1947).
Wilstach, Paul: *The Hudson River Landings*. Indianapolis: Bobbs-Merrill; 1933.

Chapter Five   THE VIRGIN DREAM

Barfield, Owen: *Romanticism Comes of Age*. London: Anthroposophic Press; 1944.
Beach, Joseph Warren: *The Concept of Nature in Nineteenth-Century English Poetry*. New York: Macmillan; 1936.
Berman, Elinor D.: *Thomas Jefferson Among the Arts*. New York: Philosophical Library; 1947.
Biese, Alfred: *The Development of the Feeling for Nature in the Middle Ages and Modern Time*. London: George Routledge; 1905.
Boas, George, ed.: *Romanticism in America*. Baltimore: Johns Hopkins University Press; 1940.
Boase, T. S. R.: "English Artists and the Val D'Aosta," *Journal of the Warburg and Courtauld Institutes*, XIX: 283 (1956).
Born, Wolfgang: *American Landscape Painting, an Interpretation*. New Haven: Yale University Press; 1948.
Brandes, George: *Main Currents in Nineteenth-Century Literature*. New York: Macmillan; 1902.
Bryant, William Cullen: *Poems*. Boston: Russel, Odiorne and Metcalf; 1834.
Burke, Edmund: *A Philosophical Enquiry into the Origin of Our Idea of the Sublime and the Beautiful*. London; 1757.
Burnet, Thomas: *The Theory of the Earth*. London; 1684.
Cooper, Anthony Ashley (Lord Shaftsbury): *The Moralists; a Philosophical Rhapsody*. London; 1709.
Dennis, John: *Miscellanies in Verse and Prose*. London; 1698.
Durand, John: *Life and Times of Ashur B. Durand*. New York: Scribner; 1898.
Dyer, John: *Works*. Edinburgh; 1794.
Ellis, Havelock: "The Love of Wild Nature," *Contemporary Review*, LXIII: 538 (1898).
Fairchild, Hoxie Neale: *The Noble Savage, a Study in Romantic Naturalism*. New York: Columbia University Press; 1929.
————: *The Romantic Quest*. New York: Columbia University Press; 1931.
Geikie, Sir Archibald: *Landscape in History and Other Essays*. New York: Macmillan; 1905.

Gesner, Conrad: *On the Admiration of Mountains* [1555], trans. H. B. D. Soulé, ed. W. Dock. San Francisco: Grabhorn Press; 1937.

Gillispie, Charles C.: *Genesis and Geology*. Cambridge, Mass.: Harvard University Press; 1951.

Hawthorne, Nathaniel: *The American Note Books* [1838], ed. Randall Stewart. New Haven: Yale University Press; 1932.

Herford, C. H.: "Romanticism in the Modern World," in *Essays and Studies by Members of the English Association*, VIII, ed. G. C. Moore Smith. Oxford: Oxford; 1922.

Hipple, Walter John, Jr.: *The Beautiful, the Sublime and the Picturesque in Eighteenth-Century British Aesthetic Theory*. Carbondale, Ill.: Southern Illinois University Press; 1957.

Hyde, Walter Woodburn: "The Development of the Appreciation of Mountain Scenery in Modern Times," *Geographical Review*, III: 107 (1917).

Jones, Howard Mumford: "Prose and Pictures: James Fennimore Cooper," *Tulane Studies in English*, III: 133 (1952).

Magoon, E. L.: *The Home Book of the Picturesque*. New York: Leavitt and Allen; 1852.

Monk, Samuel H.: *The Sublime, a Study of Critical Theories in Eighteenth-Century England*. New York: Modern Language Association of America; 1935.

Newton, Eric: *The Romantic Rebellion*. London: St. Martin's; 1963.

Nicolson, Marjorie: *Mountain Gloom and Mountain Glory*. Ithaca, N.Y.: Cornell University Press; 1959.

Petrarch, Francesca: *De Vita Solitaria*. 1346.

———: *Petrarch at Vaucluse*, trans. Ernest Hatch Wilkins. Chicago: University of Chicago Press; 1958.

Radcliffe, Ann: *The Romance of the Forest*. London; 1791.

———: *Mysteries of Udolpho, a Romance Interspersed with Some Pieces of Poetry*. London: G. G. & J. Robinson; 1794.

Railo, Eino: *The Haunted Castle*. New York: Dutton; 1927.

Ray, John: *The Wisdom of God Manifested in the Works of the Creation*. London; 1691.

Reynolds, Myra: *The Treatment of Nature in English Poetry Between Pope and Wordsworth*. Chicago: University of Chicago Press; 1896.

Robbe-Grillet, Alain: "Old Values and the New Novel (Nature, Humanism and Tragedy)," *Evergreen Review*, I:3 (1957).

Robertson, J. G.: *Studies in the Genesis of Romantic Theory in the Eighteenth Century*. New York: Macmillan; 1923.

Sauer, Carl: *Agricultural Origins and Dispersals*. New York: American Geographical Society; 1952.

Soby, James Thrall, and Dorothy C. Miller: *Romantic Painting in America*. New York: Museum of Modern Art; 1943.

Spengler, Oswald: *The Decline of the West*. London: Allen and Unwin; 1918.
Summers, Montague: *Essays in Petto*. London: The Fortune Press; n.d.
Taylor, E. G. R.: "English Worldmakers of the Seventeenth Century and their Influence on the Earth Sciences," *Geographical Review*, XXXVIII: 104 (1948).
Tuan, Yi-Fu: "Mountains, Ruins, and the Sentiment of Melancholy," *Landscape*, XIV: 1 (1964).
Von Simpson, Otto: *The Gothic Cathedral*. New York: Pantheon; 1956.
Woolley, Mary: "Development of the Love of Romantic Scenery in America," *American Historical Review*, III: 1 (1898).

Chapter Six   FELLOW CREATURES

Abell, Walter: *The Collective Dream in Art*. Cambridge, Mass.: Harvard University Press; 1957.
Chase, Richard: *Quest for Myth*. Baton Rouge, La.: Louisiana State University Press; 1949.
Clarke, C. H. D.: "Autumn Thoughts of a Hunter," *Journal of Wildlife Management*, XXII: 4 (1958).
Franck, Frederick: *Days With Albert Schweitzer: a Lambaréné Landscape*. New York: Holt; 1959.
Frazer, Sir James G.: *The Golden Bough, II: Spirits of the Corn and of the Wild*. London; 1912.
Gary, Roman: *The Roots of Heaven*. New York: Simon and Schuster; 1958.
Kelsen, Hans: *Society and Nature*. Chicago: University of Chicago Press; 1943.
Krutch, Joseph Wood: "Sportsman or Predator," *Saturday Review*, Aug. 17, 1957.
Lorenz, Konrad: *On Aggression*. New York: Harcourt, Brace; 1963.
Piddington, Robert A.: *The Limits of Mankind: a Philosophy of Population*. London: Macmillan; 1956.
Raphael, Max: *Prehistoric Cave Paintings*. New York: Pantheon; 1945.
Schweitzer, Albert: *Out of My Life and Thought*. New York: Holt; 1933.
———: *The Animal World of Albert Schweitzer*, ed. and trans. Charles R. Joy. Boston: Beacon Press; 1951.
———: *On the Edge of the Primeval Forest*. New York: Macmillan; 1952.

Shepard, Paul: "Reverence for Life at Lambaréné," *Landscape*, VIII: 2 (1958–9).

———: "A Theory of the Value of Hunting," Washington, D.C.: Trans. 24th N. A. Wildlife Conference, Wildlife Management Institute; 1959.

Steward, J. H.: "Problems of Cultural Evolution," *Evolution*, XII: 206 (1958).

Wheelright, Philip: *The Burning Fountain, a Study in the Language of Symbolism*. Bloomington, Ind.: University of Indiana Press; 1954.

Wilbur, Richard: *Ceremony and Other Poems*. New York: Harcourt, Brace & World; 1948.

Chapter Seven VARIETIES OF NATURE HATING

Arnheim, Rudolf: "The Myth of the Bleating Lamb," *Toward a Psychology of Art*. Berkeley, Calif.: University of California Press; 1966.

Babbitt, Irving: *Rousseau and Romanticism*. Boston: Houghton Mifflin; 1919.

Bernheimer, Richard: *Wild Men in the Middle Ages, a Study in Art, Sentiment and Demonology*. Cambridge, Mass.: Harvard University Press; 1952.

Bidwell, John: *A Journey to California with Observations About Country, Climate, and the Route to This Country* [1841]. Berkeley, Calif.: University of California Press; 1937.

Bury, J. B.: *The Idea of Progress*. New York: Macmillan; 1932.

Collier, John: *Indians of the Americas*. New York: Norton; 1947.

———: *On the Gleaming Way*. Denver, Col.: Sage; 1949.

De Voto, Bernard: *Across the Wide Missouri*. Boston: Houghton Mifflin; 1947.

Dewey, John: "Antinaturalism in Extremis," in Y. H. Krikorian: *Naturalism and the Human Spirit*. New York: Columbia University Press; 1944.

Dixon, R. A.: "Origin and Development of Property," in *Economic Institutions and Cultural Change*. New York: McGraw Hill; 1941.

Fromm, Erich: *The Forgotten Language*. New York: Rinehart; 1951.

Glackens, Clarence: "Origins of the Conservation Philosophy," *Journal of Soil and Water Conservation*, XI: 2 (1956).

———: "Changing Ideas of the Habitable World," in William L. Thomas, ed.: *Man's Role in Changing the Face of the Earth*. Chicago: University of Chicago Press; 1956.

Gray, L. C., et al.: "The Causes: Traditional Attitudes and

Institutions," *Soils and Men, Yearbook of Agriculture.* Washington, D.C.: U.S.D.A.; 1938.

Hale, Israel F.: "Diary of Trip to California in 1849," *Quarterly of Society of California Pioneers,* II: June 1926.

Hedges, Cornelius: "Journal of Judge Cornelius Hedges," *Contributions to the Historical Society of Montana,* V: 370 (1904).

Jackson, J. B.: "Notes and Comments," *Landscape,* III: 2 (1953–4).

———: "The Westward Moving House," *Landscape,* II: 3 (1953).

James, William: *A Pluralistic Universe.* New York: Longmans; 1943.

Johnson, Overton, and William H. Winter: *Route Across the Rocky Mountains, With a Description of Oregon and California, the Geographical Features, Their Resources, Soil, Climate, Productions, and Etc.* Lafayette, Ind.: John B. Semans; 1946.

Krutch, Joseph Wood: "Conservation is Not Enough," *American Scholar,* XXIII: 295 (1954).

Lowenthal, David: "Geography, Experience, and Imagination: Towards a Geographical Epistemology," *Annals of the Association of American Geographers,* LI:241 (1961).

———: "Is Wilderness Paradise Enow?" *Columbia University Forum,* VII: 2 (1964).

Malinowski, Bronislaw: *Coral Gardens and Their Magic, a Study of Methods of Tilling the Soil and of Agricultural Rites in the Trobriand Islands.* New York: American Book Co.; 1935.

Potter, David M.: *People of Plenty, Economic Abundance and the American Character.* Chicago: University of Chicago Press; 1954.

Price, Lucian: *Dialogues of Alfred North Whitehead.* Boston: Little, Brown; 1945.

Raven, Charles: *Natural Religion and Christian Theology.* Cambridge: The University Press; 1953.

Rust, Eric: *Nature and Man in Biblical Thought.* London: Lutterworth; 1953.

Smith, Homer: *Man and His Gods.* Boston: Little, Brown; 1952.

Spilhaus, Athielstan: "Control of the World Environment," *Geographical Review,* XLVI: 451 (1956).

Thurnwald, R.: *Economics in Primitive Communities.* London: International African Institute; 1932.

Van Dresser, Peter: "The Coming Solar Age," *Landscape,* II: 3 (1953).

Van Hise, C. R.: *The Conservation of Natural Resources in the United States.* New York: Macmillan; 1910.

Velikovsky, Immanuel: *Worlds in Collision.* Garden City, N.Y.: Doubleday; 1950.

Watts, Alan: *Nature, Man and Woman.* New York: Pantheon; 1958.

Whittlesly, Derwent: "Impress of Effective Central Authority Upon the Landscape," *Annals of the Association of American Geographers,* XXV: 2 (1935).

Wiener, Norbert: *The Human Use of Human Beings: Cybernetics and Society.* Boston: Houghton Mifflin; 1955.

Williams, George H.: *Wilderness and Paradise in Christian Thought.* New York: Harper; 1962.

Chapter Eight   THE AMERICAN WEST

Augspurger, Marie M.: *Yellowstone National Park.* Middletown, Ohio: privately published; 1948.

Bryant, Edwin: *What I Saw in California, Being a Journal of a Tour by the Emigrant Route and South Pass of the Rocky Mountains Across the Continent of North America, the Great Desert Basin, and Through California, in the Years 1846–47.* Philadelphia: Carey and Hart; 1847.

Bunnell, Lafayette Houghton: *Discovery of the Yosemite.* Chicago: Fleming and Revell; 1880.

Catlin, George: *Letters, Notes on the North American Indians.* London; 1841.

Cramton, Louis C.: *Early History of Yellowstone National Park and its Relation to National Park Policy.* Washington, D.C.: U.S. National Park Service, Department of the Interior; 1932.

Delano, A.: *Life on the Plains and Among the Diggings.* Auburn and Buffalo: Miller, Orton and Mulligan; 1854.

Doane, Gustavus C.: *Executive Document No. 51.* Washington, D.C.: 41st Congress, 3rd Session; 1875.

Everts, Trueman C.: *Thirty-Seven Days of Peril.* New York: Scribner; 1871.

Folsom, David E.: "The Valley of the Upper Yellowstone," *Western Monthly,* July 1870.

Langford, Nathaniel Pitt: *A Diary of the Washburn Expedition to the Yellowstone and Firehole Rivers.* 1905.

Lugn, A. L.: *The Pleistocene Geology of Nebraska.* Lincoln, Nebr.: *Nebraska Geological Survey, Bulletin No. 10,* 2nd Series; 1935.

Olmsted, Frederick Law: "The Yosemite Valley and Mariposa Big Trees," *Landscape Architecture,* XLIII: 1 (1953).

Parker, Rev. Samuel: *Journal of an Exploring Tour Beyond the Rocky Mountains, Under the Direction of A.B.C.F.M., Per-*

formed in the Years 1835, 36, and 37, Containing a Description of the Geography, Geology, Climate, and Productions; And the Number, Manners, and Customs of the Natives, With a Map of Oregon Territory. Ithaca; 1839.

Shepard, Paul: "Dead Cities in the American West," *Landscape*, VI: 2 (1956–7).

Smith, Henry Nash: *Virgin Land*. Cambridge, Mass.: Harvard University Press; 1950.

Thornton, J. Quinn: *Oregon and California in 1845*. New York; 1849.

Townsend, John K.: *Journey Across the Rocky Mountains*. Philadelphia: Henry Perkins; 1839.

Watson, William J.: *Journal of an Overland Journey to Oregon, Made in the Year 1849, with Full and Accurate Account of the Route, its Distances, Scenery, Streams, Mountains, Game, and Everything of Use or of Interest Which Meets the Traveler in the Overland Route to Oregon and California.* Jacksonville, Ala.: E. R. Roe; 1851.

Index